Epilogue 27>> Unease

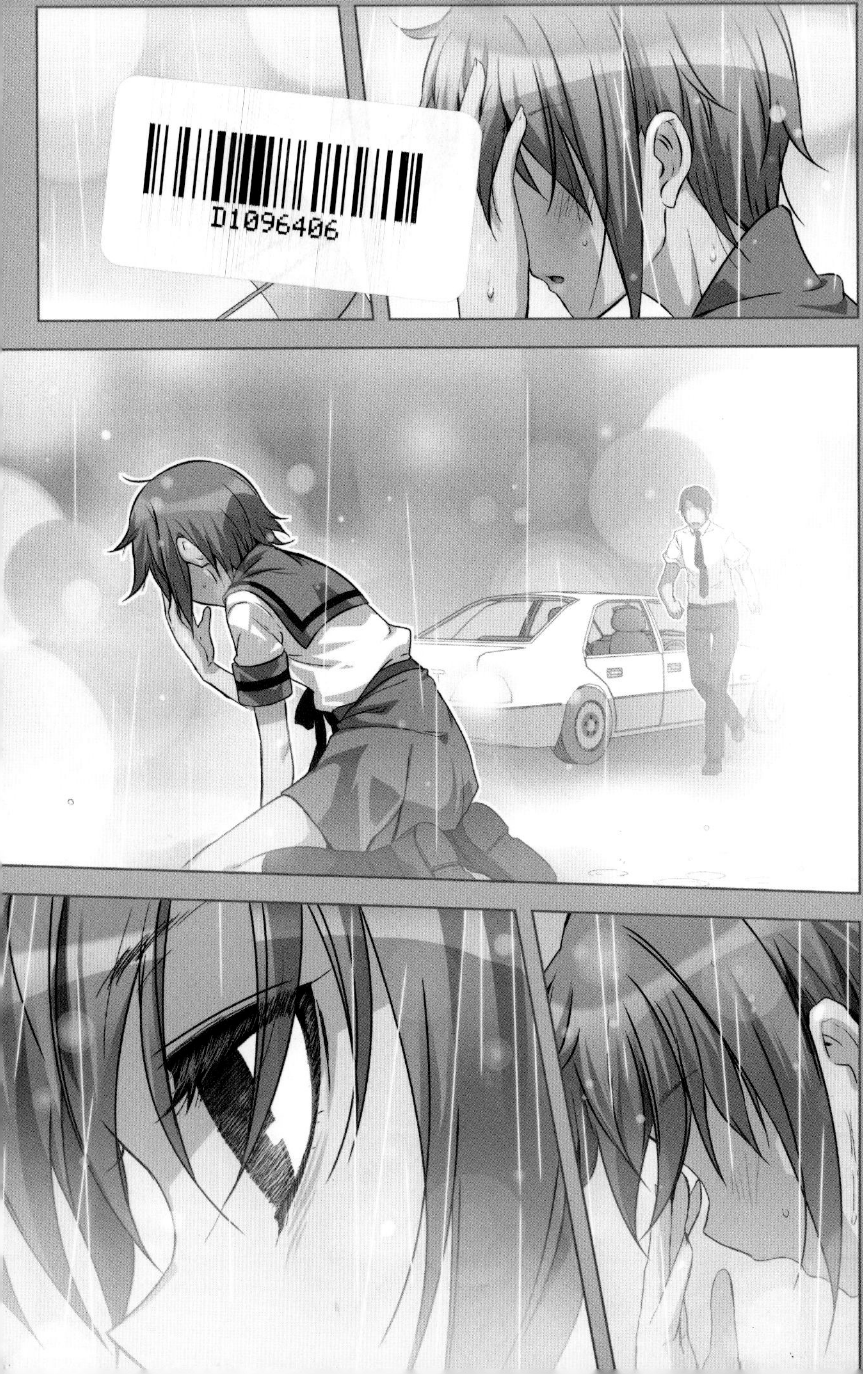

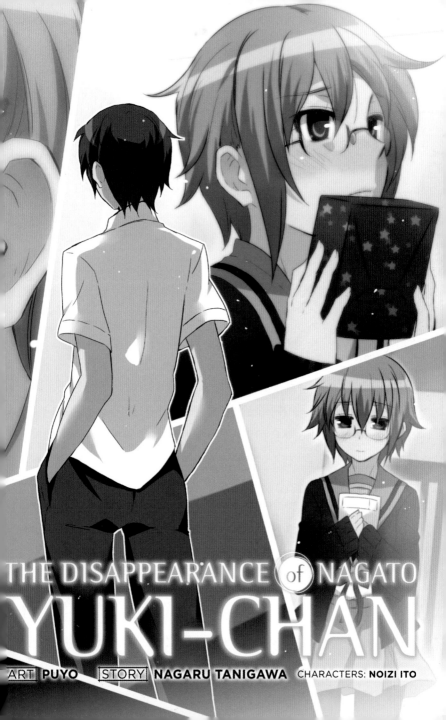

THE DISAPPEARANCE of NAGATO
YUKI-CHAN

ART PUYO   STORY NAGARU TANIGAWA   CHARACTERS: NOIZI ITO

Epilogue 27>> Unease

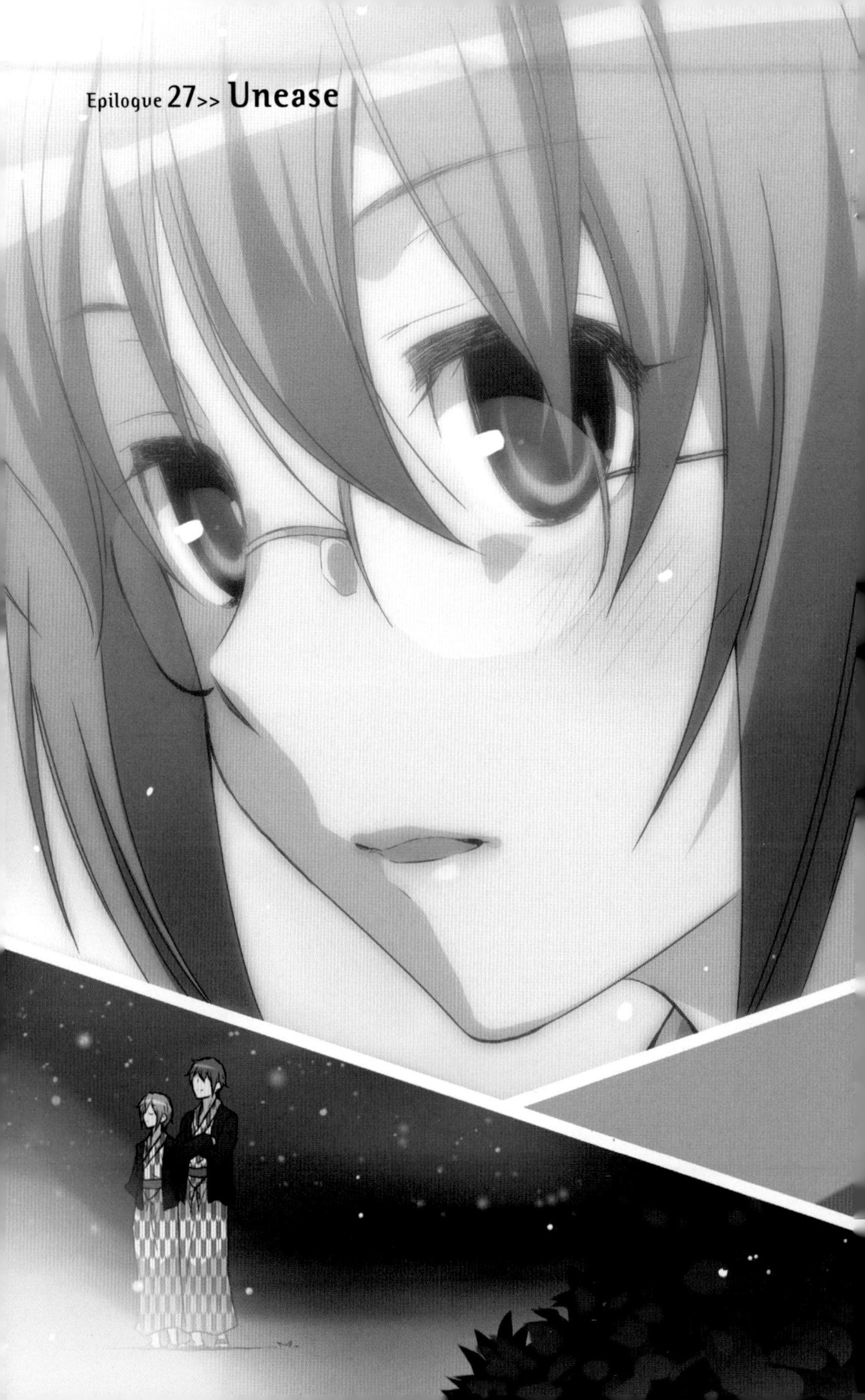

001
Epilogue 27   Unease

021
Epilogue 28   Memory

053
Epilogue 29   Daily Life

077
Epilogue 30   Library

093
Epilogue 31   Library Card

117
Epilogue 32   End of Testing

141
Epilogue 33   Confession

163
Bonus Material

CON-
TENTS!

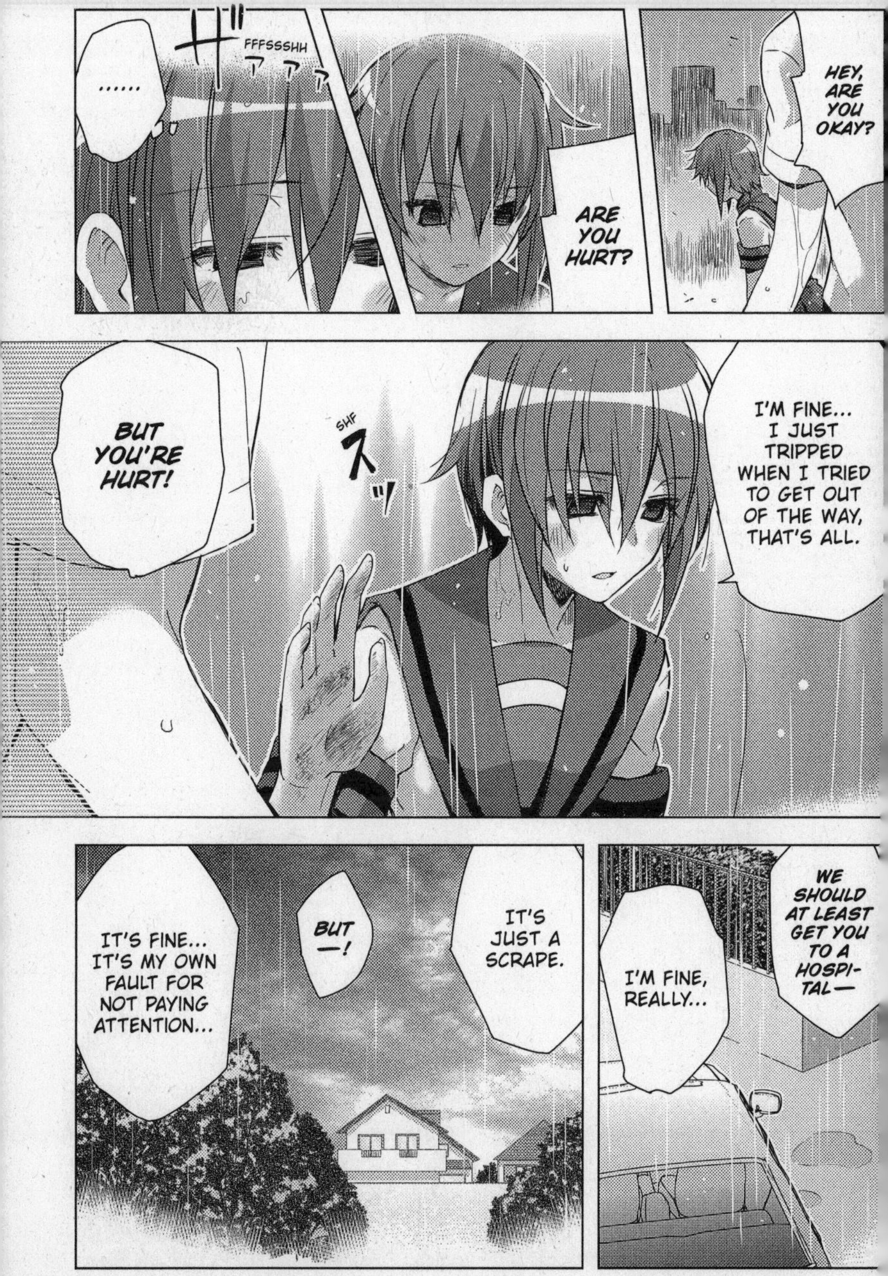
HEY, ARE YOU OKAY?
ARE YOU HURT?
ザァァァ
FFFSSSHH
......
I'M FINE... I JUST TRIPPED WHEN I TRIED TO GET OUT OF THE WAY, THAT'S ALL.
スッ
SHF
BUT YOU'RE HURT!
WE SHOULD AT LEAST GET YOU TO A HOSPI-TAL—
I'M FINE, REALLY...
IT'S JUST A SCRAPE.
BUT—!
IT'S FINE... IT'S MY OWN FAULT FOR NOT PAYING ATTENTION...

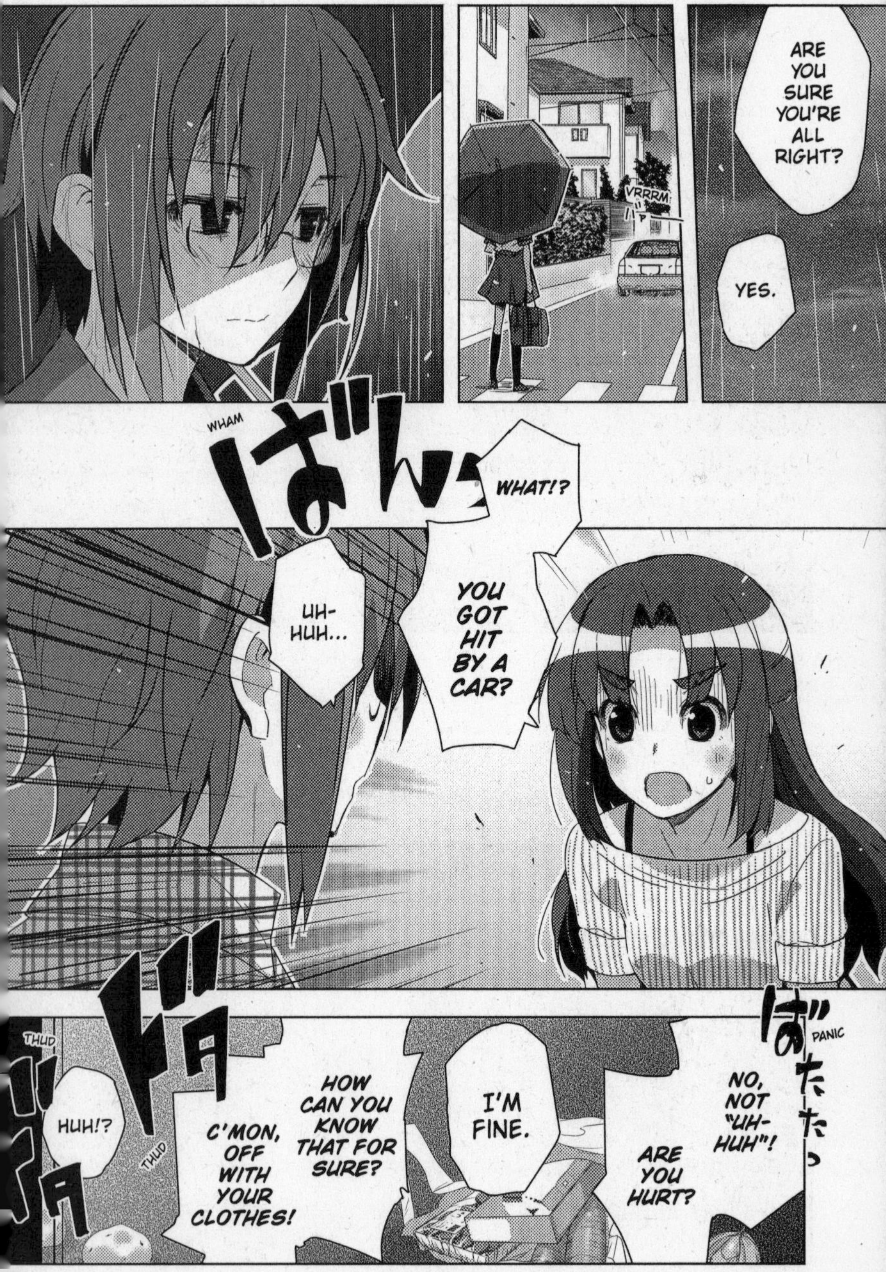
ARE YOU SURE YOU'RE ALL RIGHT?
YES.
VRRRM
WHAM
ばん
WHAT!?
YOU GOT HIT BY A CAR?
UH-HUH...
ぱたたっ
PANIC
NO, NOT "UH-HUH"!
ARE YOU HURT?
I'M FINE.
HOW CAN YOU KNOW THAT FOR SURE?
C'MON, OFF WITH YOUR CLOTHES!
ドタ
THUD
ドタ
THUD
HUH!?

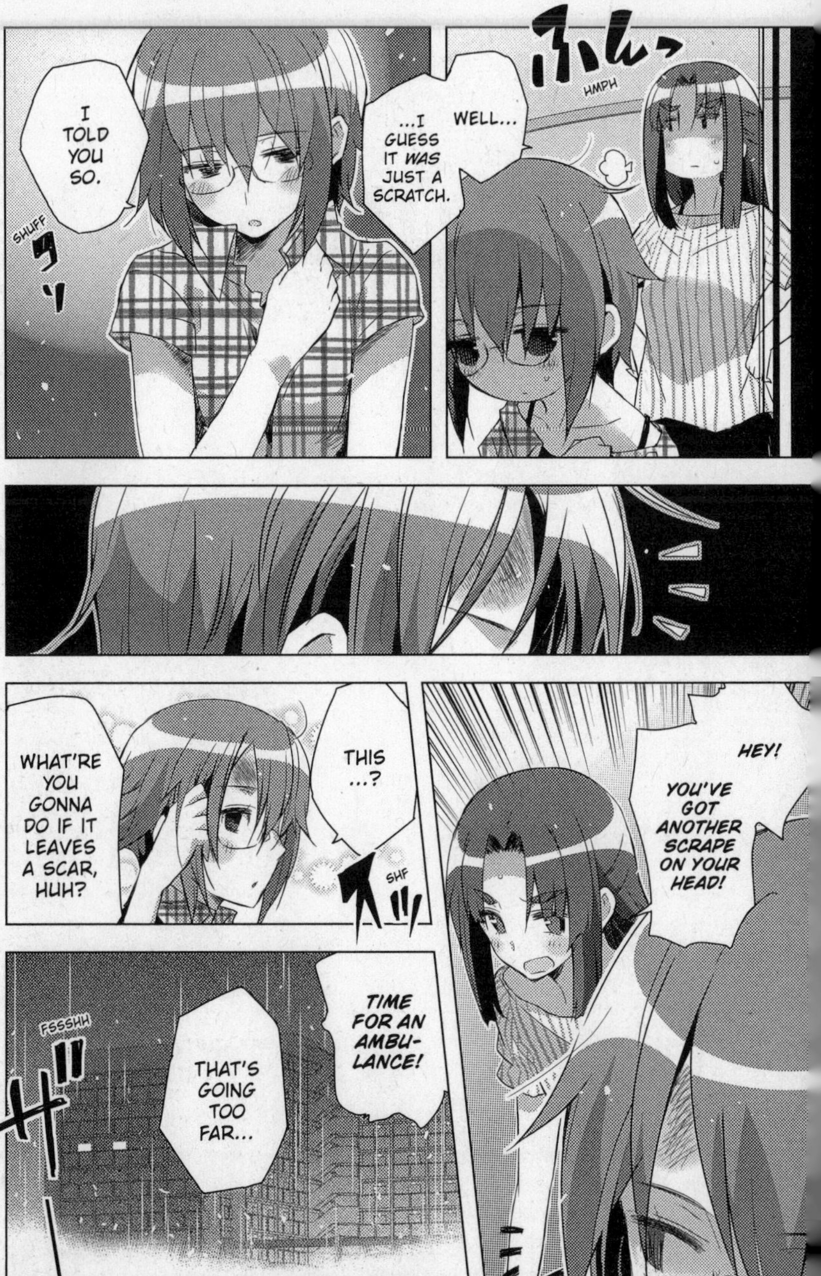
ふんっ
HMPH
WELL...
...I GUESS IT WAS JUST A SCRATCH.
SHUFF
I TOLD YOU SO.
HEY!
YOU'VE GOT ANOTHER SCRAPE ON YOUR HEAD!
TIME FOR AN AMBU-LANCE!
THIS ...?
SHF
WHAT'RE YOU GONNA DO IF IT LEAVES A SCAR, HUH?
FSSSHH
THAT'S GOING TOO FAR...

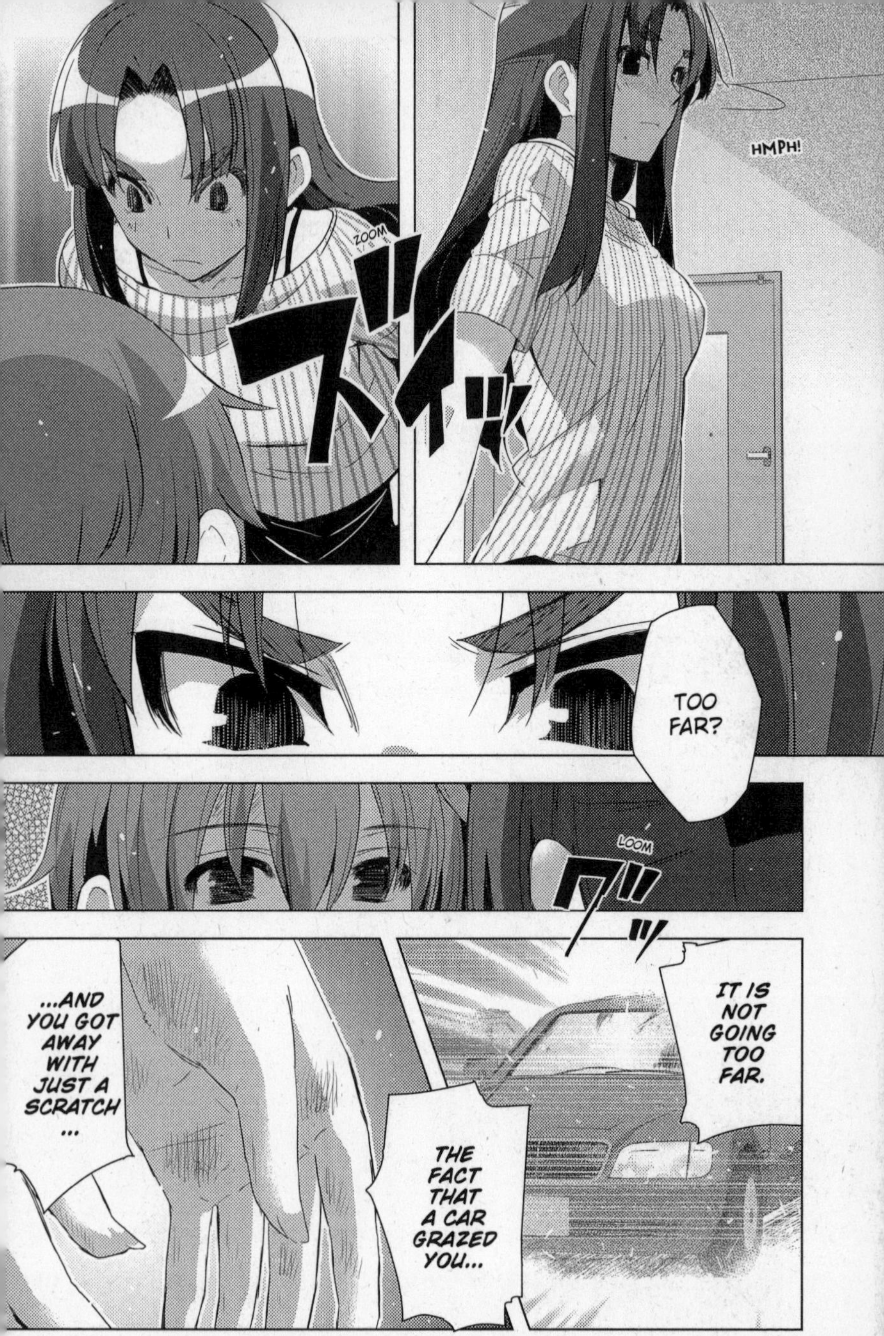
HMPH!
ZOOM
TOO FAR?
LOOM
IT IS NOT GOING TOO FAR.
THE FACT THAT A CAR GRAZED YOU...
...AND YOU GOT AWAY WITH JUST A SCRATCH ...

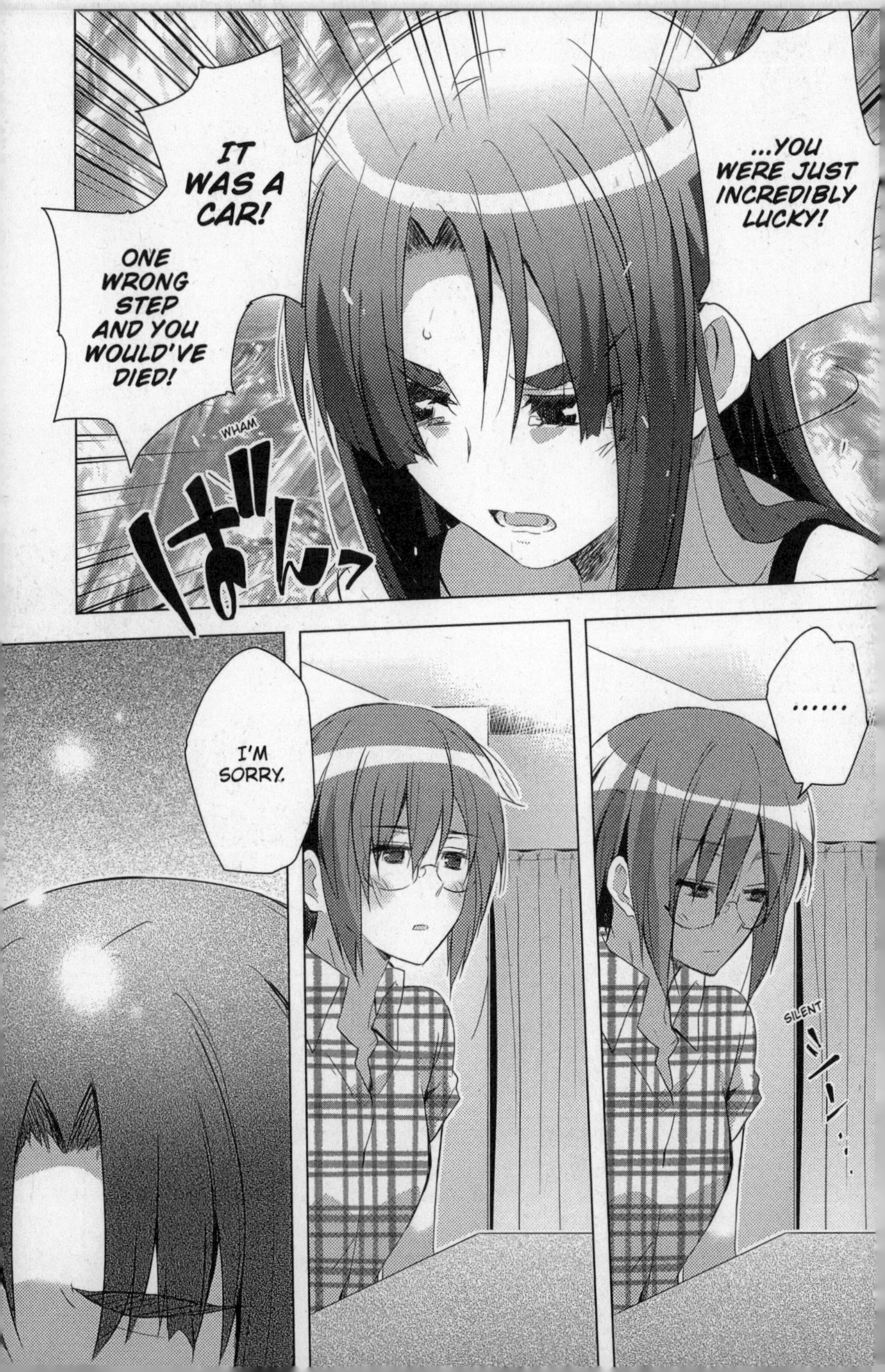
...YOU WERE JUST INCREDIBLY LUCKY!
IT WAS A CAR!
ONE WRONG STEP AND YOU WOULD'VE DIED!
WHAM
ばんっ
......
SILENT
I'M SORRY.

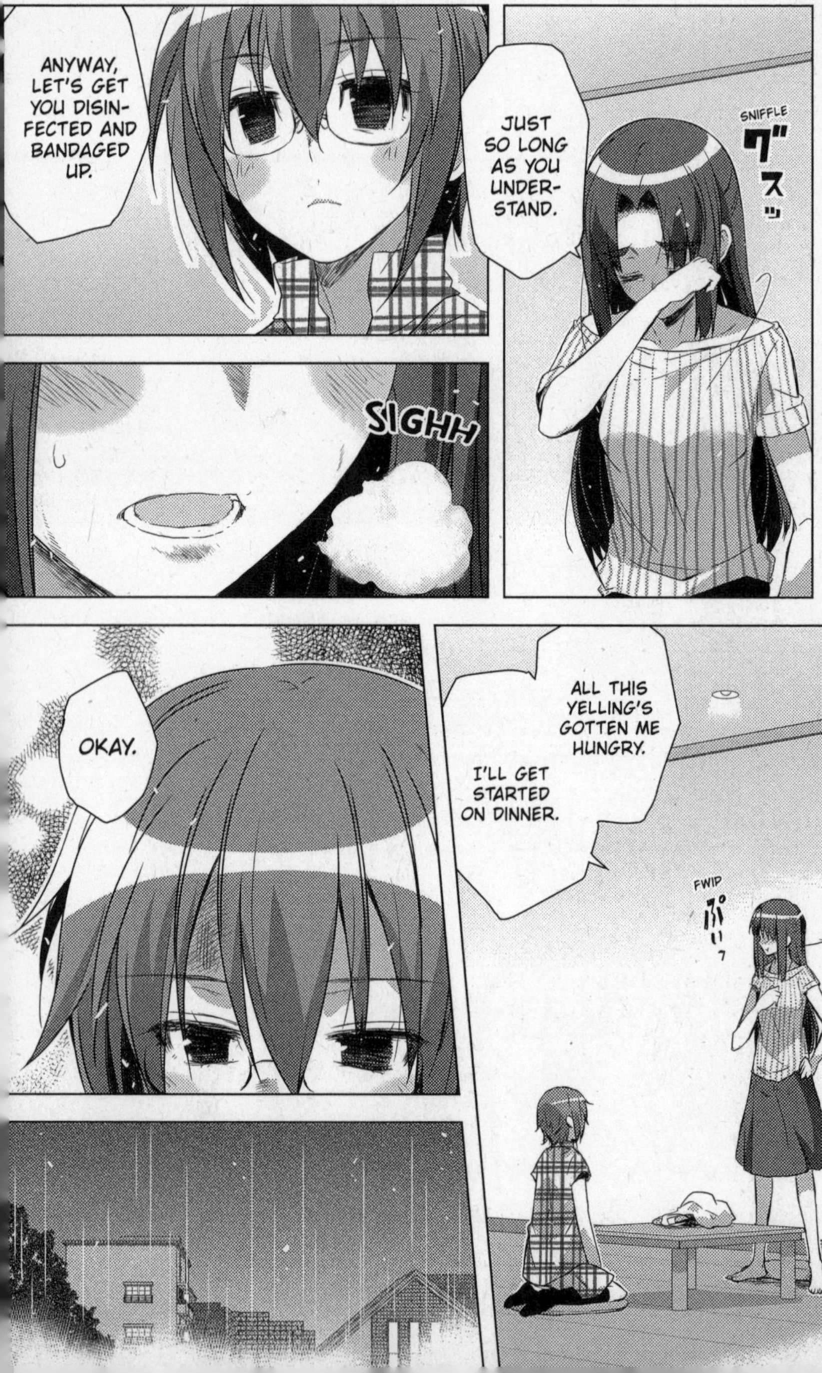
JUST SO LONG AS YOU UNDER-STAND.
SNIFFLE
グスッ
ANYWAY, LET'S GET YOU DISIN-FECTED AND BANDAGED UP.
SIGHH
ALL THIS YELLING'S GOTTEN ME HUNGRY.
I'LL GET STARTED ON DINNER.
FWIP
ぷいっ
OKAY.

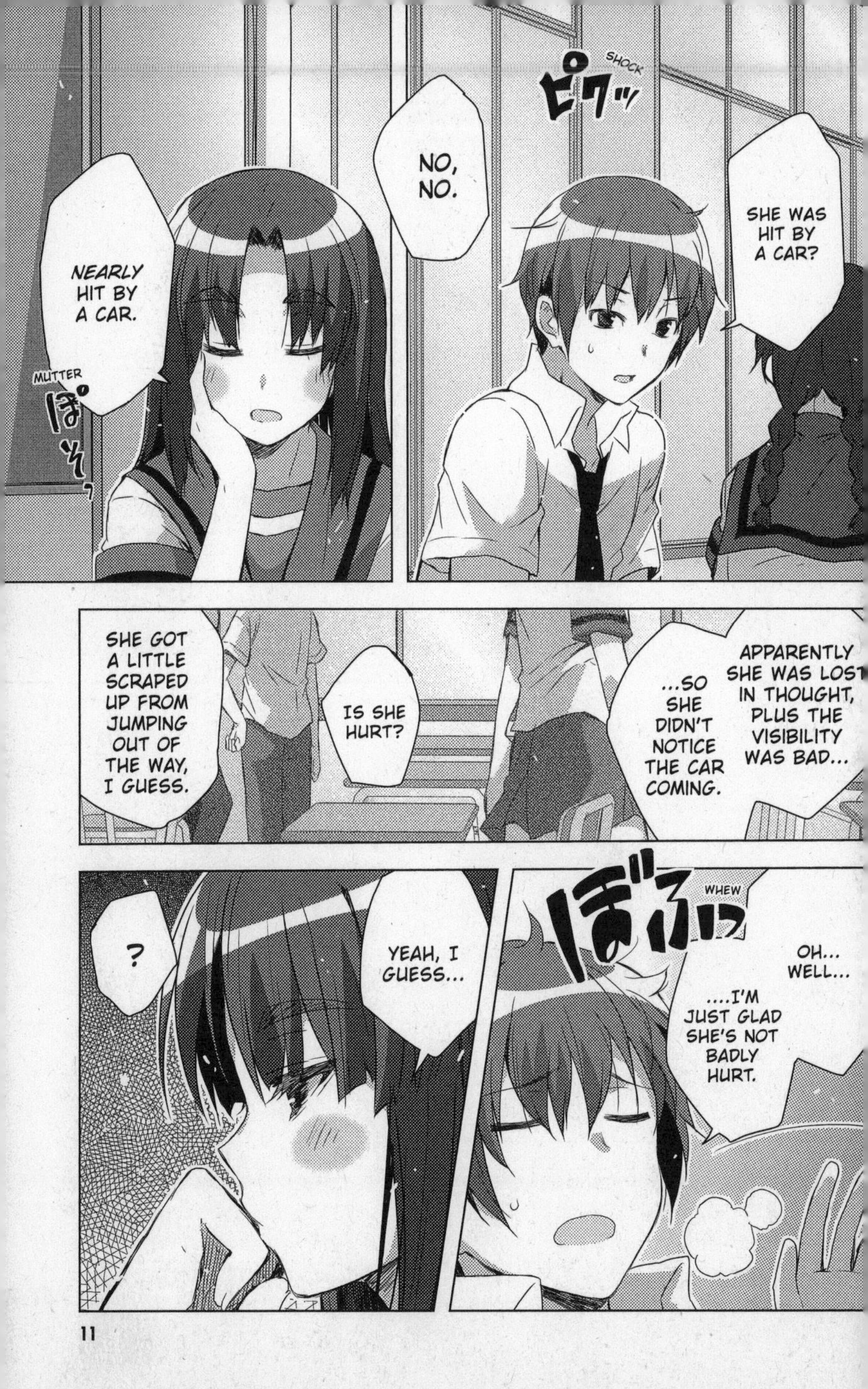
SHOCK
ピクッ
SHE WAS HIT BY A CAR?
NO, NO.
NEARLY HIT BY A CAR.
MUTTER
ぼそっ
APPARENTLY SHE WAS LOST IN THOUGHT, PLUS THE VISIBILITY WAS BAD...
...SO SHE DIDN'T NOTICE THE CAR COMING.
IS SHE HURT?
SHE GOT A LITTLE SCRAPED UP FROM JUMPING OUT OF THE WAY, I GUESS.
WHEW
ぼふっ
OH... WELL...
....I'M JUST GLAD SHE'S NOT BADLY HURT.
YEAH, I GUESS...
?

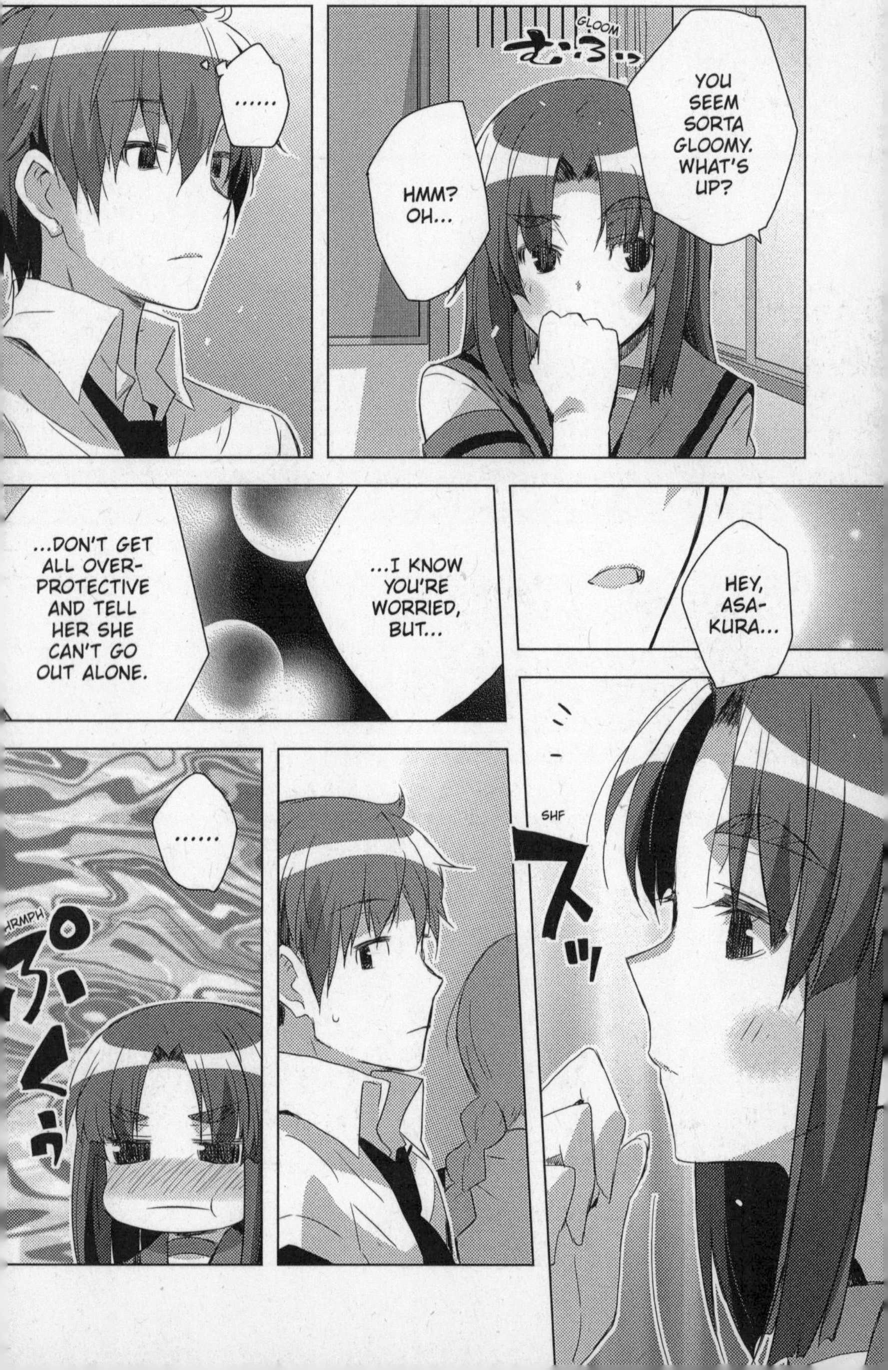
GLOOM
YOU SEEM SORTA GLOOMY. WHAT'S UP?
HMM? OH...
......
HEY, ASA-KURA...
...I KNOW YOU'RE WORRIED, BUT...
...DON'T GET ALL OVER-PROTECTIVE AND TELL HER SHE CAN'T GO OUT ALONE.
SHF
......
HRMPH

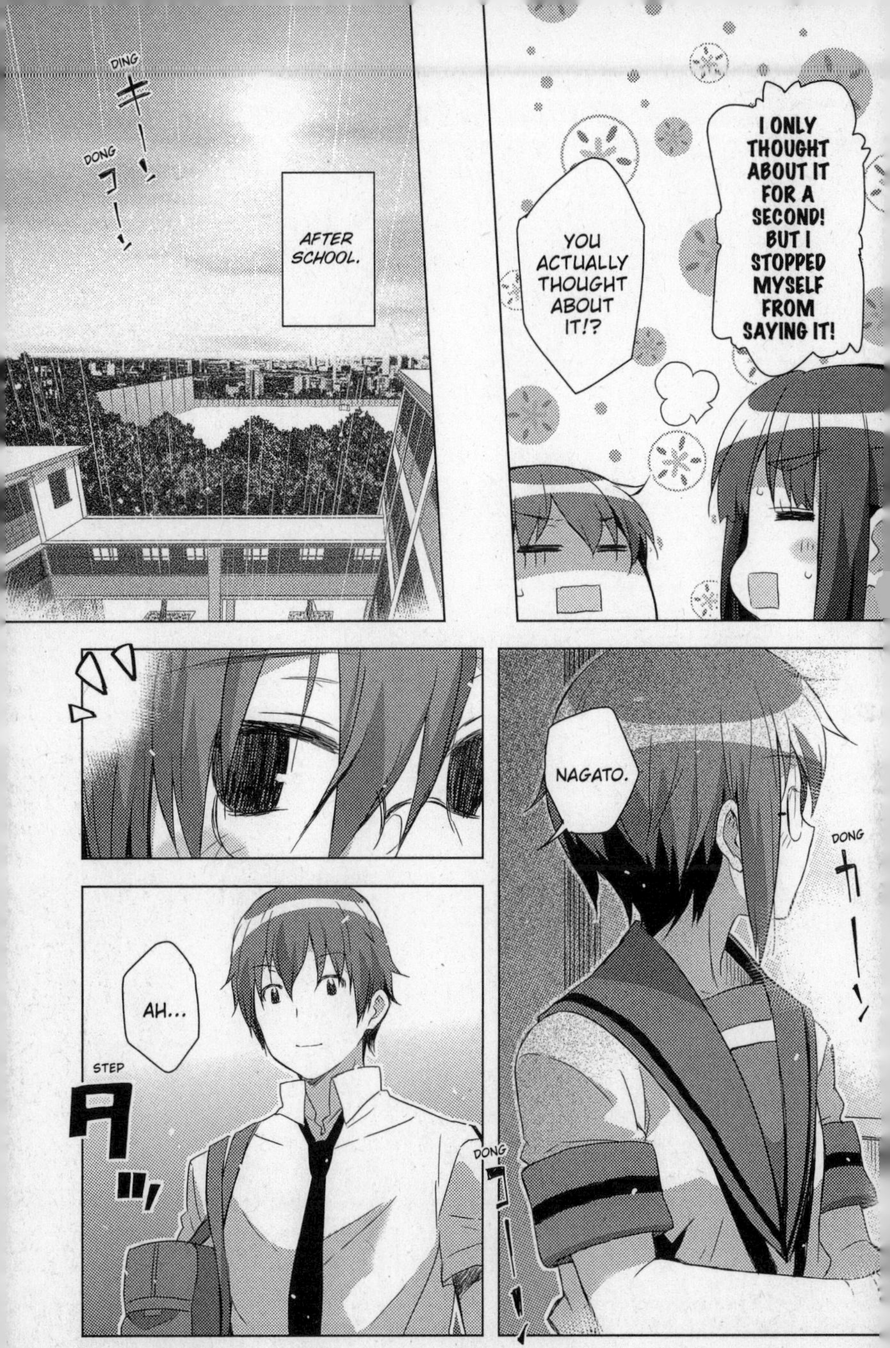
I ONLY THOUGHT ABOUT IT FOR A SECOND! BUT I STOPPED MYSELF FROM SAYING IT!
YOU ACTUALLY THOUGHT ABOUT IT!?
DING
DONG
AFTER SCHOOL.
NAGATO.
DONG
DONG
AH...
STEP

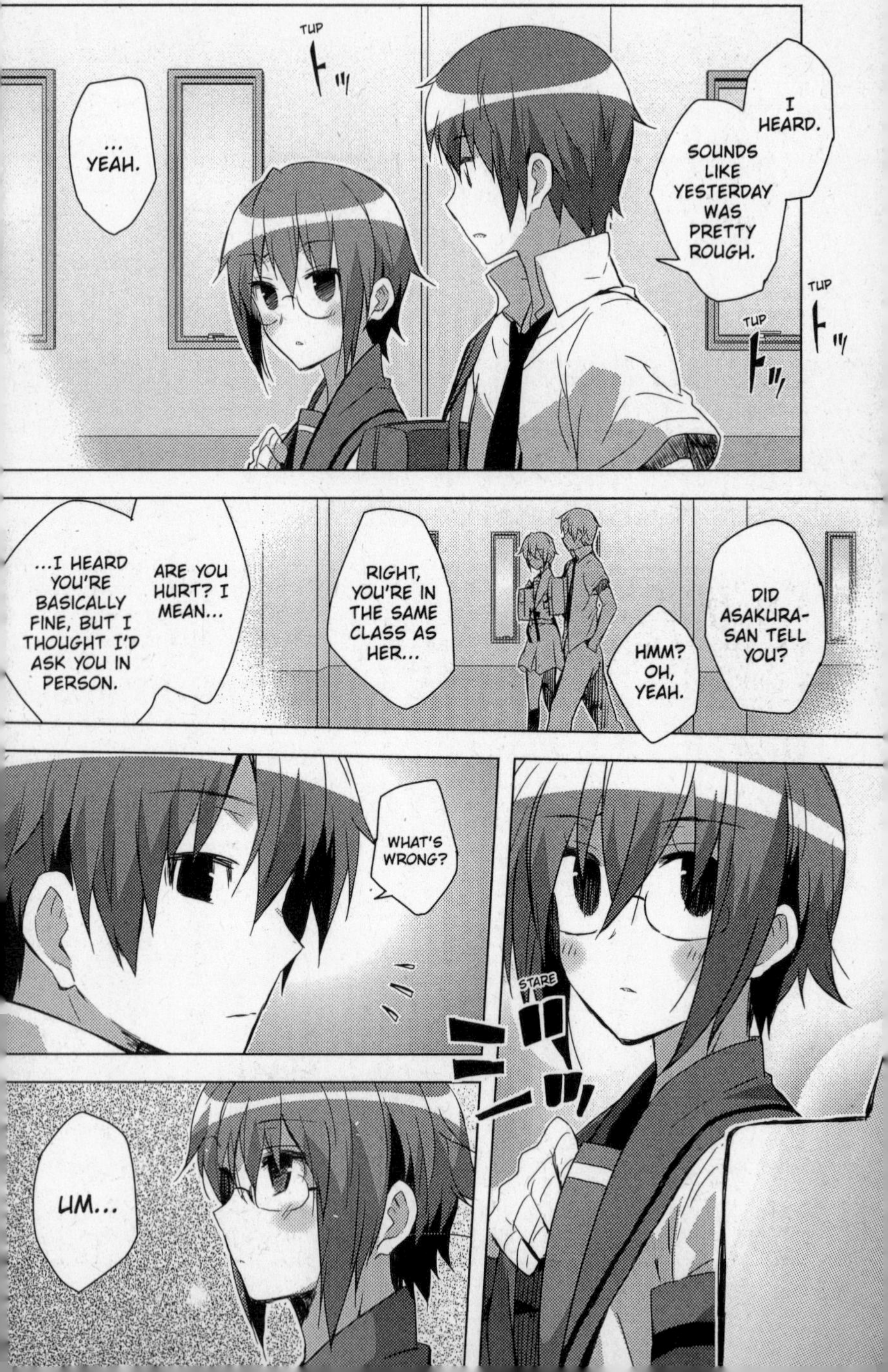
I HEARD. SOUNDS LIKE YESTERDAY WAS PRETTY ROUGH.
TUP
TUP
TUP
... YEAH.
DID ASAKURA-SAN TELL YOU?
HMM? OH, YEAH.
RIGHT, YOU'RE IN THE SAME CLASS AS HER...
ARE YOU HURT? I MEAN...
...I HEARD YOU'RE BASICALLY FINE, BUT I THOUGHT I'D ASK YOU IN PERSON.
STARE
WHAT'S WRONG?
UM...

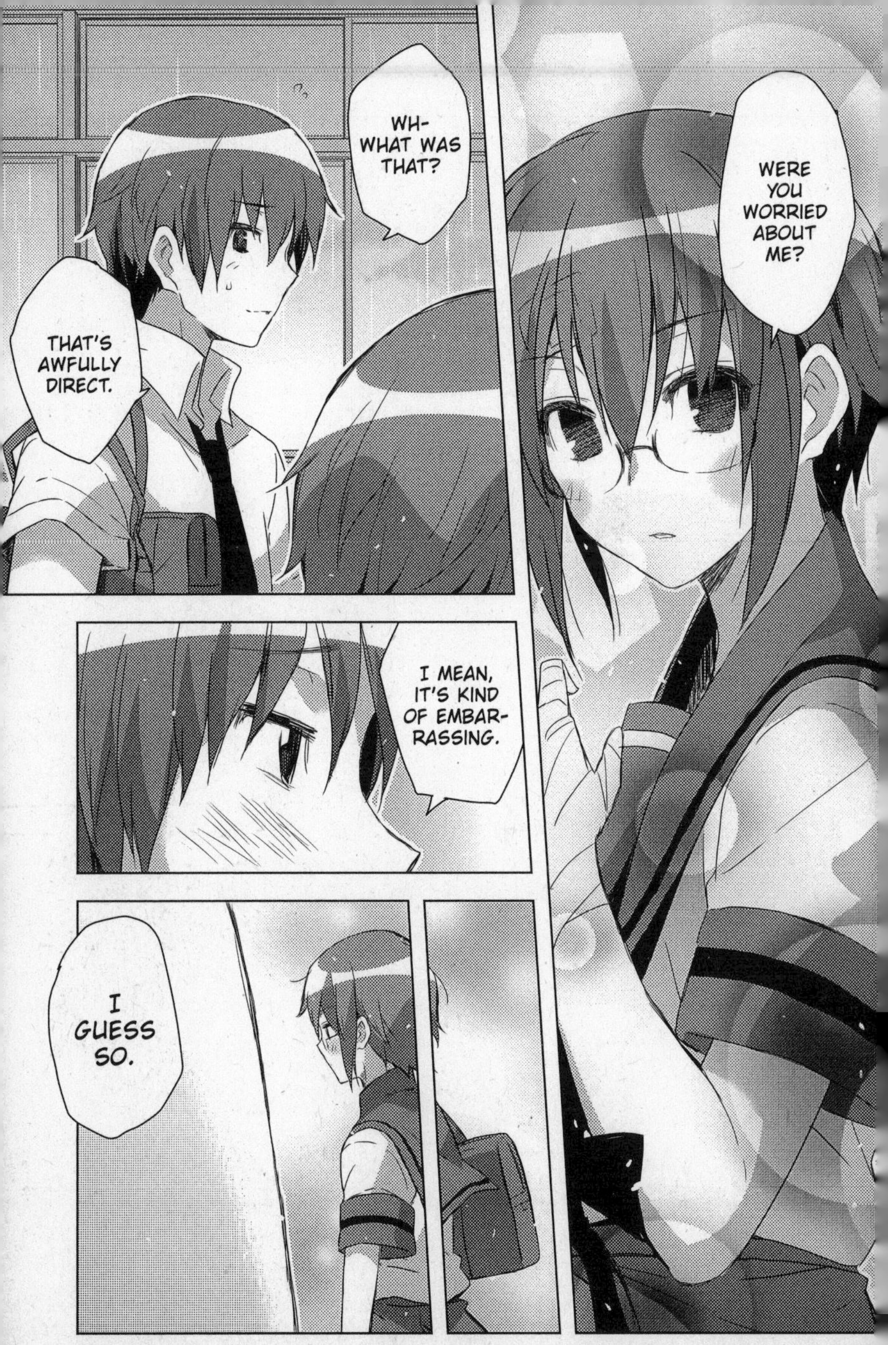
WERE YOU WORRIED ABOUT ME?
WH- WHAT WAS THAT?
THAT'S AWFULLY DIRECT.
I MEAN, IT'S KIND OF EMBAR- RASSING.
I GUESS SO.

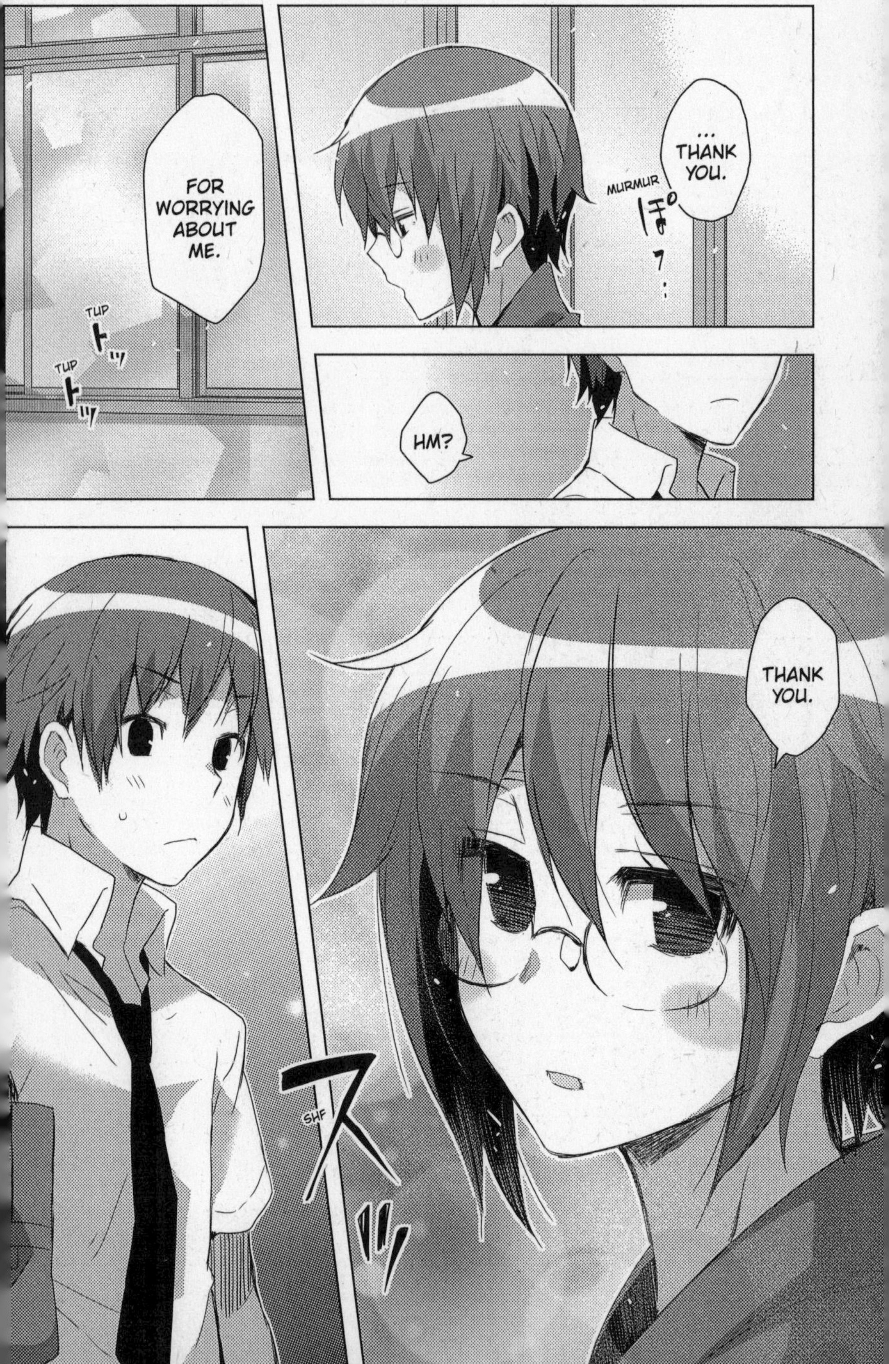
...THANK YOU.
MURMUR
HM?
FOR WORRYING ABOUT ME.
TUP
TUP
THANK YOU.
SHF

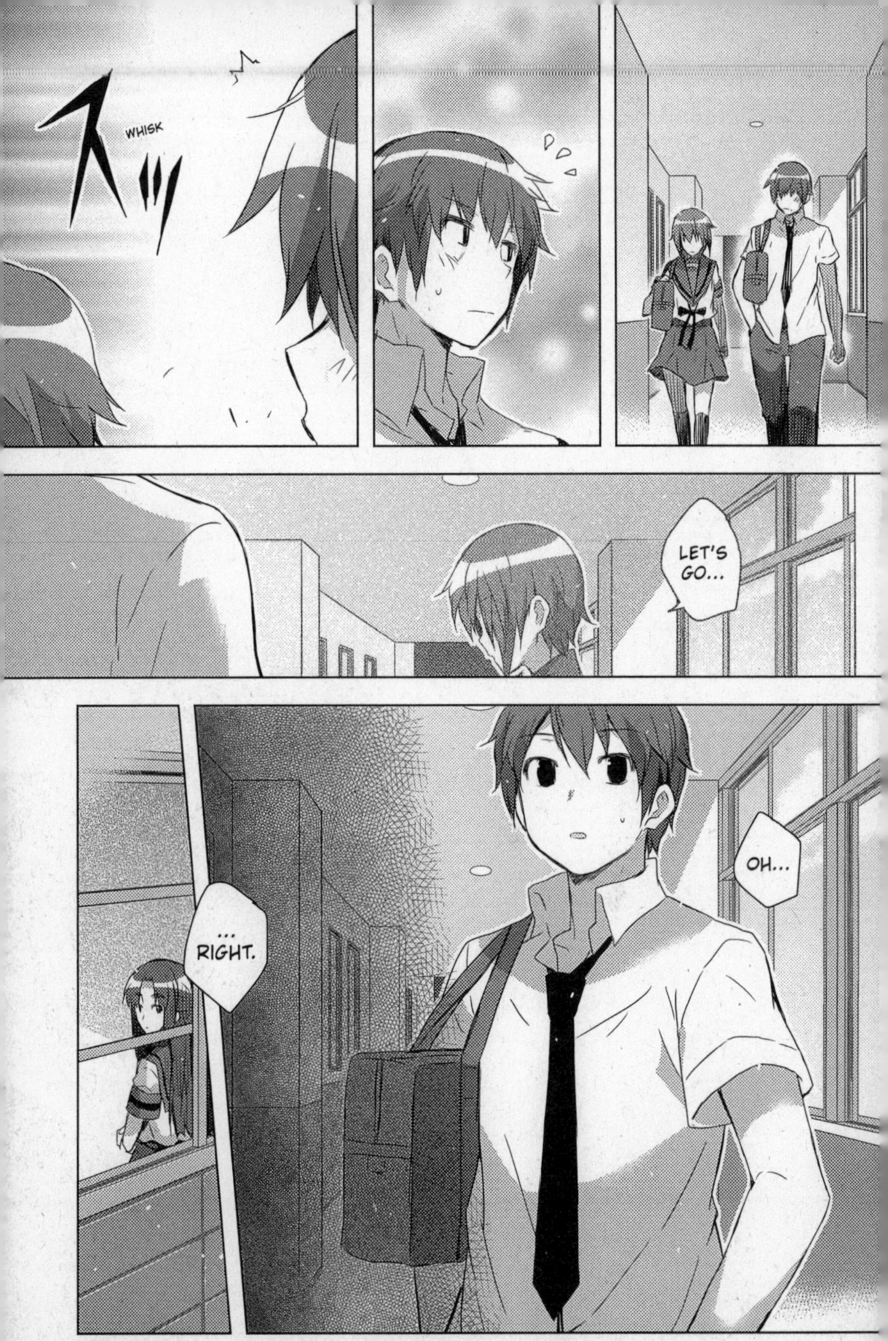
スッ
WHISK
LET'S GO...
OH...
...RIGHT.

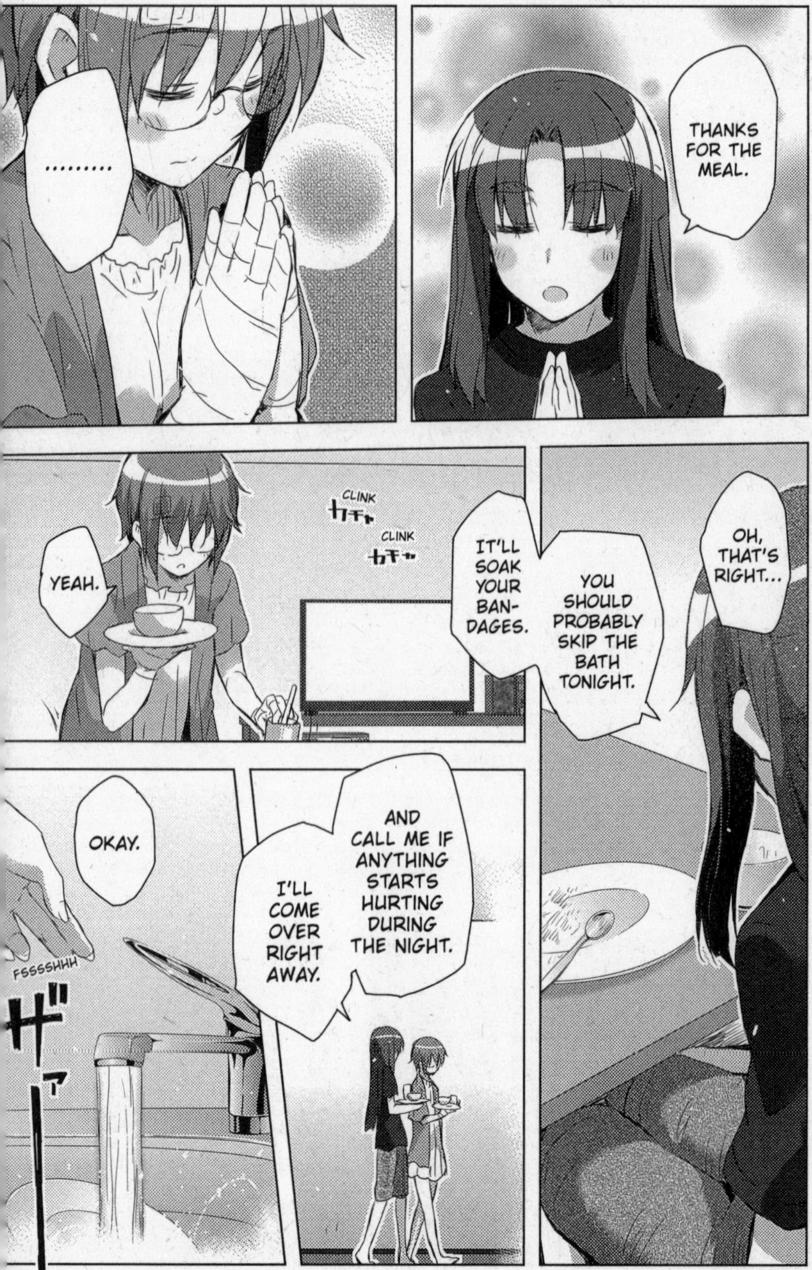
THANKS FOR THE MEAL.
....
OH, THAT'S RIGHT...
YOU SHOULD PROBABLY SKIP THE BATH TONIGHT.
IT'LL SOAK YOUR BAN-DAGES.
CLINK
カチャ
CLINK
カチャ
YEAH.
AND CALL ME IF ANYTHING STARTS HURTING DURING THE NIGHT.
I'LL COME OVER RIGHT AWAY.
OKAY.
FSSSSHHH
ザァー

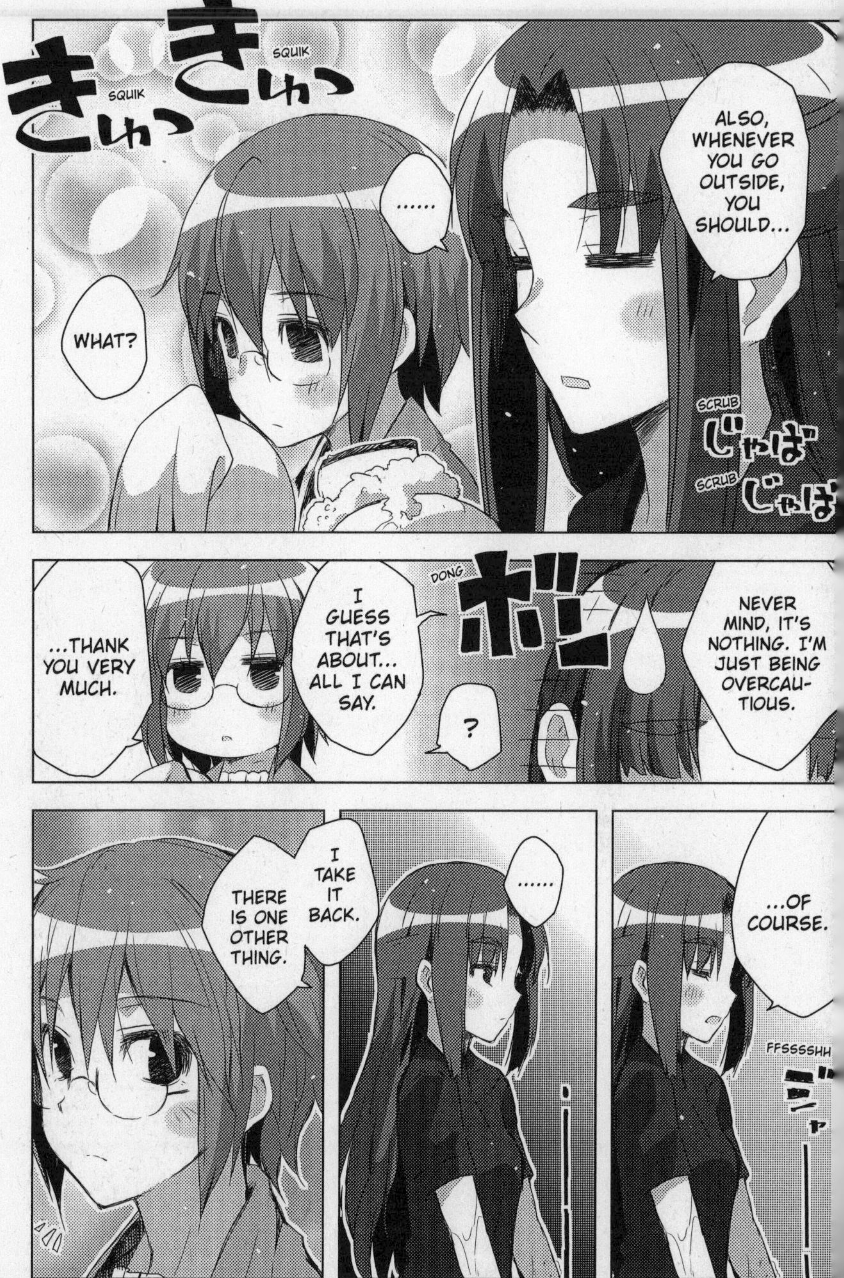
ALSO, WHENEVER YOU GO OUTSIDE, YOU SHOULD...
SCRUB
じゃぼ
SCRUB
じゃぼ
......
SQUIK
きゅっ
SQUIK
きゅっ
WHAT?
NEVER MIND, IT'S NOTHING. I'M JUST BEING OVERCAUTIOUS.
?
DONG
ボン
I GUESS THAT'S ABOUT... ALL I CAN SAY.
...THANK YOU VERY MUCH.
...OF COURSE.
FFSSSSHH
ジャー
......
I TAKE IT BACK.
THERE IS ONE OTHER THING.

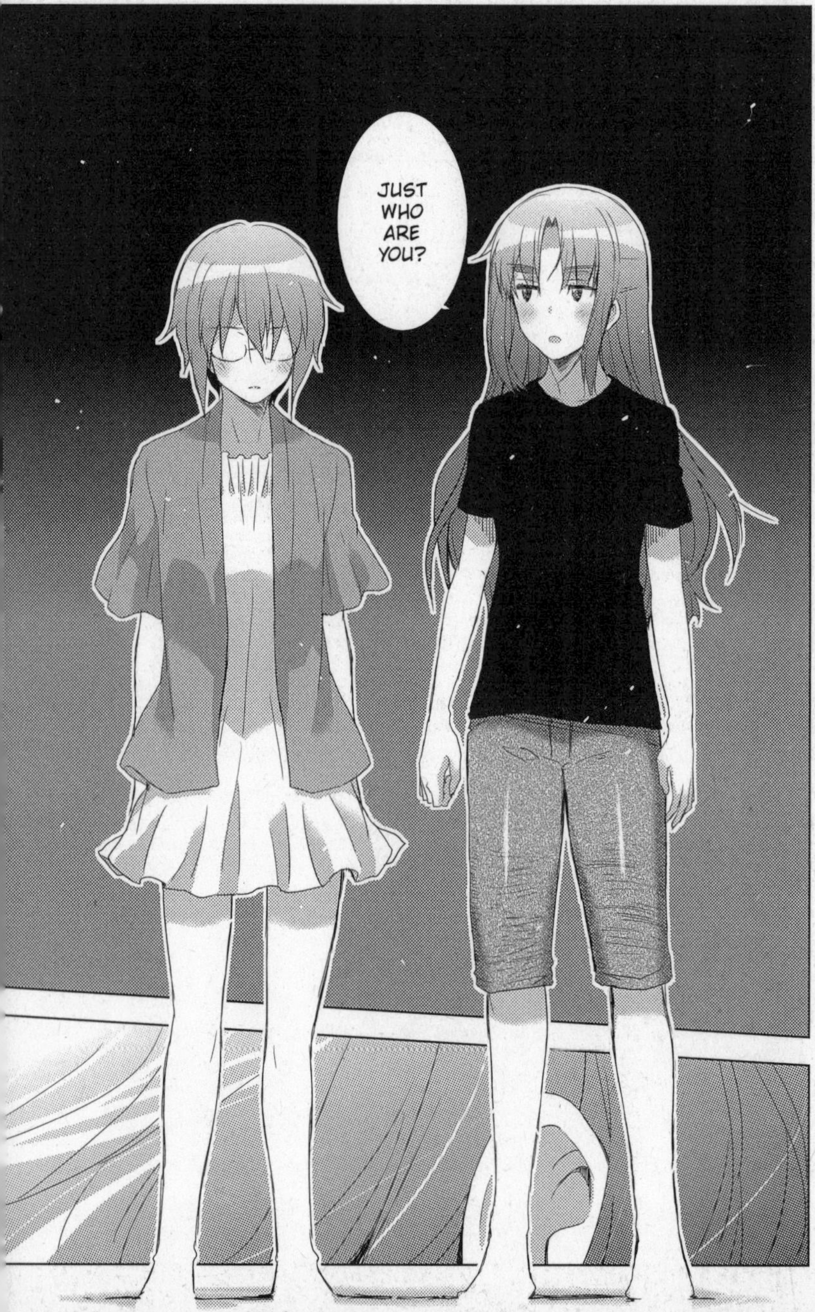
JUST WHO ARE YOU?

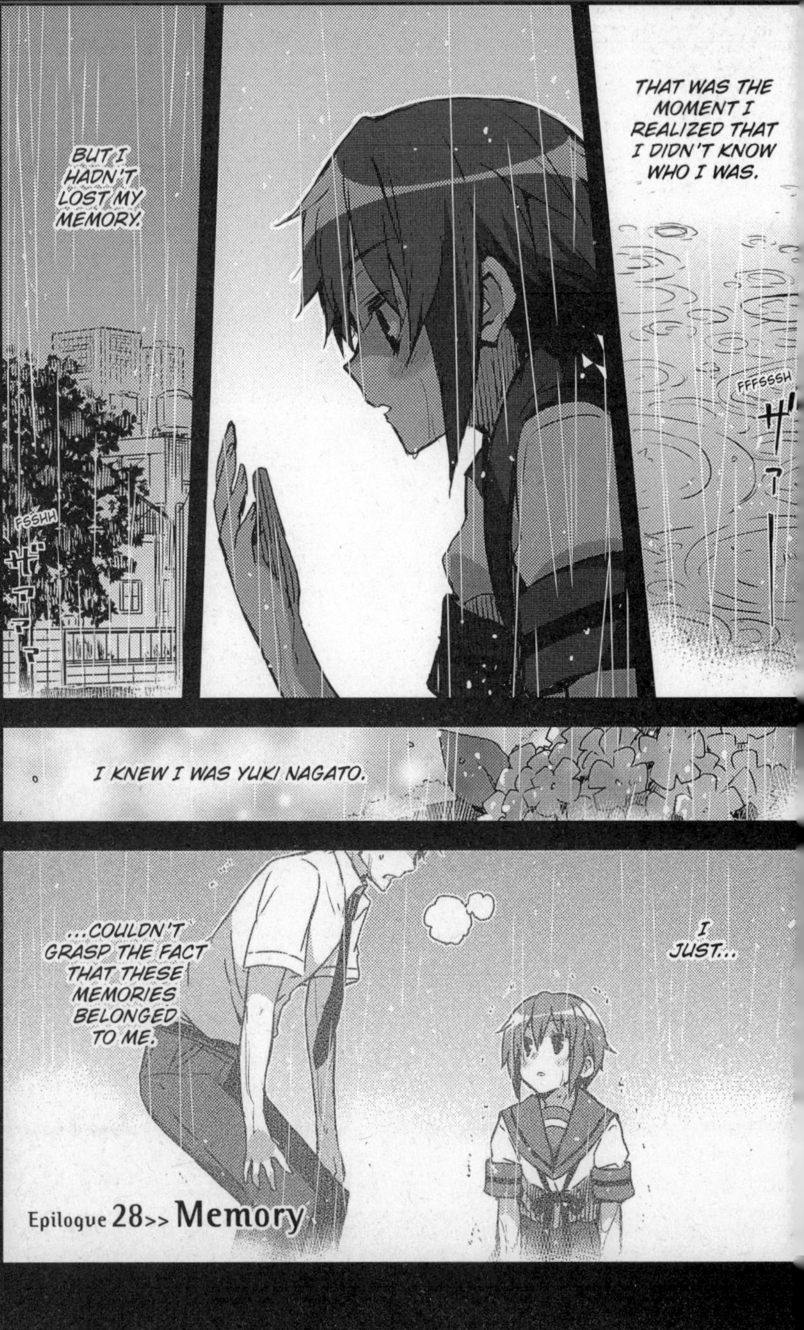

THAT WAS THE MOMENT I REALIZED THAT I DIDN'T KNOW WHO I WAS.
FFFSSSH
ザァー
BUT I HADN'T LOST MY MEMORY.
FSSHH
ザァァァ
I KNEW I WAS YUKI NAGATO.
I JUST...
...COULDN'T GRASP THE FACT THAT THESE MEMORIES BELONGED TO ME.

Epilogue 28>> Memory

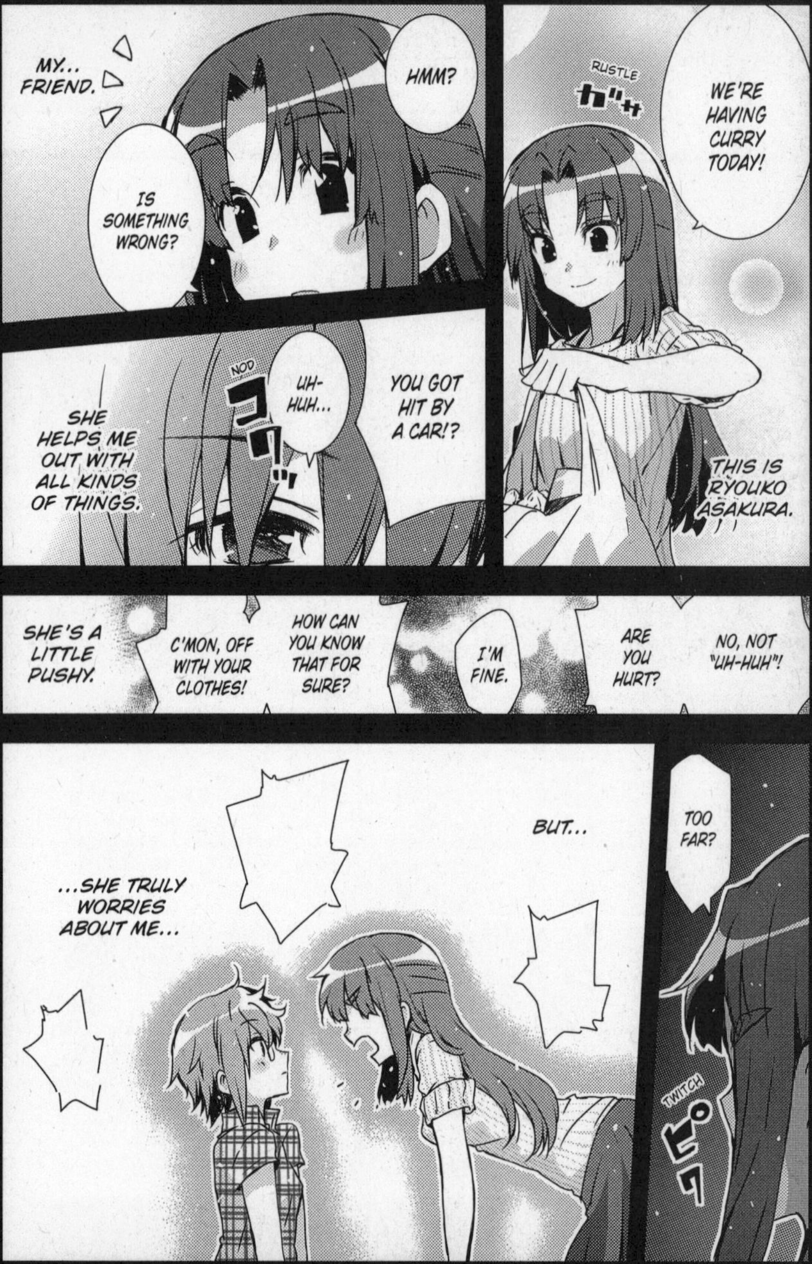
WE'RE HAVING CURRY TODAY!
RUSTLE
THIS IS RYOUKO ASAKURA.
HMM?
IS SOMETHING WRONG?
MY... FRIEND.
YOU GOT HIT BY A CAR!?
UH-HUH...
NOD
SHE HELPS ME OUT WITH ALL KINDS OF THINGS.
NO, NOT "UH-HUH"!
ARE YOU HURT?
I'M FINE.
HOW CAN YOU KNOW THAT FOR SURE?
C'MON, OFF WITH YOUR CLOTHES!
SHE'S A LITTLE PUSHY.
TOO FAR?
TWITCH
BUT...
...SHE TRULY WORRIES ABOUT ME...

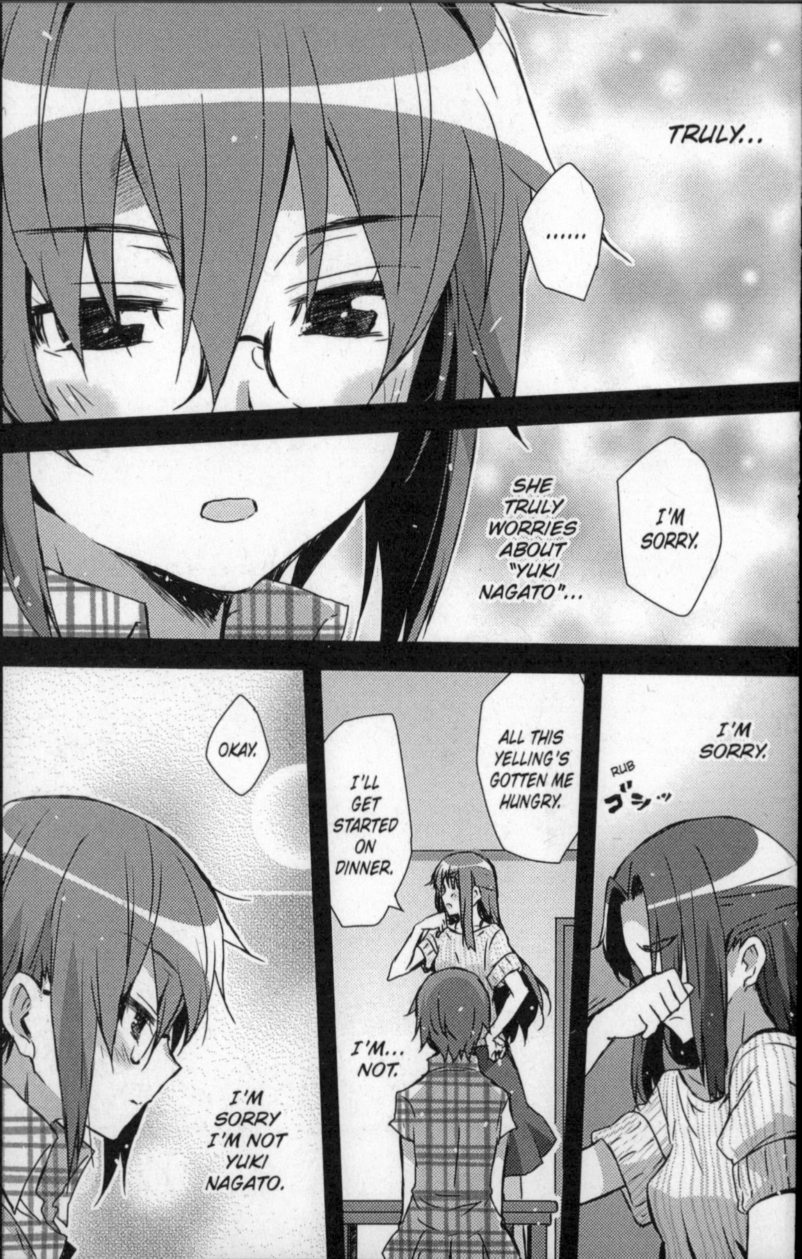
TRULY...
......
I'M SORRY.
SHE TRULY WORRIES ABOUT "YUKI NAGATO"...
I'M SORRY.
RUB
ゴシッ
ALL THIS YELLING'S GOTTEN ME HUNGRY.
I'LL GET STARTED ON DINNER.
I'M... NOT.
OKAY.
I'M SORRY I'M NOT YUKI NAGATO.

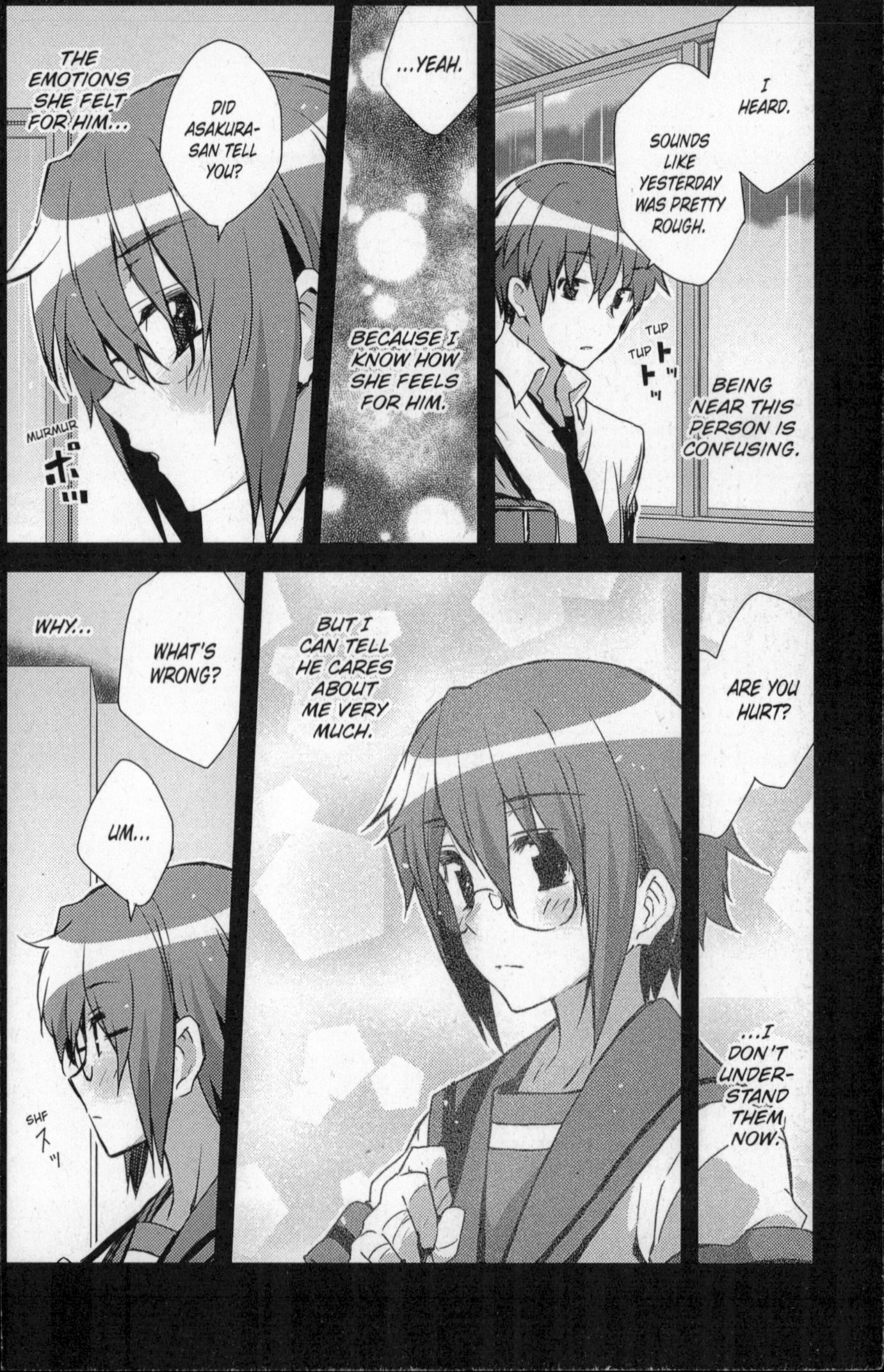
I HEARD.
SOUNDS LIKE YESTERDAY WAS PRETTY ROUGH.
TUP TUP
BEING NEAR THIS PERSON IS CONFUSING.
...YEAH.
BECAUSE I KNOW HOW SHE FEELS FOR HIM.
DID ASAKURA-SAN TELL YOU?
THE EMOTIONS SHE FELT FOR HIM...
MURMUR
ARE YOU HURT?
...I DON'T UNDER-STAND THEM NOW.
BUT I CAN TELL HE CARES ABOUT ME VERY MUCH.
WHAT'S WRONG?
WHY...
UM...
SHF

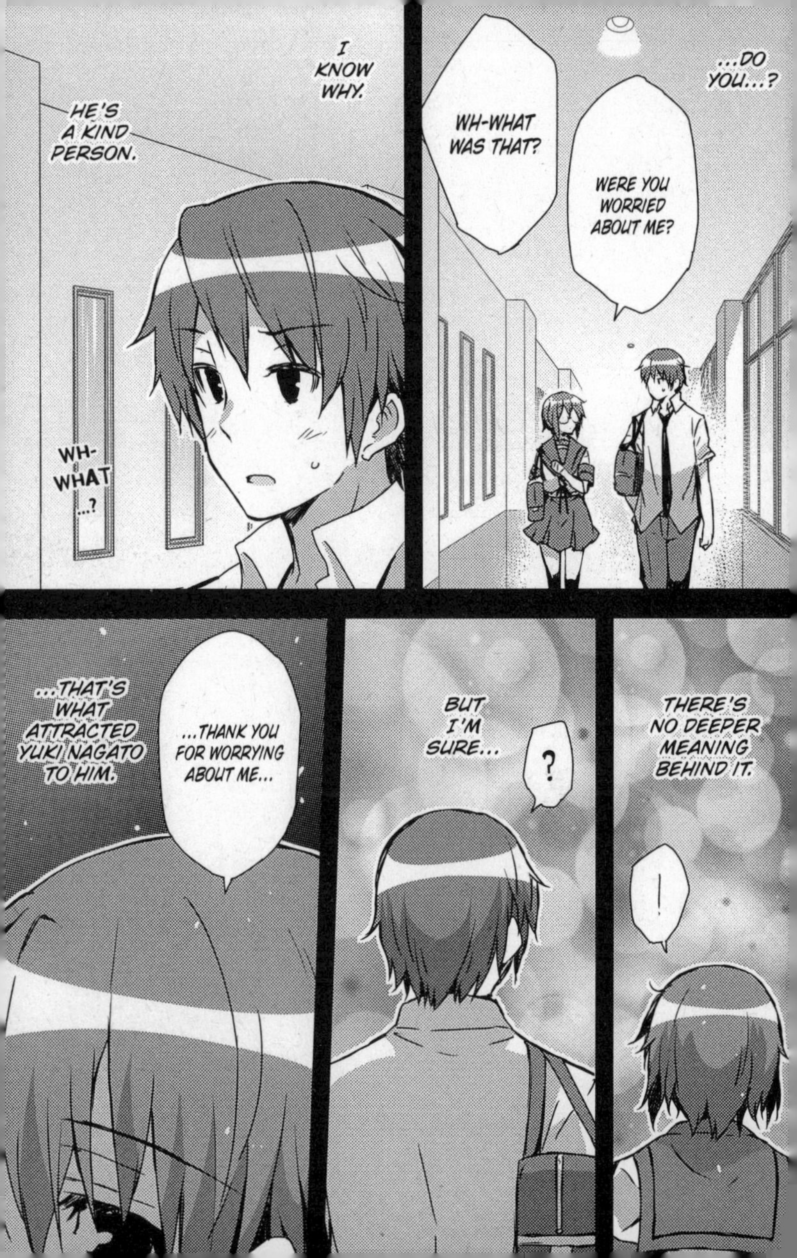
...DO YOU...?
WERE YOU WORRIED ABOUT ME?
WH-WHAT WAS THAT?
I KNOW WHY.
HE'S A KIND PERSON.
WH-WHAT ...?
THERE'S NO DEEPER MEANING BEHIND IT.
!
BUT I'M SURE...
?
...THANK YOU FOR WORRYING ABOUT ME...
...THAT'S WHAT ATTRACTED YUKI NAGATO TO HIM.

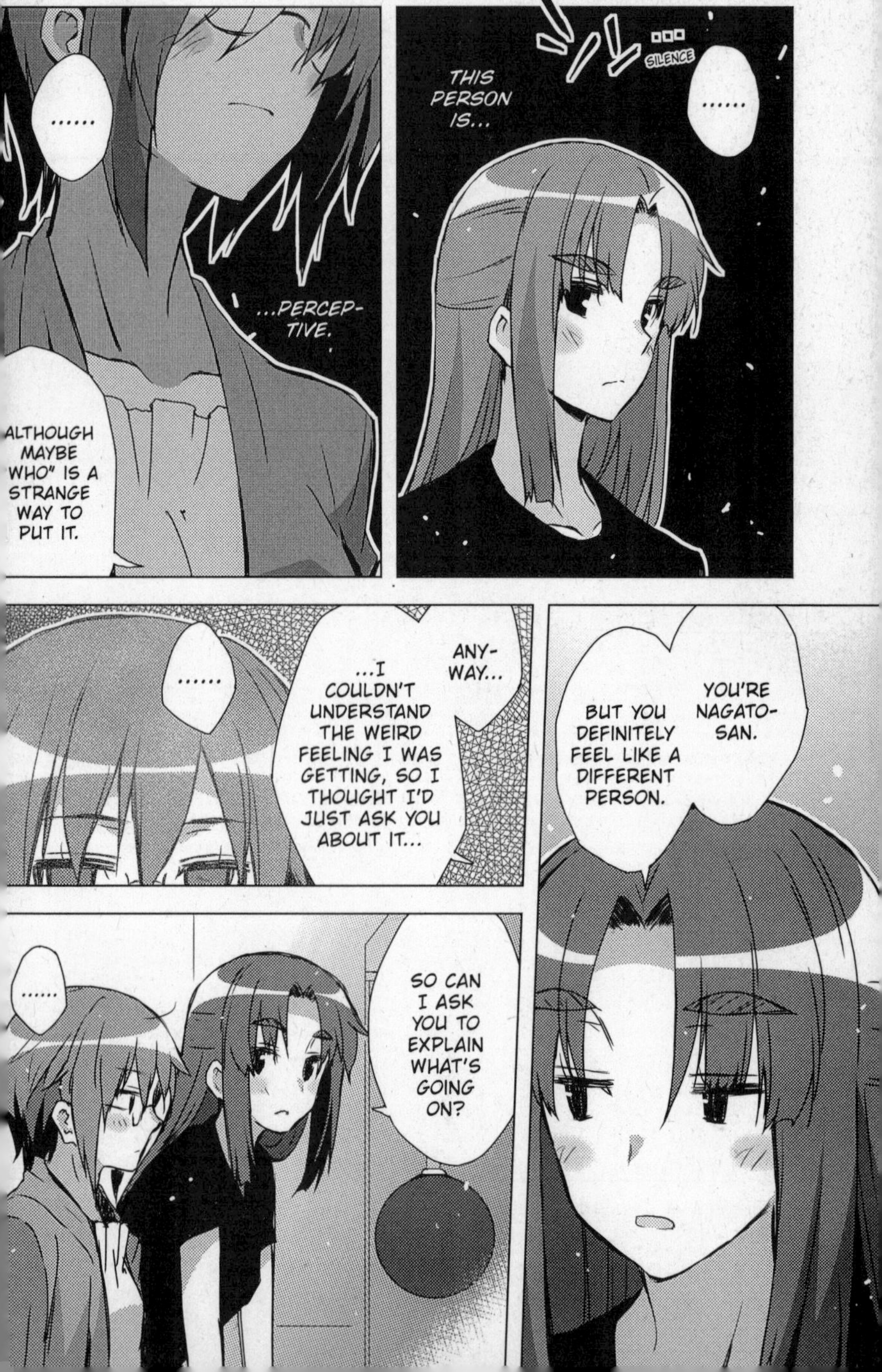
SILENCE
......
THIS PERSON IS...
......
...PERCEP-TIVE.
ALTHOUGH MAYBE "WHO" IS A STRANGE WAY TO PUT IT.
YOU'RE NAGATO-SAN.
BUT YOU DEFINITELY FEEL LIKE A DIFFERENT PERSON.
ANY-WAY...
...I COULDN'T UNDERSTAND THE WEIRD FEELING I WAS GETTING, SO I THOUGHT I'D JUST ASK YOU ABOUT IT...
......
SO CAN I ASK YOU TO EXPLAIN WHAT'S GOING ON?
......

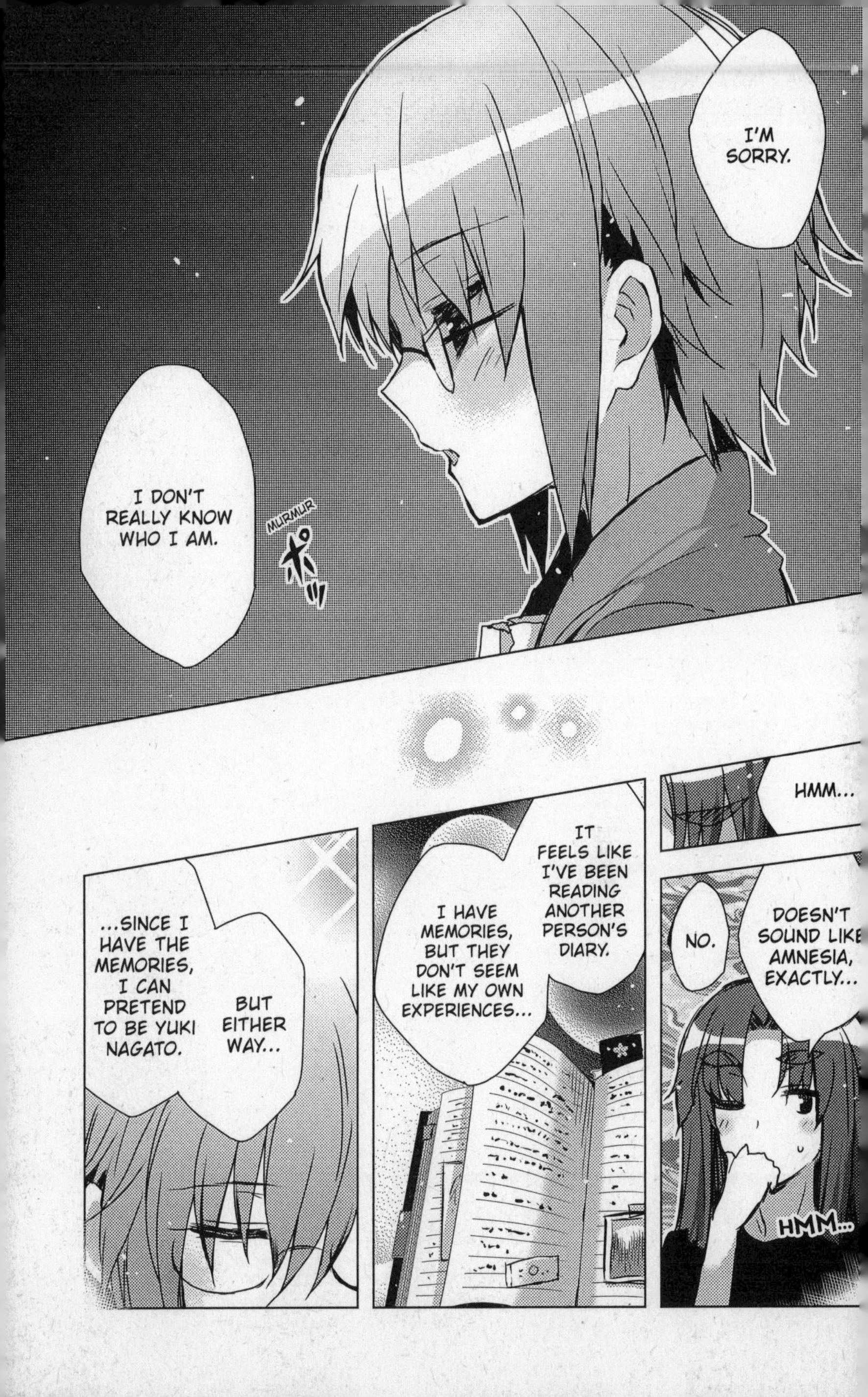
I'M SORRY.
MURMUR
I DON'T REALLY KNOW WHO I AM.
HMM...
DOESN'T SOUND LIKE AMNESIA, EXACTLY...
NO.
HMM...
IT FEELS LIKE I'VE BEEN READING ANOTHER PERSON'S DIARY.
I HAVE MEMORIES, BUT THEY DON'T SEEM LIKE MY OWN EXPERIENCES...
BUT EITHER WAY...
...SINCE I HAVE THE MEMORIES, I CAN PRETEND TO BE YUKI NAGATO.

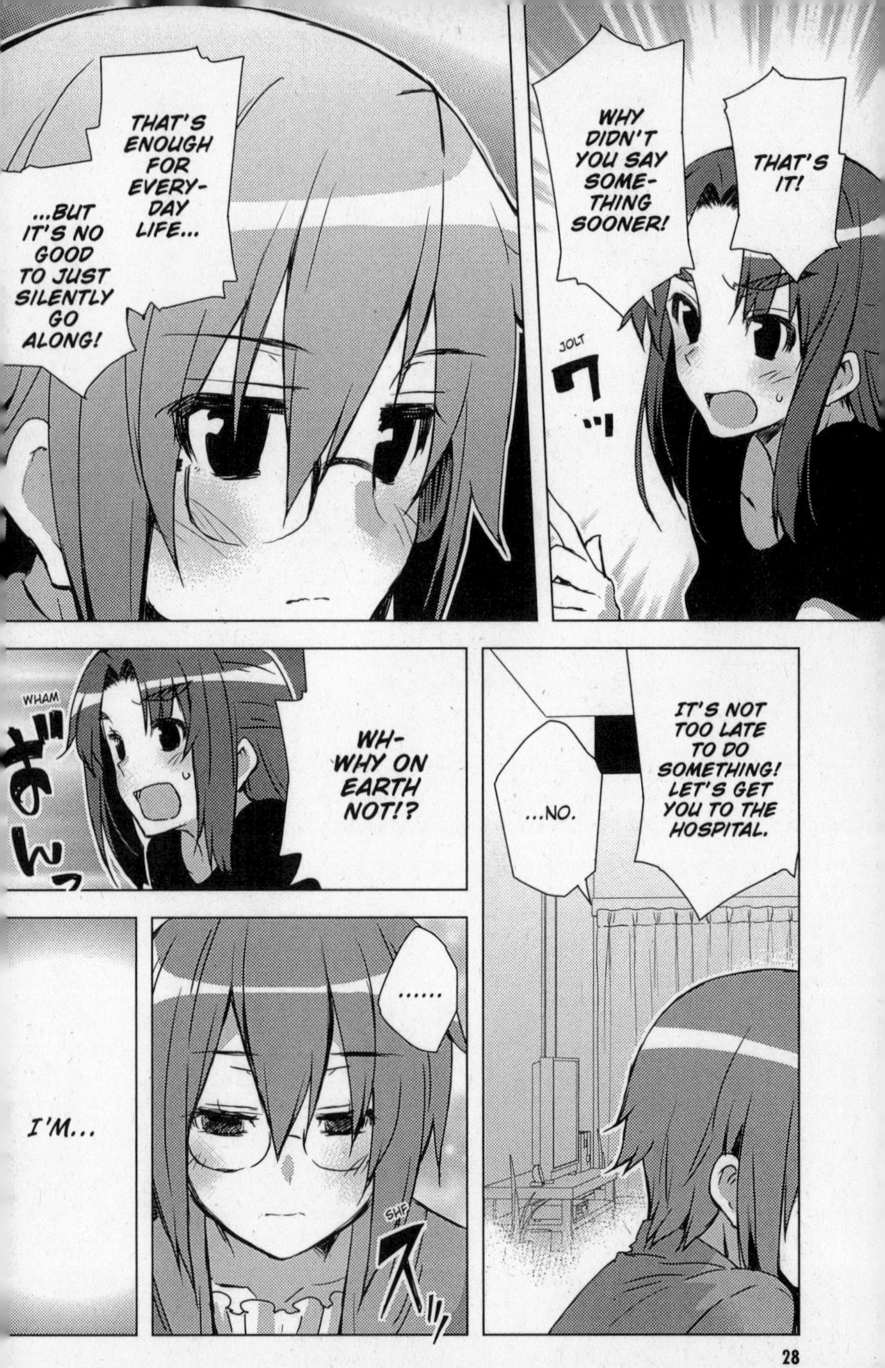
THAT'S IT!
WHY DIDN'T YOU SAY SOME-THING SOONER!
JOLT
ワッ
THAT'S ENOUGH FOR EVERY-DAY LIFE...
...BUT IT'S NO GOOD TO JUST SILENTLY GO ALONG!
IT'S NOT TOO LATE TO DO SOMETHING! LET'S GET YOU TO THE HOSPITAL.
...NO.
WH-WHY ON EARTH NOT!?
WHAM
ばんっ
......
SHF
スッ
I'M...

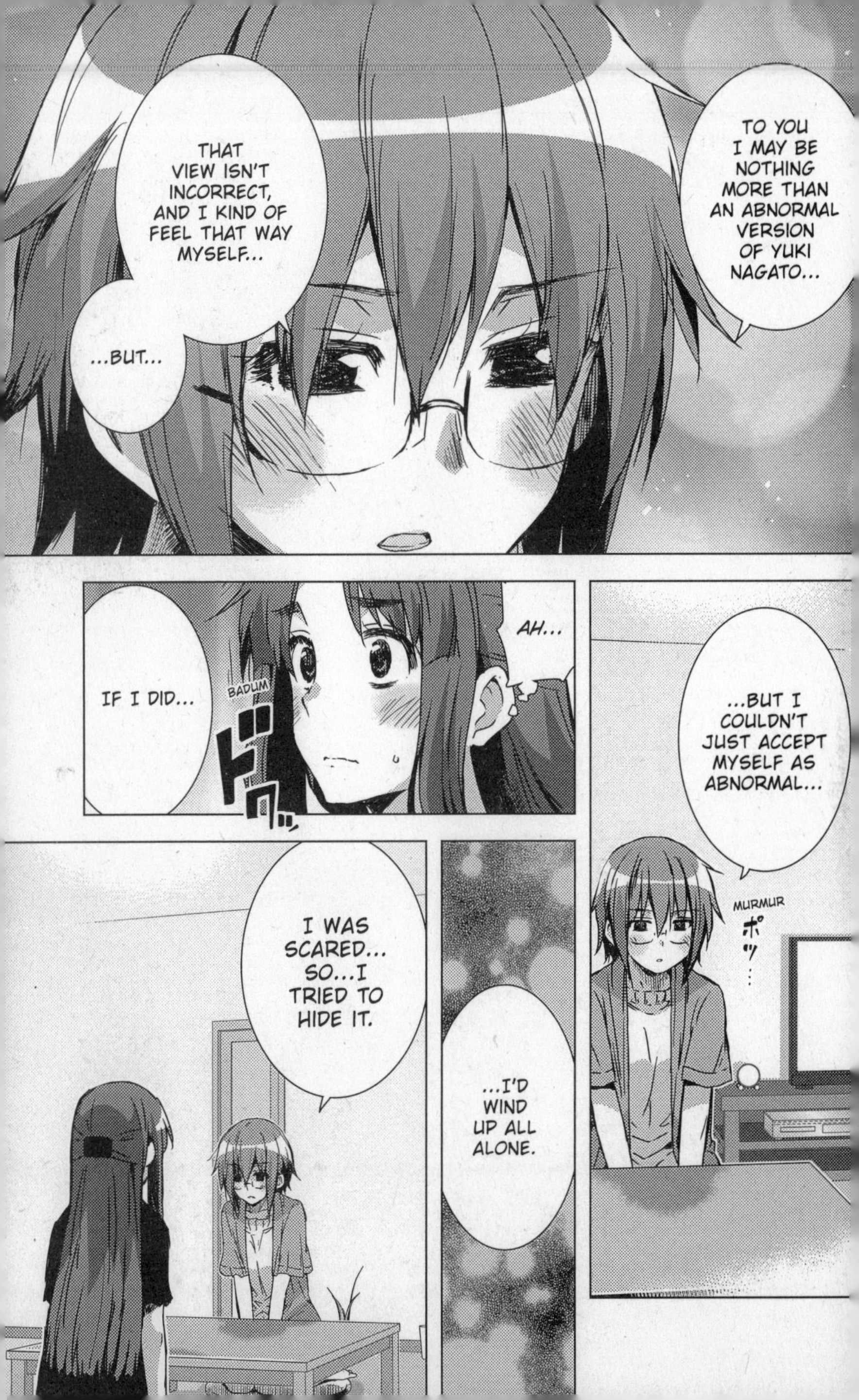
TO YOU I MAY BE NOTHING MORE THAN AN ABNORMAL VERSION OF YUKI NAGATO...
THAT VIEW ISN'T INCORRECT, AND I KIND OF FEEL THAT WAY MYSELF...
...BUT...
...BUT I COULDN'T JUST ACCEPT MYSELF AS ABNORMAL...
MURMUR
ポツ...
AH...
BADUM
ドクン
IF I DID...
...I'D WIND UP ALL ALONE.
I WAS SCARED... SO...I TRIED TO HIDE IT.

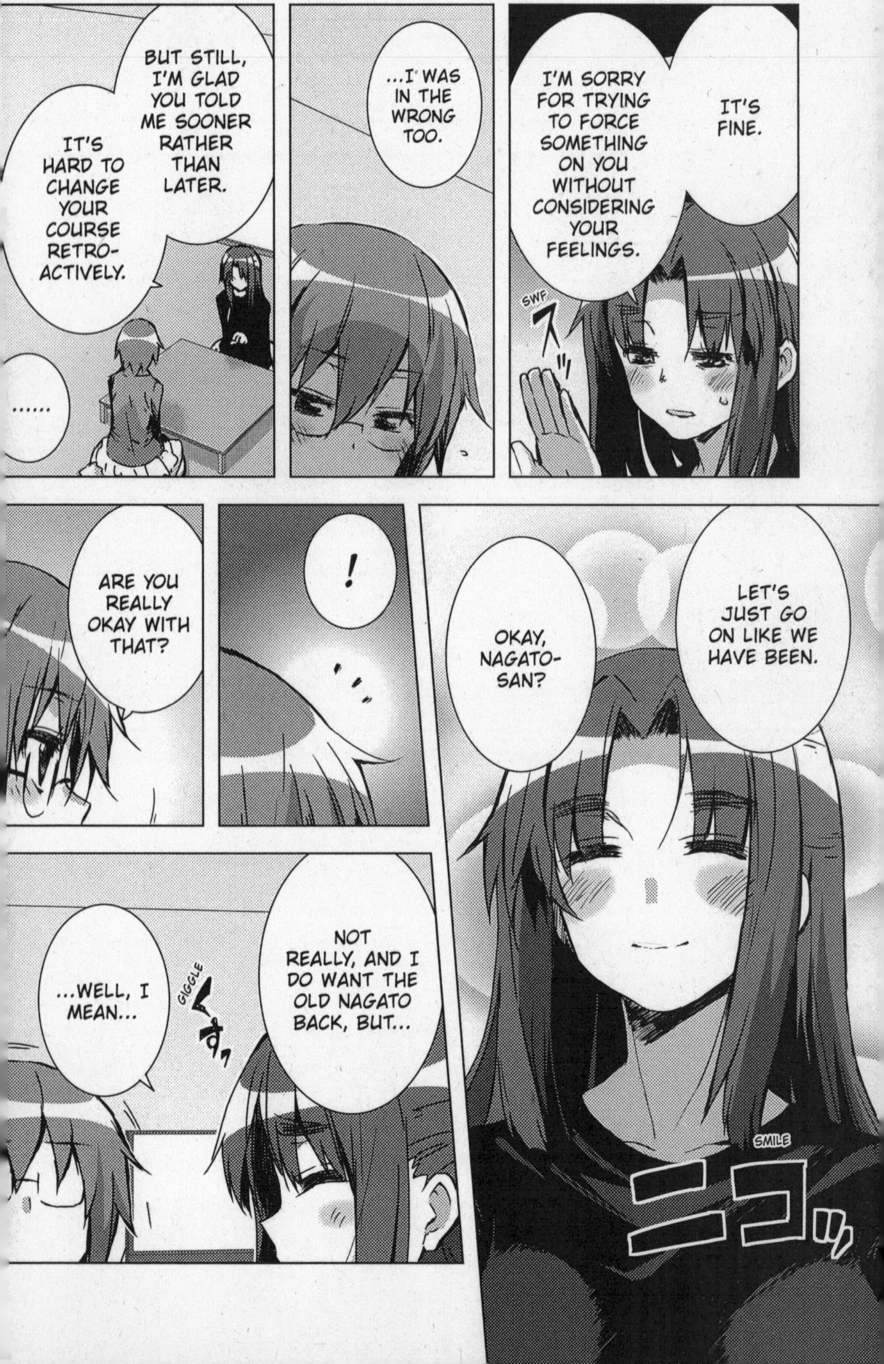
IT'S FINE.
I'M SORRY FOR TRYING TO FORCE SOMETHING ON YOU WITHOUT CONSIDERING YOUR FEELINGS.
SWF
...I WAS IN THE WRONG TOO.
BUT STILL, I'M GLAD YOU TOLD ME SOONER RATHER THAN LATER.
IT'S HARD TO CHANGE YOUR COURSE RETRO-ACTIVELY.
......
LET'S JUST GO ON LIKE WE HAVE BEEN.
OKAY, NAGATO-SAN?
SMILE
!
ARE YOU REALLY OKAY WITH THAT?
NOT REALLY, AND I DO WANT THE OLD NAGATO BACK, BUT...
GIGGLE
...WELL, I MEAN...

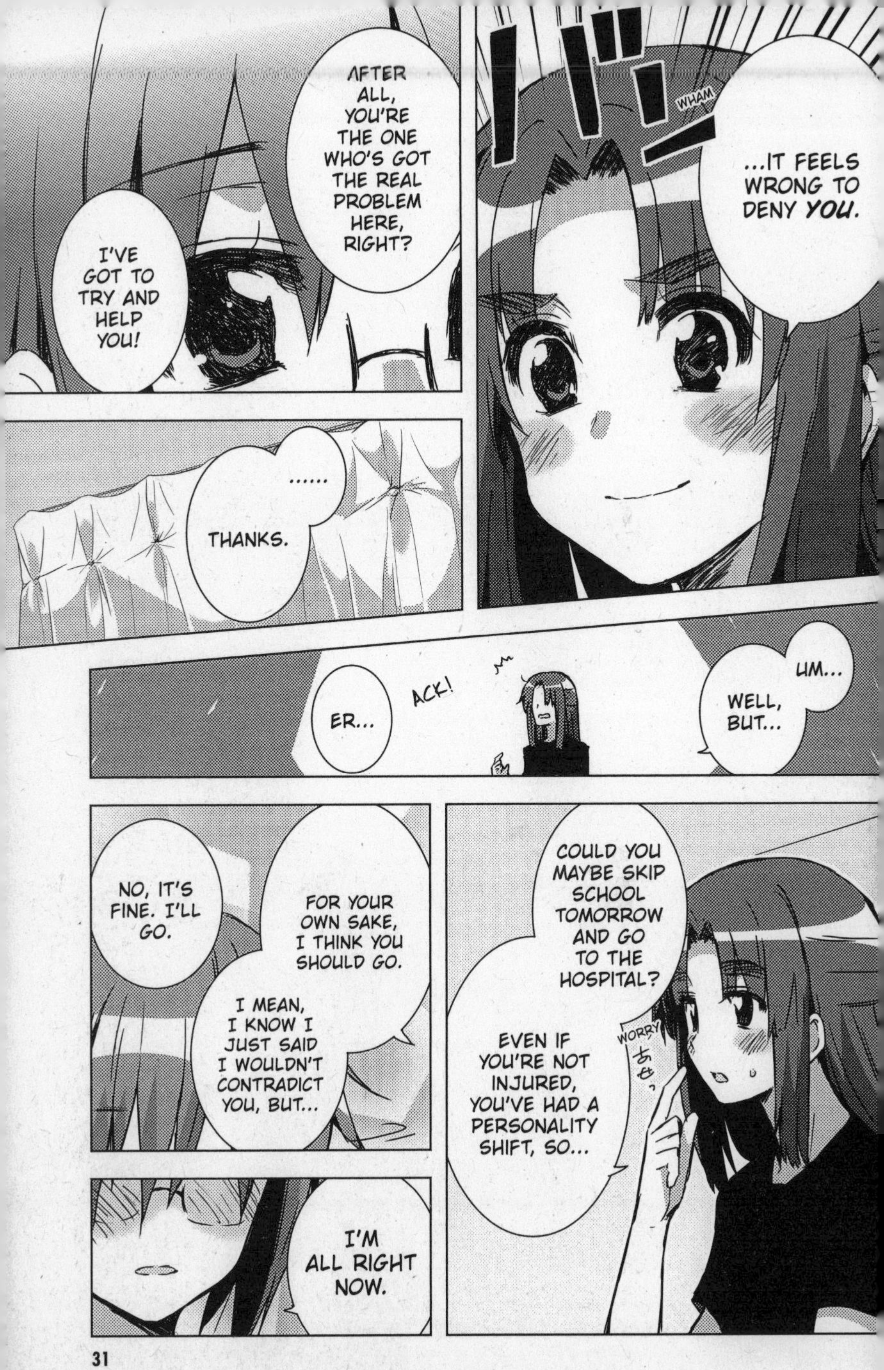
WHAM
...IT FEELS WRONG TO DENY *YOU*.
AFTER ALL, YOU'RE THE ONE WHO'S GOT THE REAL PROBLEM HERE, RIGHT?
I'VE GOT TO TRY AND HELP YOU!
......
THANKS.
UM...
WELL, BUT...
ACK!
ER...
COULD YOU MAYBE SKIP SCHOOL TOMORROW AND GO TO THE HOSPITAL?
WORRY
EVEN IF YOU'RE NOT INJURED, YOU'VE HAD A PERSONALITY SHIFT, SO...
FOR YOUR OWN SAKE, I THINK YOU SHOULD GO.
I MEAN, I KNOW I JUST SAID I WOULDN'T CONTRADICT YOU, BUT...
NO, IT'S FINE. I'LL GO.
I'M ALL RIGHT NOW.

UTH HOSPITAL

......

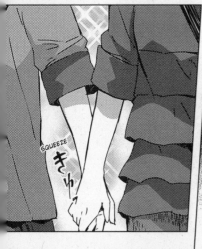

SQUEEZE
キゅ

ガ"
アァァァ
WHHSSH

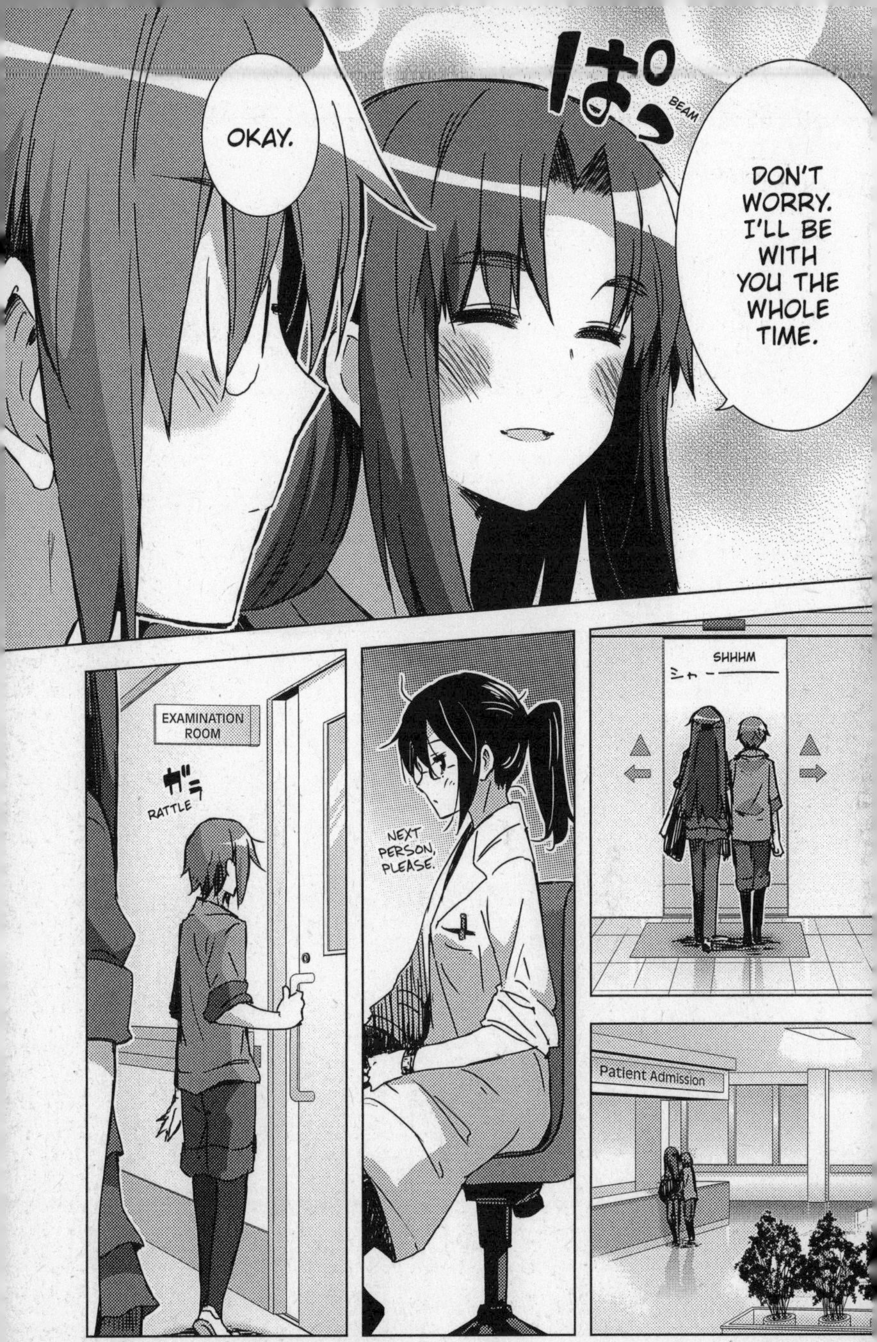
DON'T WORRY. I'LL BE WITH YOU THE WHOLE TIME.
ぱっ
BEAM
OKAY.
シャー
SHHHM
Patient Admission
NEXT PERSON, PLEASE.
EXAMINATION ROOM
ガラ
RATTLE

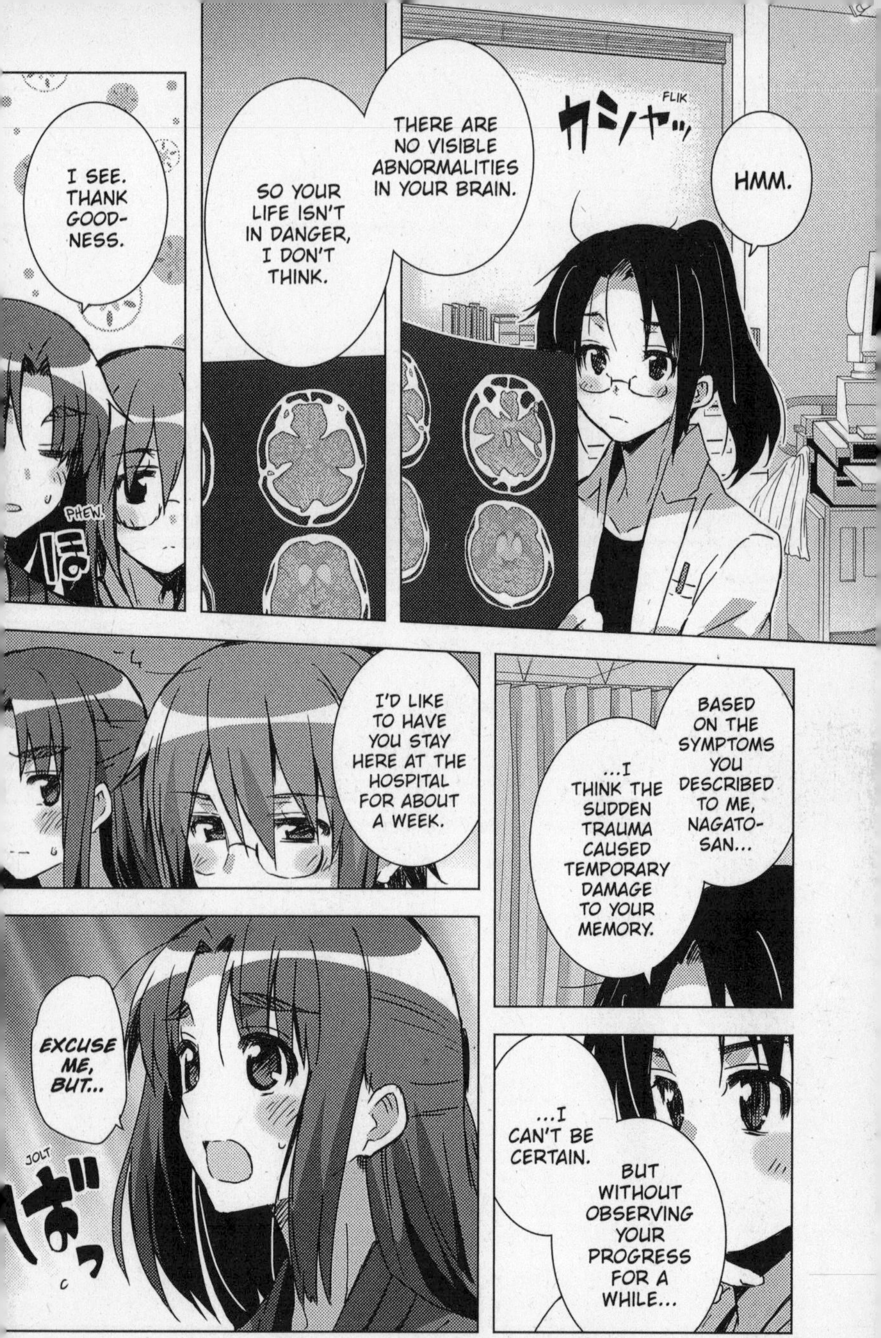
FLIK
HMM.
THERE ARE NO VISIBLE ABNORMALITIES IN YOUR BRAIN.
SO YOUR LIFE ISN'T IN DANGER, I DON'T THINK.
I SEE. THANK GOOD-NESS.
PHEW.
BASED ON THE SYMPTOMS YOU DESCRIBED TO ME, NAGATO-SAN...
...I THINK THE SUDDEN TRAUMA CAUSED TEMPORARY DAMAGE TO YOUR MEMORY.
I'D LIKE TO HAVE YOU STAY HERE AT THE HOSPITAL FOR ABOUT A WEEK.
...I CAN'T BE CERTAIN.
BUT WITHOUT OBSERVING YOUR PROGRESS FOR A WHILE...
EXCUSE ME, BUT...
JOLT

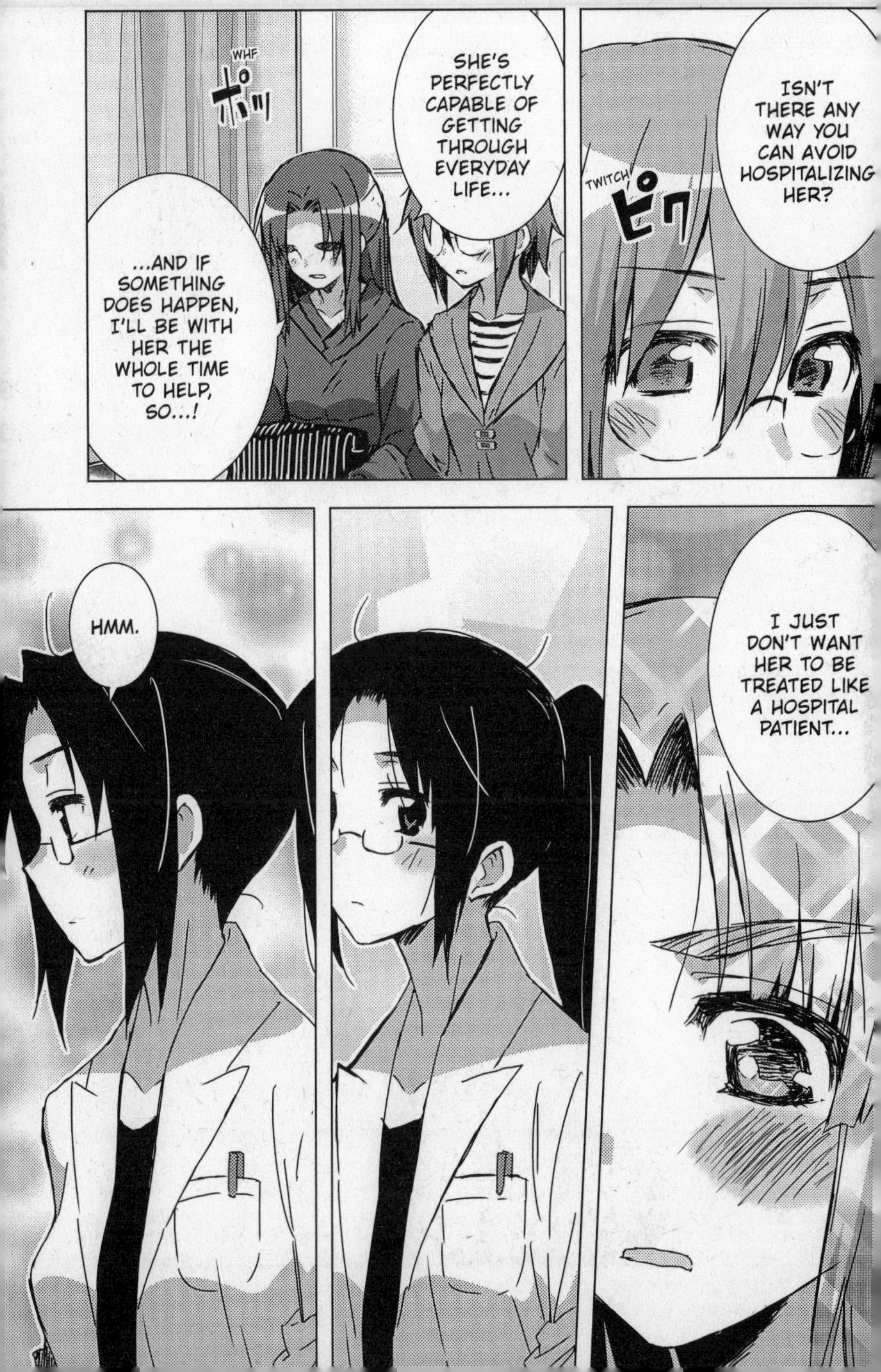
ISN'T THERE ANY WAY YOU CAN AVOID HOSPITALIZING HER?
TWITCH
ピク
SHE'S PERFECTLY CAPABLE OF GETTING THROUGH EVERYDAY LIFE...
WHF
ポッ
...AND IF SOMETHING DOES HAPPEN, I'LL BE WITH HER THE WHOLE TIME TO HELP, SO...!
I JUST DON'T WANT HER TO BE TREATED LIKE A HOSPITAL PATIENT...
HMM.

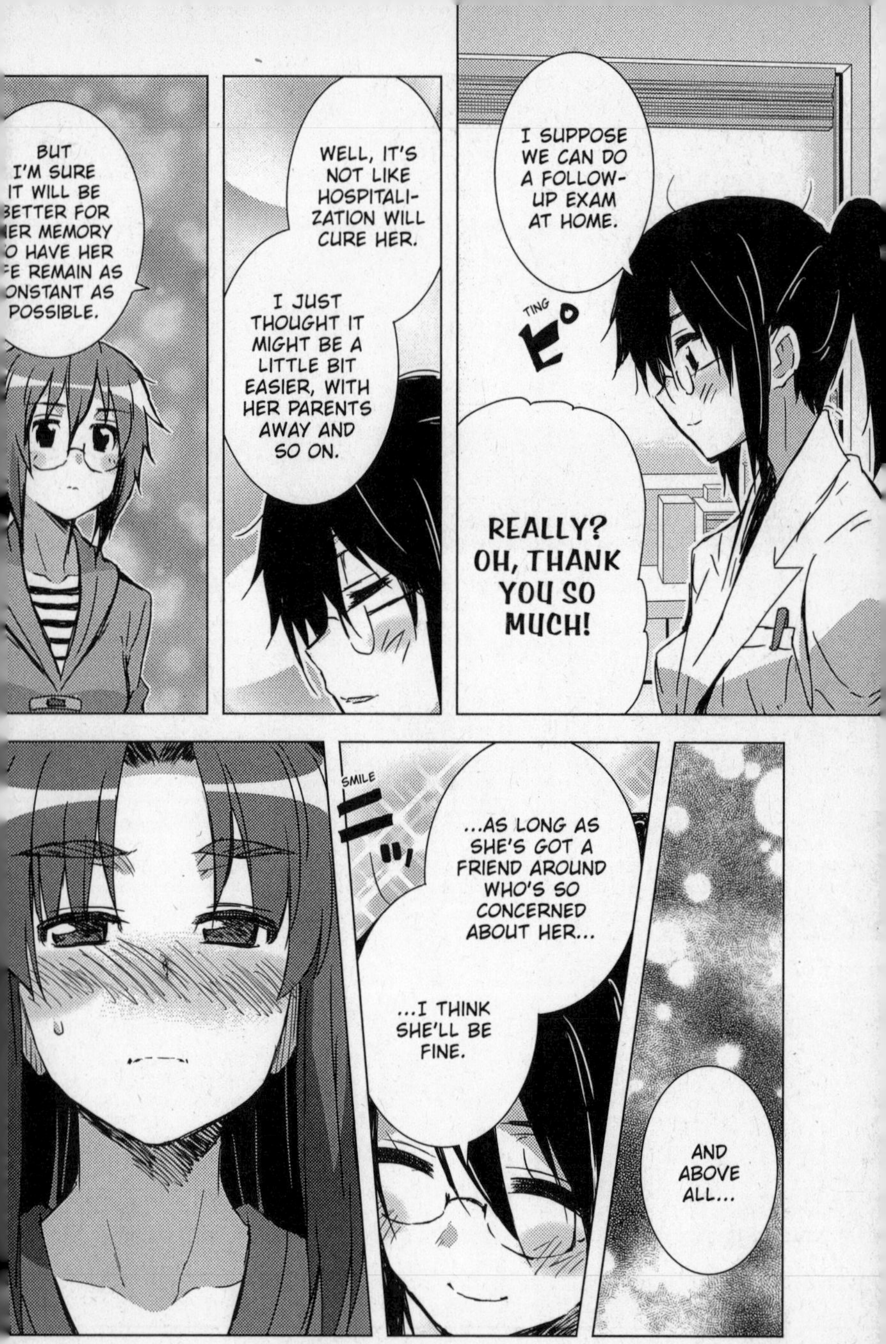
I SUPPOSE WE CAN DO A FOLLOW-UP EXAM AT HOME.
TING
REALLY? OH, THANK YOU SO MUCH!
WELL, IT'S NOT LIKE HOSPITALI-ZATION WILL CURE HER.
I JUST THOUGHT IT MIGHT BE A LITTLE BIT EASIER, WITH HER PARENTS AWAY AND SO ON.
BUT I'M SURE IT WILL BE BETTER FOR ER MEMORY O HAVE HER FE REMAIN AS ONSTANT AS POSSIBLE.
AND ABOVE ALL...
SMILE
...AS LONG AS SHE'S GOT A FRIEND AROUND WHO'S SO CONCERNED ABOUT HER...
...I THINK SHE'LL BE FINE.

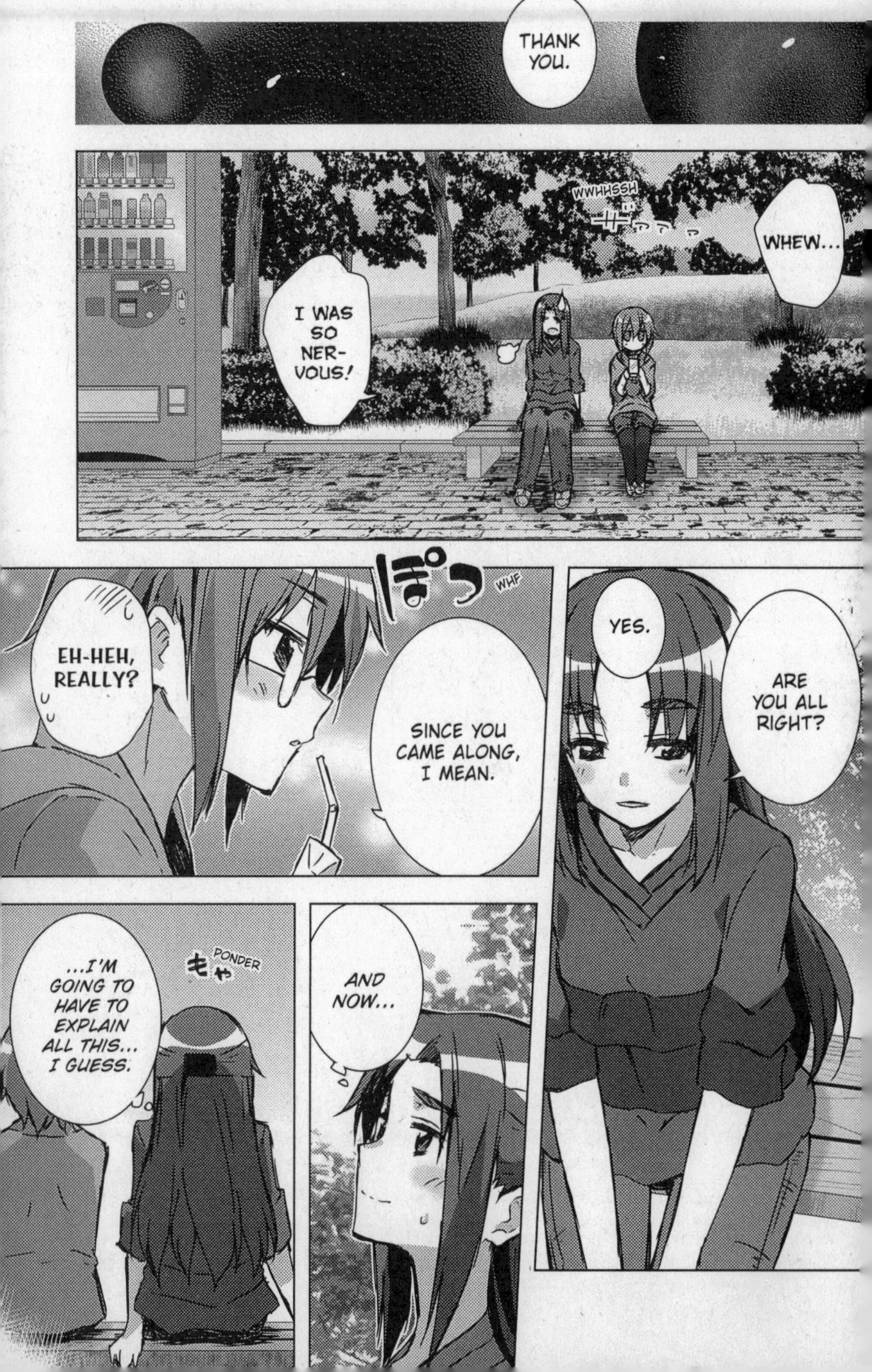
THANK YOU.
WHEW...
WWHHSSH
I WAS SO NER-VOUS!
ARE YOU ALL RIGHT?
YES.
SINCE YOU CAME ALONG, I MEAN.
ぽっ
WHF
EH-HEH, REALLY?
AND NOW...
もや
PONDER
...I'M GOING TO HAVE TO EXPLAIN ALL THIS... I GUESS.

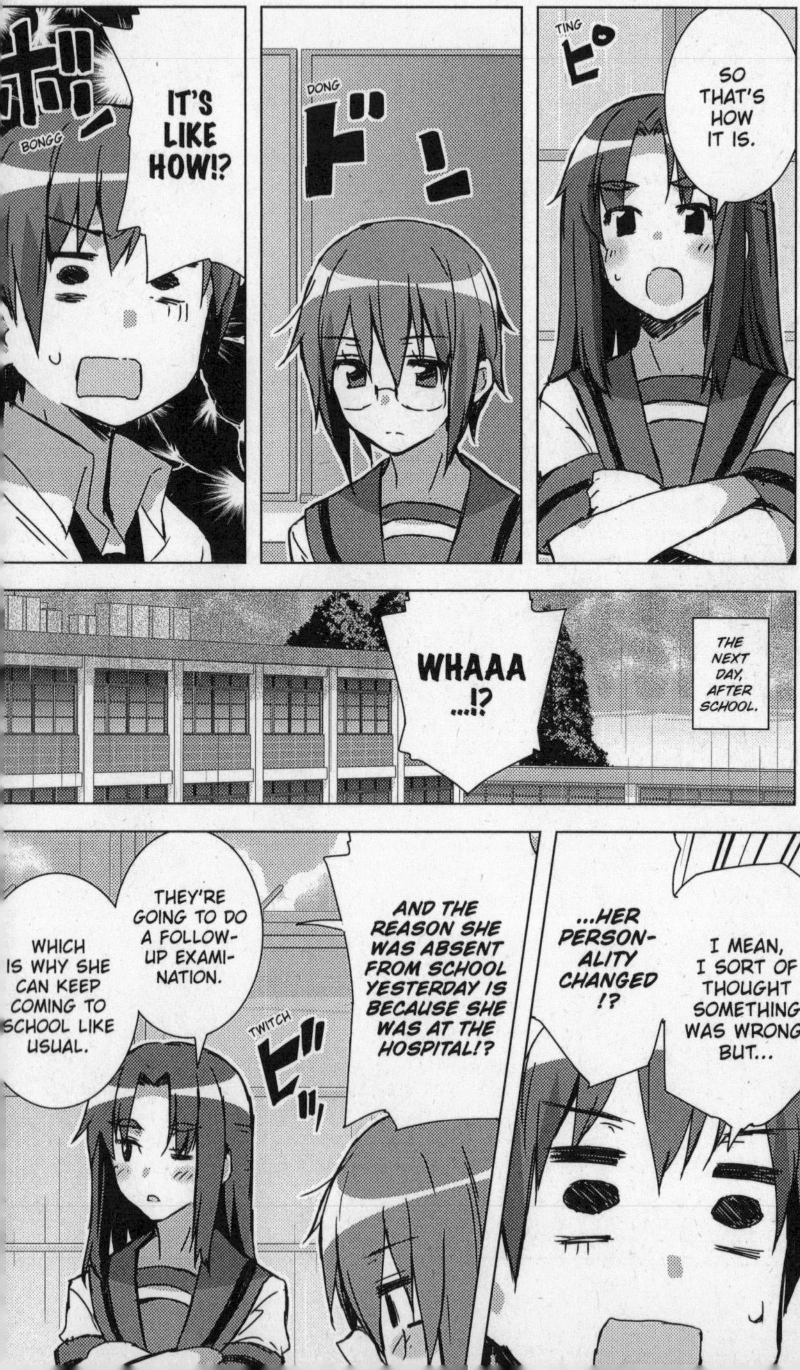
TING
SO THAT'S HOW IT IS.
DONG
BONGG
IT'S LIKE HOW!?
THE NEXT DAY, AFTER SCHOOL.
WHAAA ...!?
I MEAN, I SORT OF THOUGHT SOMETHING WAS WRONG, BUT...
...HER PERSONALITY CHANGED!?
HUH!?
AND THE REASON SHE WAS ABSENT FROM SCHOOL YESTERDAY IS BECAUSE SHE WAS AT THE HOSPITAL!?
TWITCH
THEY'RE GOING TO DO A FOLLOW-UP EXAMINATION.
WHICH IS WHY SHE CAN KEEP COMING TO SCHOOL LIKE USUAL.

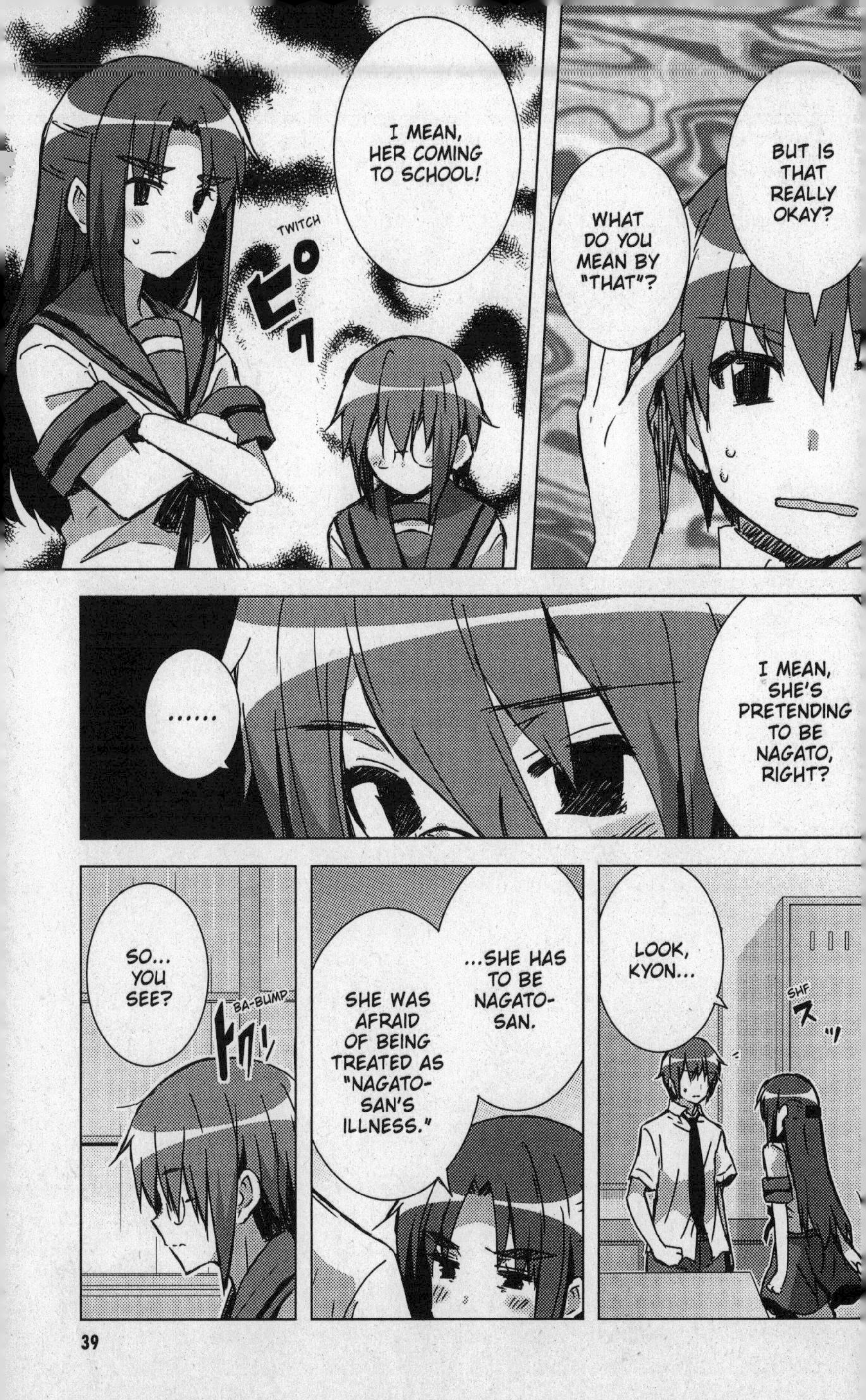
BUT IS THAT REALLY OKAY?
WHAT DO YOU MEAN BY "THAT"?
I MEAN, HER COMING TO SCHOOL!
TWITCH
I MEAN, SHE'S PRETENDING TO BE NAGATO, RIGHT?
......
LOOK, KYON...
SHF
...SHE HAS TO BE NAGATO-SAN.
SHE WAS AFRAID OF BEING TREATED AS "NAGATO-SAN'S ILLNESS."
SO... YOU SEE?
BA-BUMP

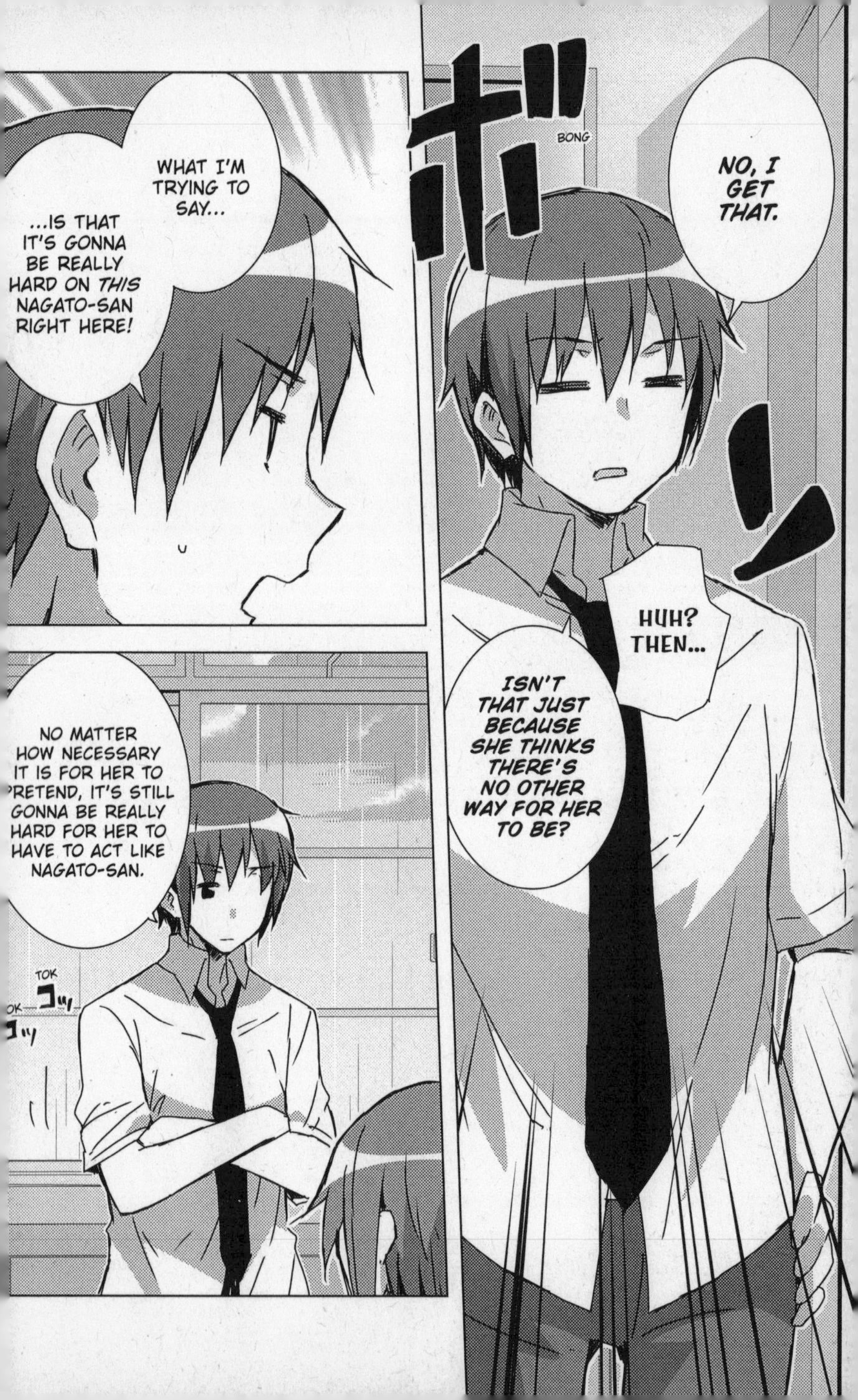
BONG
NO, I GET THAT.
HUH? THEN...
ISN'T THAT JUST BECAUSE SHE THINKS THERE'S NO OTHER WAY FOR HER TO BE?
WHAT I'M TRYING TO SAY...
...IS THAT IT'S GONNA BE REALLY HARD ON *THIS* NAGATO-SAN RIGHT HERE!
NO MATTER HOW NECESSARY IT IS FOR HER TO PRETEND, IT'S STILL GONNA BE REALLY HARD FOR HER TO HAVE TO ACT LIKE NAGATO-SAN.
TOK
TOK

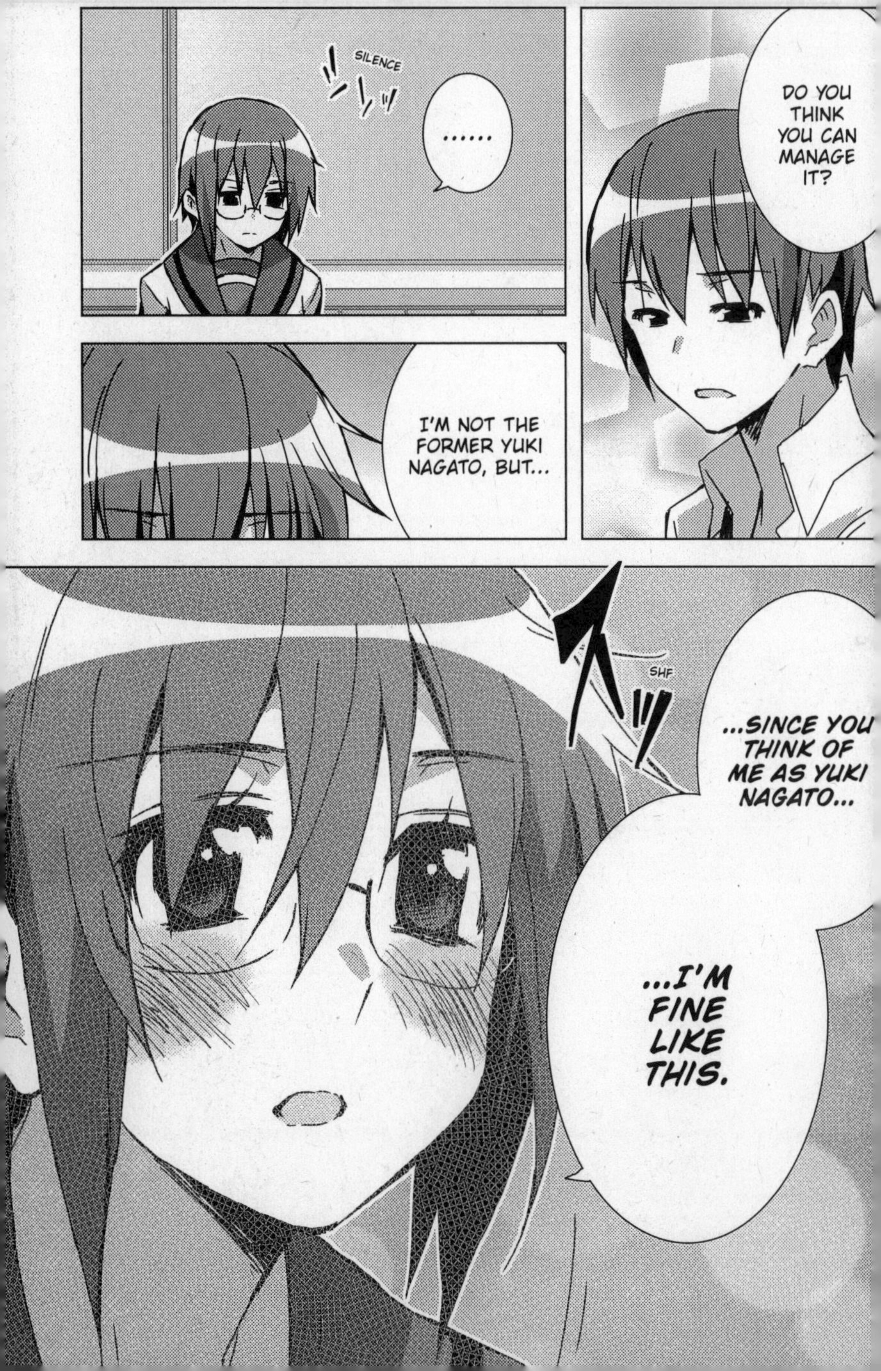
DO YOU THINK YOU CAN MANAGE IT?
SILENCE
......
I'M NOT THE FORMER YUKI NAGATO, BUT...
SHF
...SINCE YOU THINK OF ME AS YUKI NAGATO...
...I'M FINE LIKE THIS.

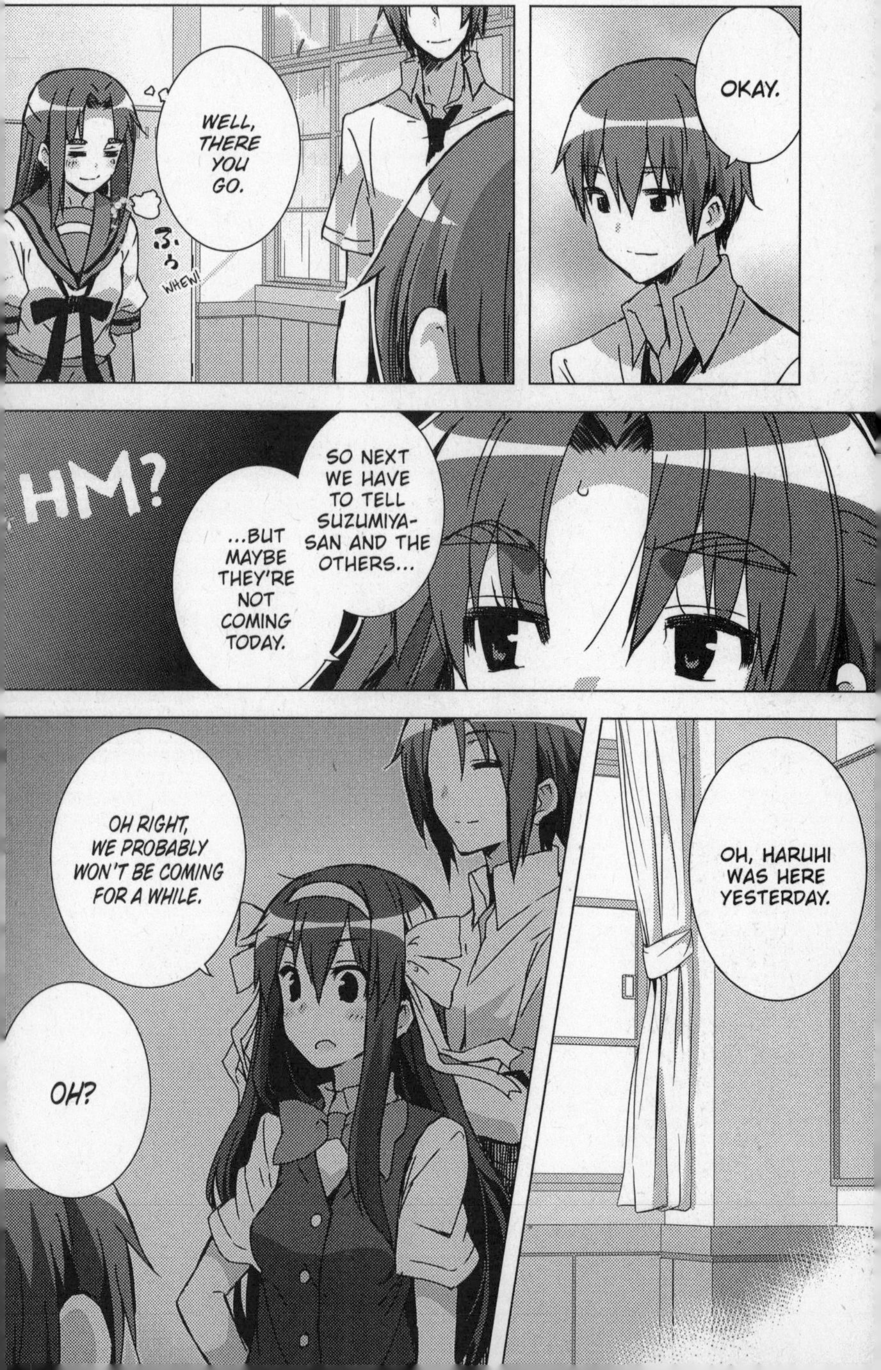
OKAY.
WELL, THERE YOU GO.
ふぅ
WHEW!
SO NEXT WE HAVE TO TELL SUZUMIYA-SAN AND THE OTHERS...
...BUT MAYBE THEY'RE NOT COMING TODAY.
HM?
OH, HARUHI WAS HERE YESTERDAY.
OH RIGHT, WE PROBABLY WON'T BE COMING FOR A WHILE.
OH?

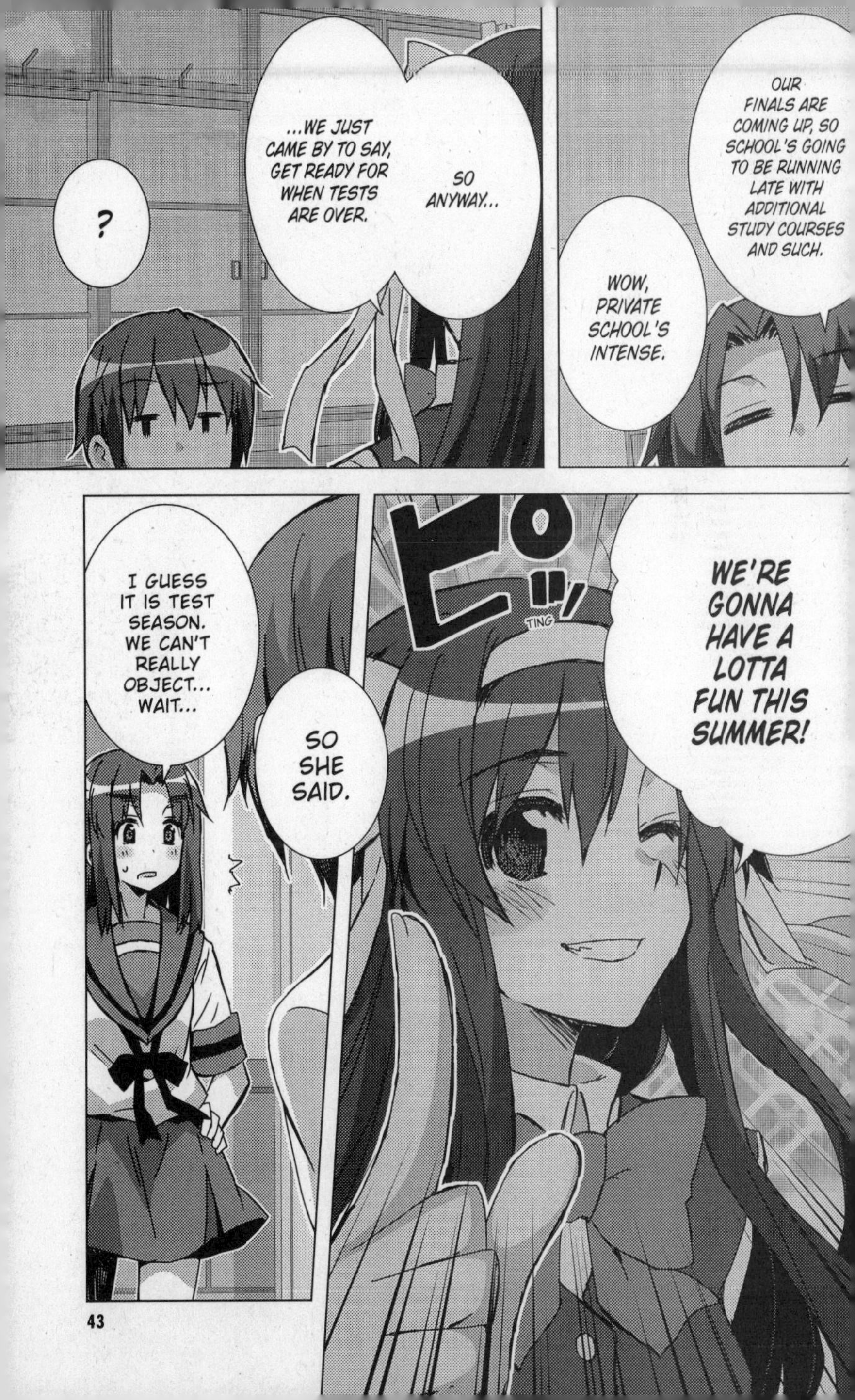
OUR FINALS ARE COMING UP, SO SCHOOL'S GOING TO BE RUNNING LATE WITH ADDITIONAL STUDY COURSES AND SUCH.
WOW, PRIVATE SCHOOL'S INTENSE.
SO ANYWAY...
...WE JUST CAME BY TO SAY, GET READY FOR WHEN TESTS ARE OVER.
?
WE'RE GONNA HAVE A LOTTA FUN THIS SUMMER!
TING
SO SHE SAID.
I GUESS IT IS TEST SEASON. WE CAN'T REALLY OBJECT... WAIT...

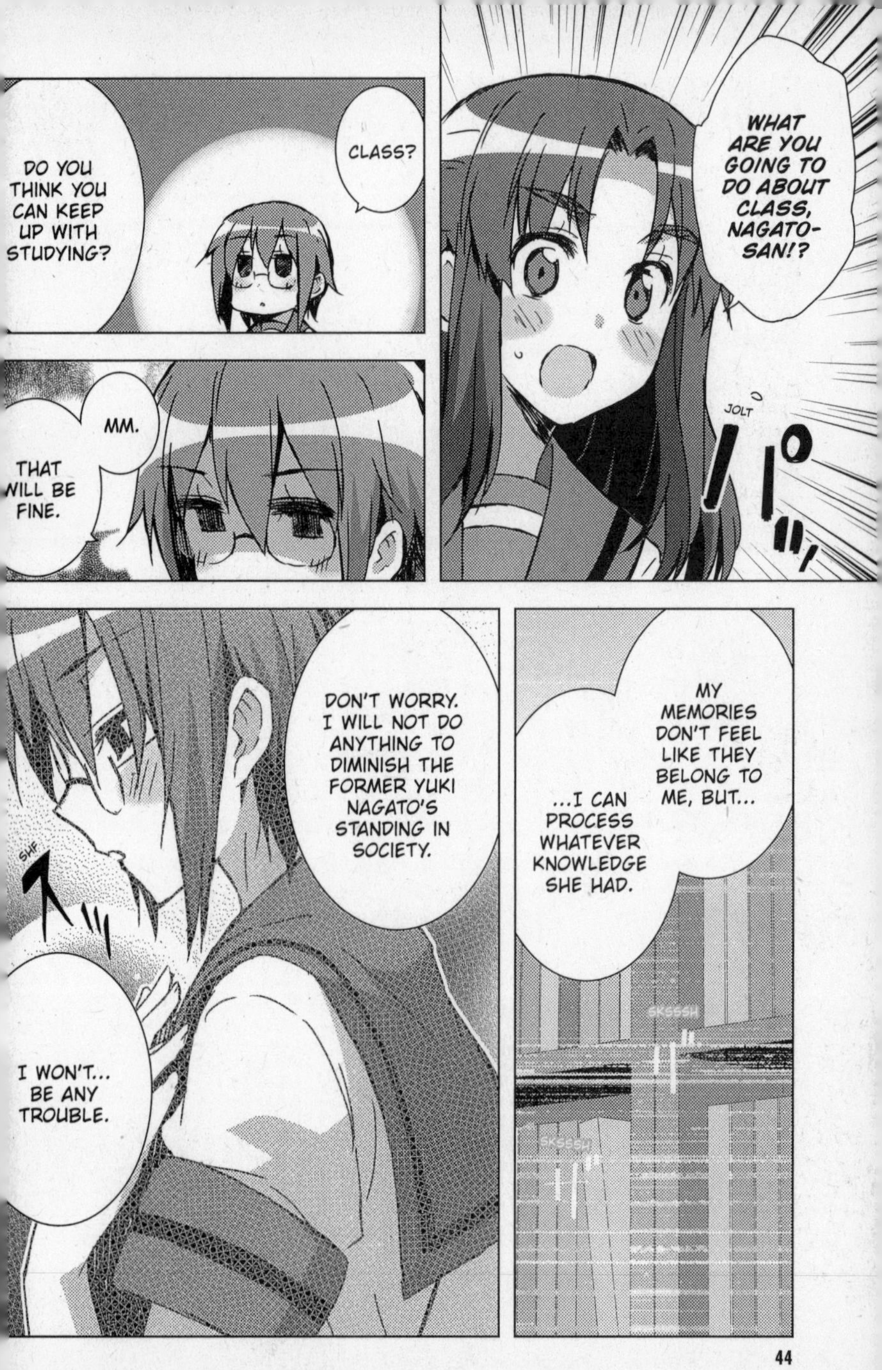
WHAT ARE YOU GOING TO DO ABOUT CLASS, NAGATO-SAN!?
JOLT
CLASS?
DO YOU THINK YOU CAN KEEP UP WITH STUDYING?
MM.
THAT WILL BE FINE.
MY MEMORIES DON'T FEEL LIKE THEY BELONG TO ME, BUT...
...I CAN PROCESS WHATEVER KNOWLEDGE SHE HAD.
SKSSSH
SKSSSH
DON'T WORRY. I WILL NOT DO ANYTHING TO DIMINISH THE FORMER YUKI NAGATO'S STANDING IN SOCIETY.
SHF
I WON'T... BE ANY TROUBLE.

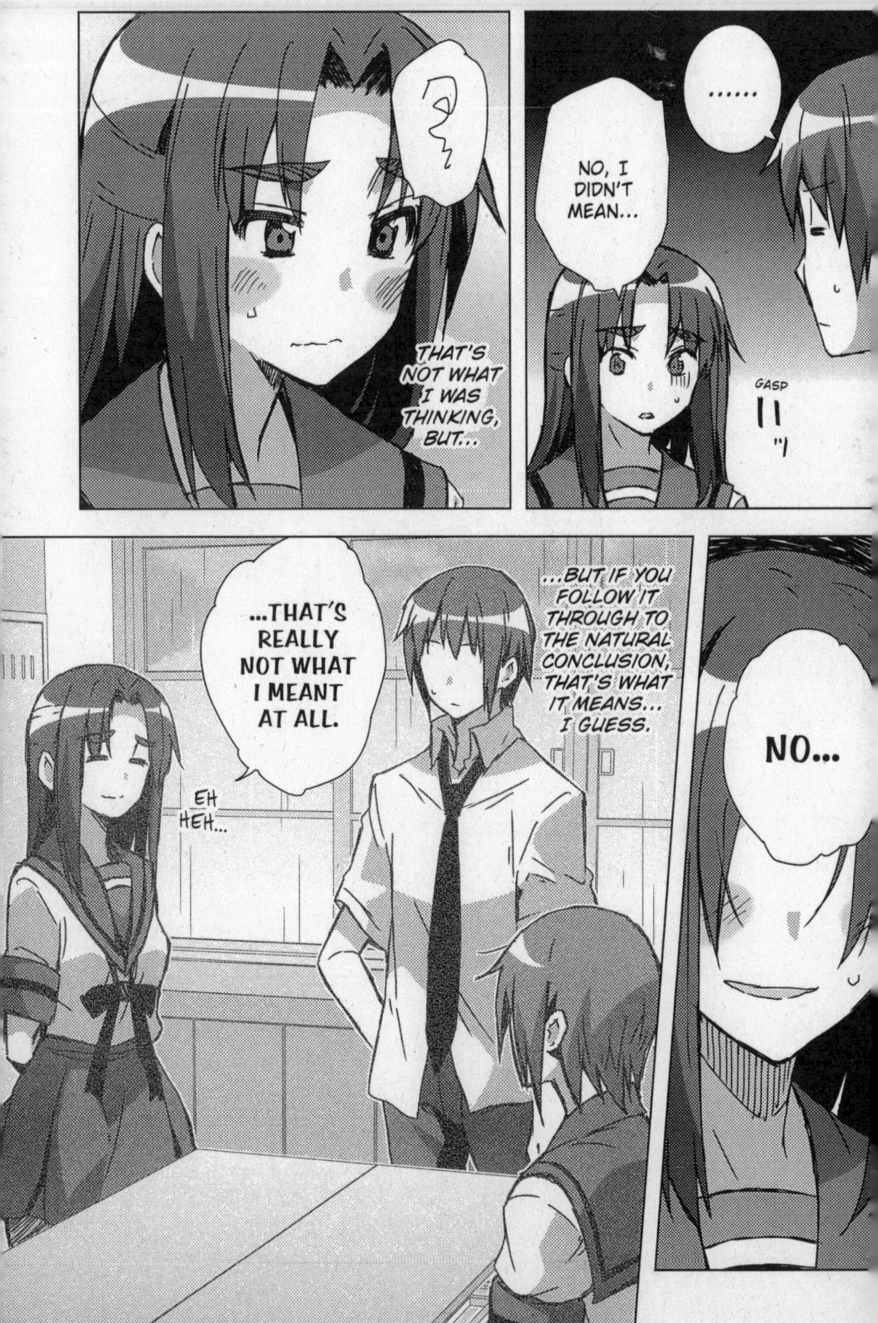
......
NO, I DIDN'T MEAN...
GASP
THAT'S NOT WHAT I WAS THINKING, BUT...
NO...
...BUT IF YOU FOLLOW IT THROUGH TO THE NATURAL CONCLUSION, THAT'S WHAT IT MEANS... I GUESS.
...THAT'S REALLY NOT WHAT I MEANT AT ALL.
EH HEH...

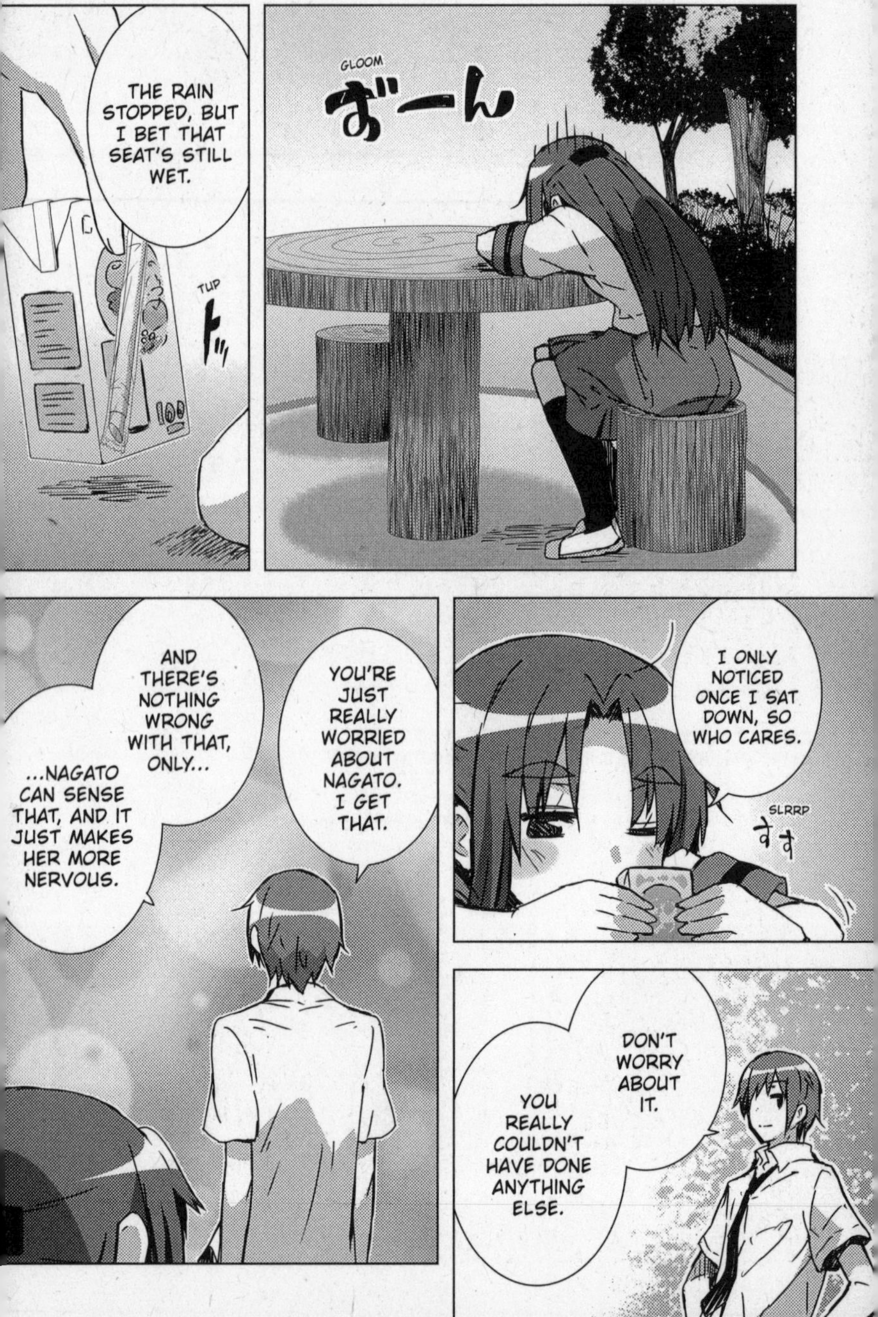
GLOOM
ずーん
THE RAIN STOPPED, BUT I BET THAT SEAT'S STILL WET.
TUP
ト
I ONLY NOTICED ONCE I SAT DOWN, SO WHO CARES.
SLRRP
すす
DON'T WORRY ABOUT IT.
YOU REALLY COULDN'T HAVE DONE ANYTHING ELSE.
YOU'RE JUST REALLY WORRIED ABOUT NAGATO. I GET THAT.
AND THERE'S NOTHING WRONG WITH THAT, ONLY...
...NAGATO CAN SENSE THAT, AND IT JUST MAKES HER MORE NERVOUS.

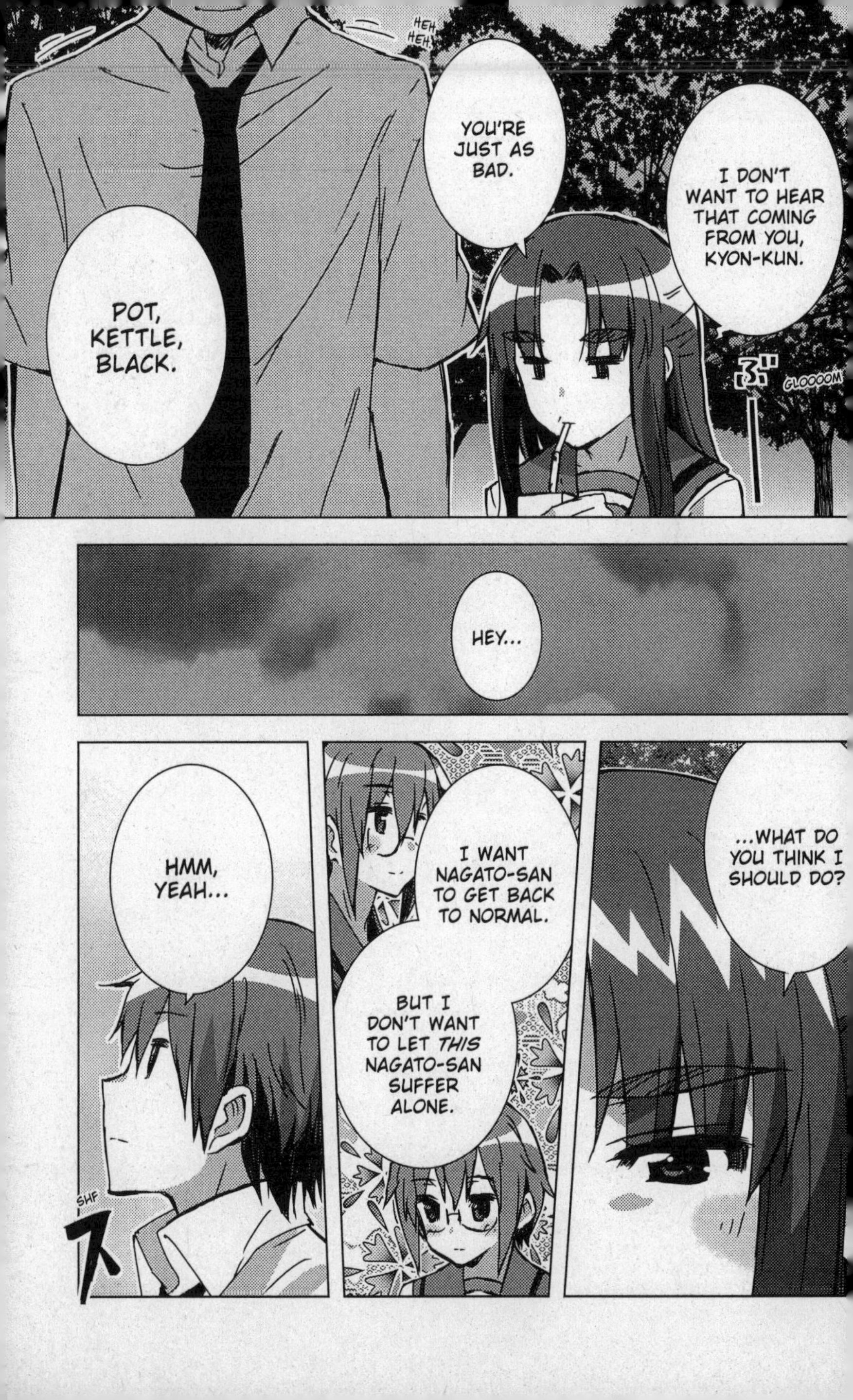
I DON'T WANT TO HEAR THAT COMING FROM YOU, KYON-KUN.
HEH HEH.
YOU'RE JUST AS BAD.
GLOOOOM
POT, KETTLE, BLACK.
HEY...
...WHAT DO YOU THINK I SHOULD DO?
I WANT NAGATO-SAN TO GET BACK TO NORMAL.
BUT I DON'T WANT TO LET *THIS* NAGATO-SAN SUFFER ALONE.
HMM, YEAH...
SHF

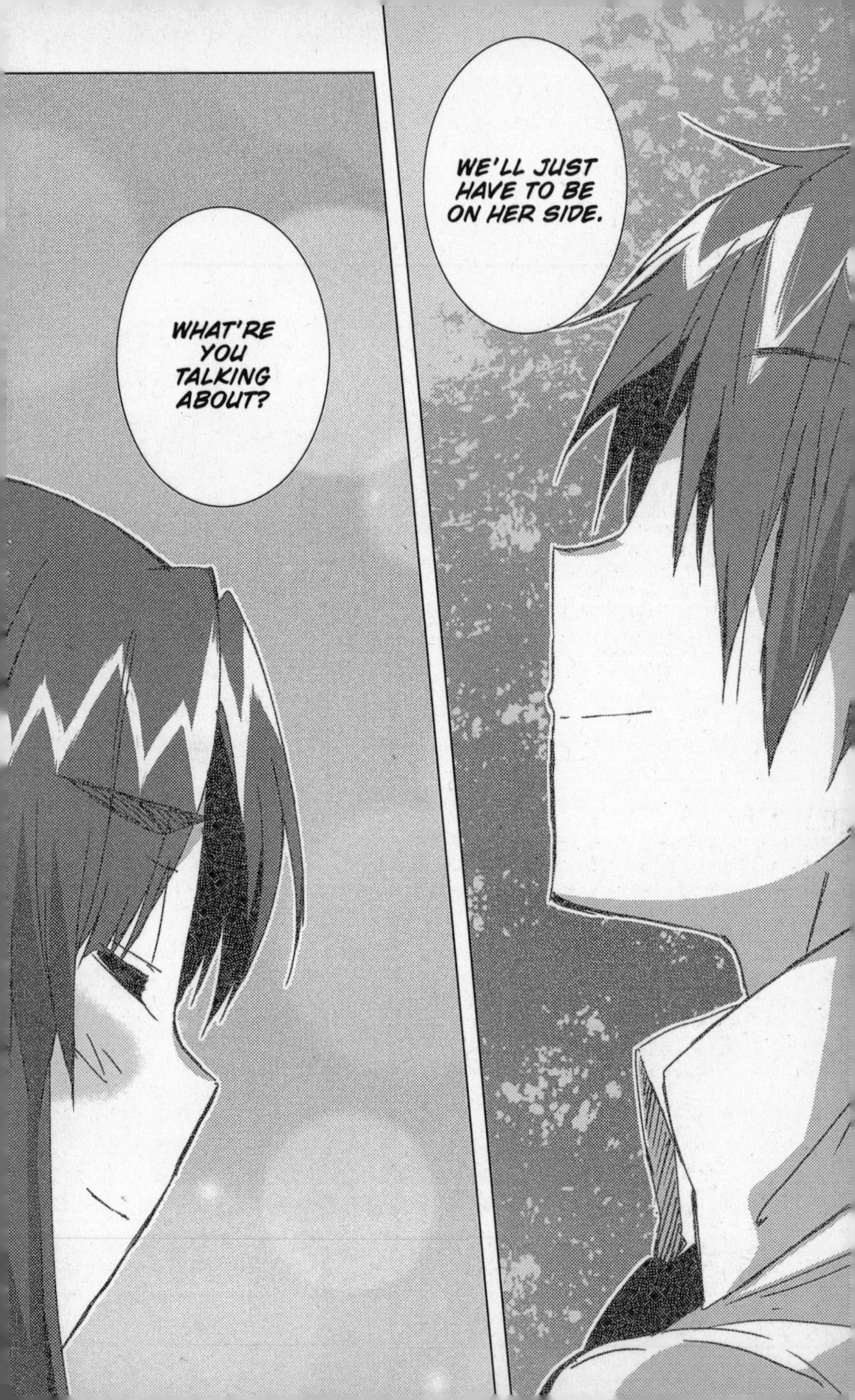
WE'LL JUST HAVE TO BE ON HER SIDE.
WHAT'RE YOU TALKING ABOUT?

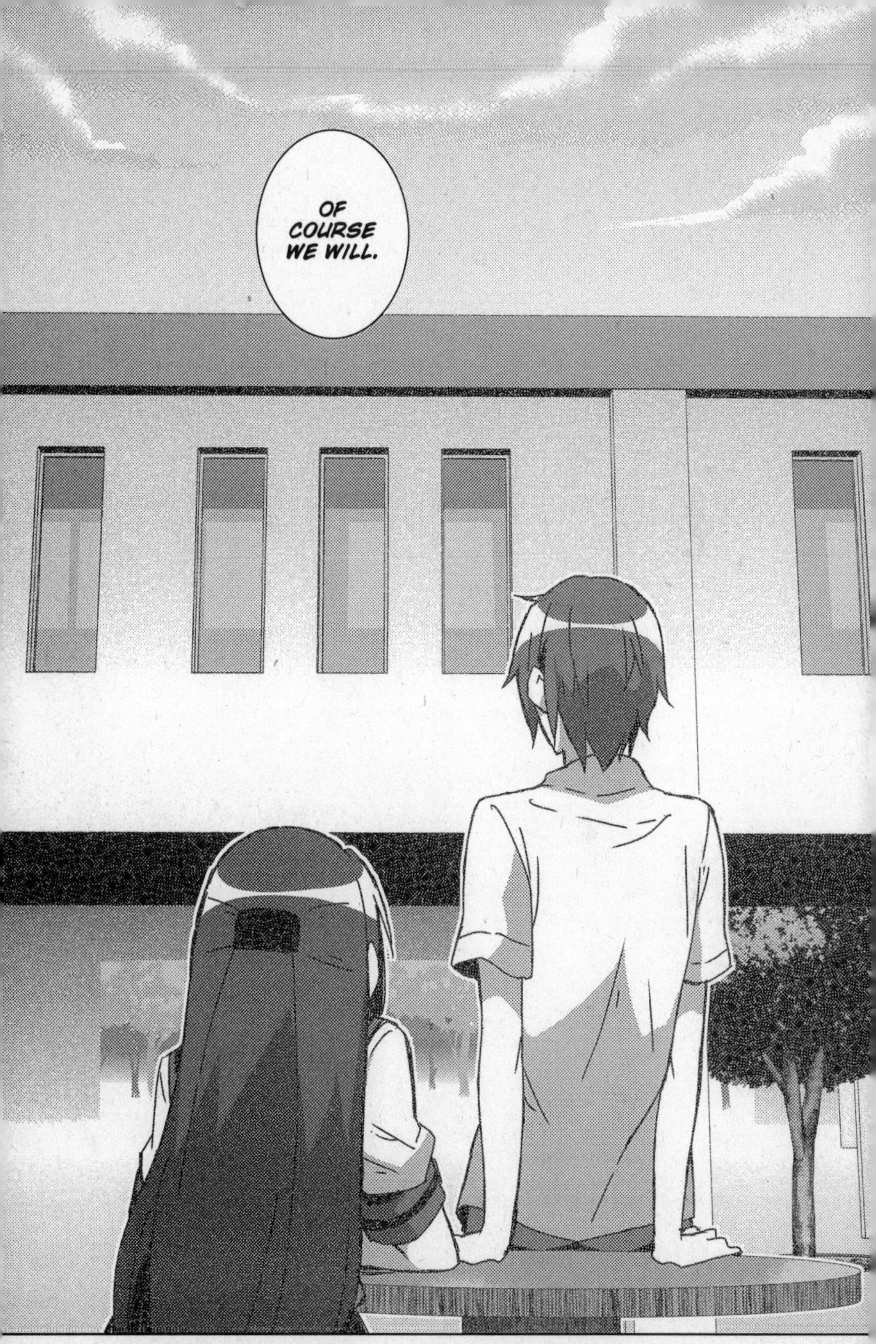
OF COURSE WE WILL.

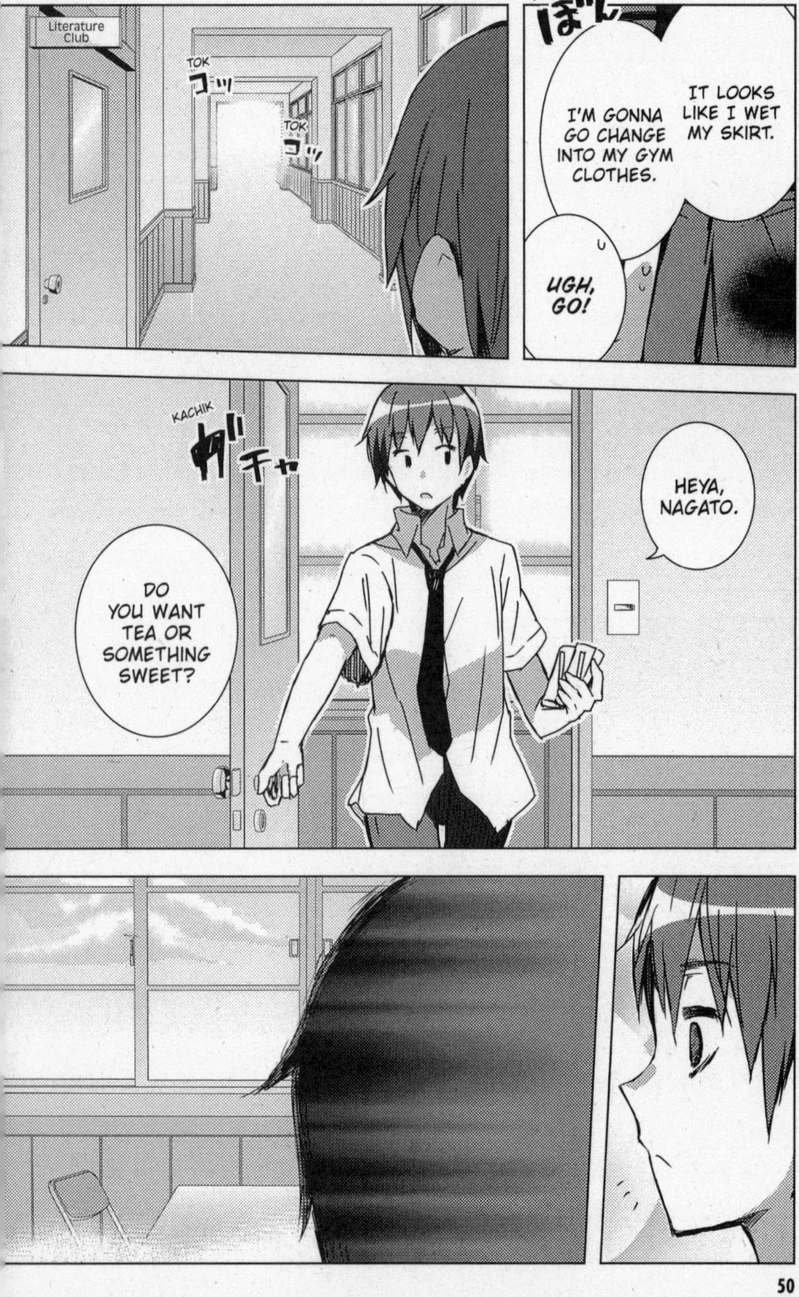
DUM
IT LOOKS LIKE I WET MY SKIRT.
I'M GONNA GO CHANGE INTO MY GYM CLOTHES.
UGH, GO!
Literature Club
TOK
TOK
HEYA, NAGATO.
KACHIK
DO YOU WANT TEA OR SOMETHING SWEET?

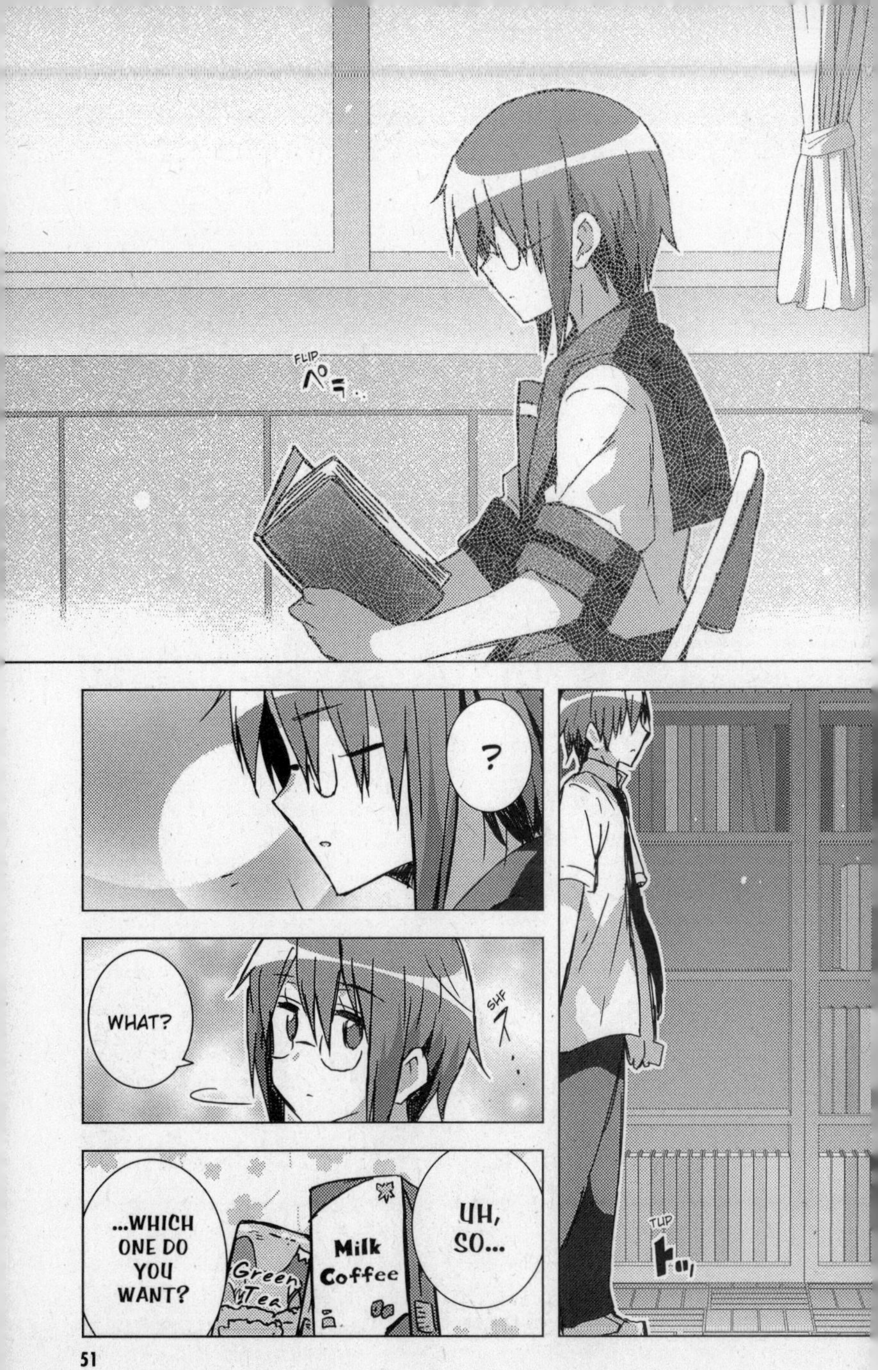
FLIP
ペラ..
TUP
トッ
?
SHF
ス
WHAT?
UH, SO...
Milk Coffee
...WHICH ONE DO YOU WANT?
Green Tea

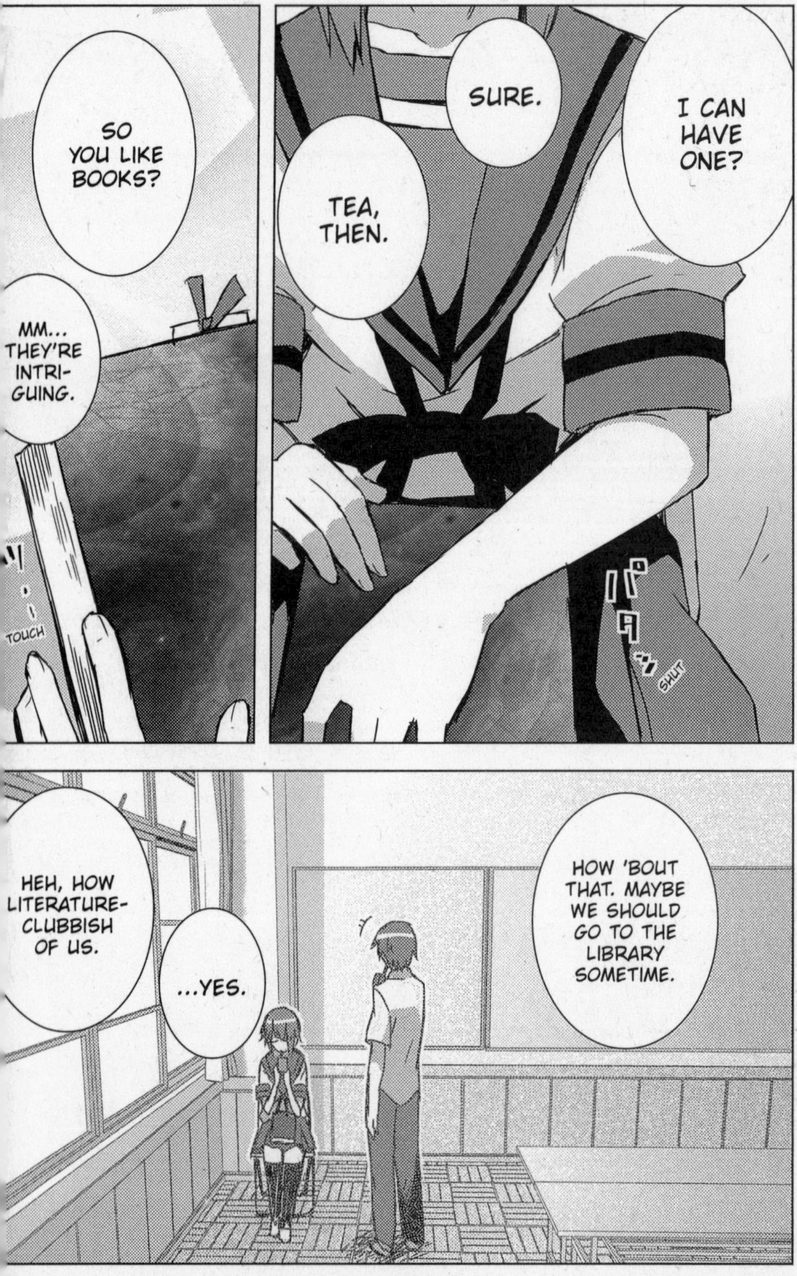
I CAN HAVE ONE?
SURE.
TEA, THEN.
SHUT
SO YOU LIKE BOOKS?
MM... THEY'RE INTRIGUING.
TOUCH
HOW 'BOUT THAT. MAYBE WE SHOULD GO TO THE LIBRARY SOMETIME.
HEH, HOW LITERATURE-CLUBBISH OF US.
...YES.

Epilogue 29 >> Daily Life

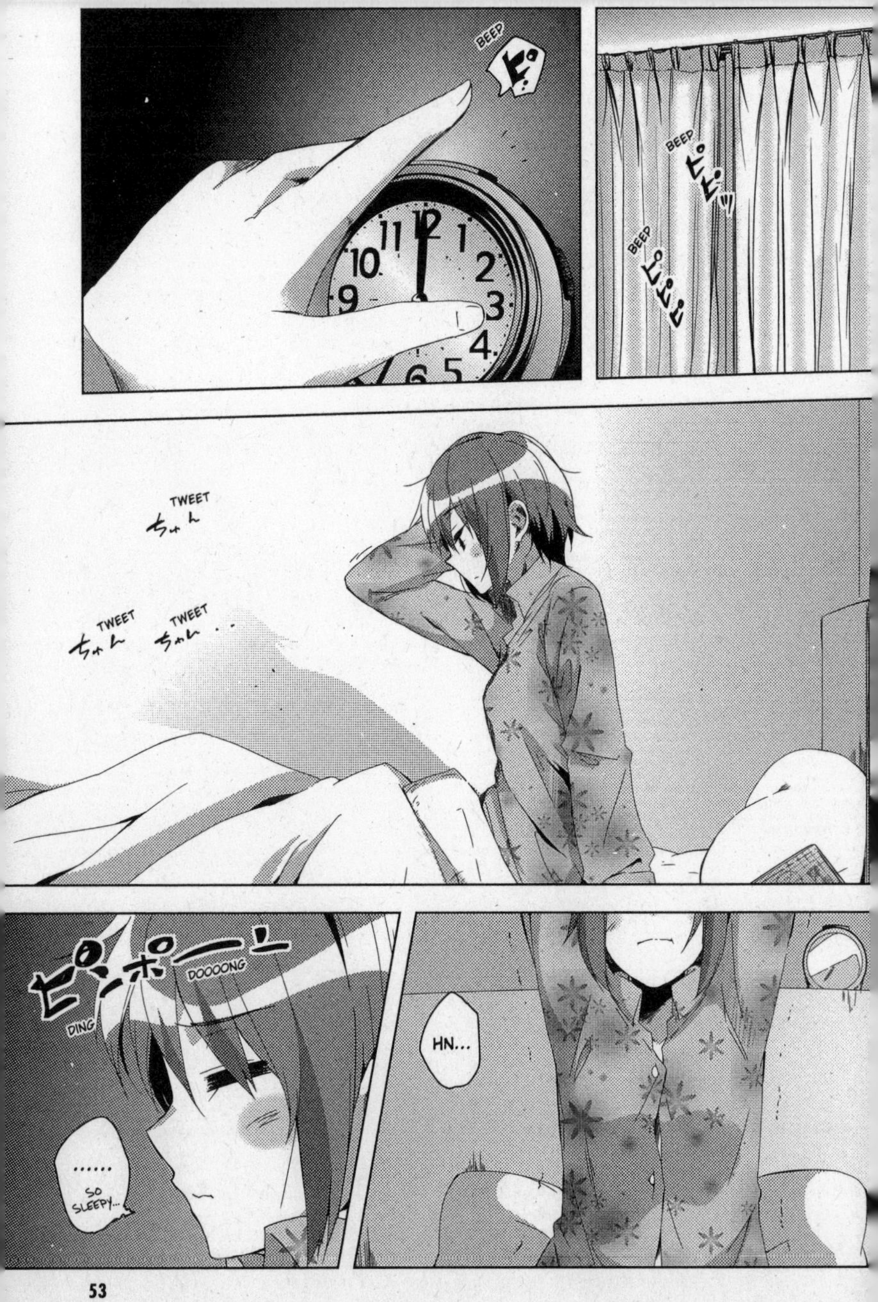
BEEP
ピピッ
BEEP
ピピピ
BEEP
ピ
TWEET
ちゅん
TWEET
ちゅん
TWEET
ちゅん
HN...
ピンポーン
DING
DOOOONG
......
SO SLEEPY...

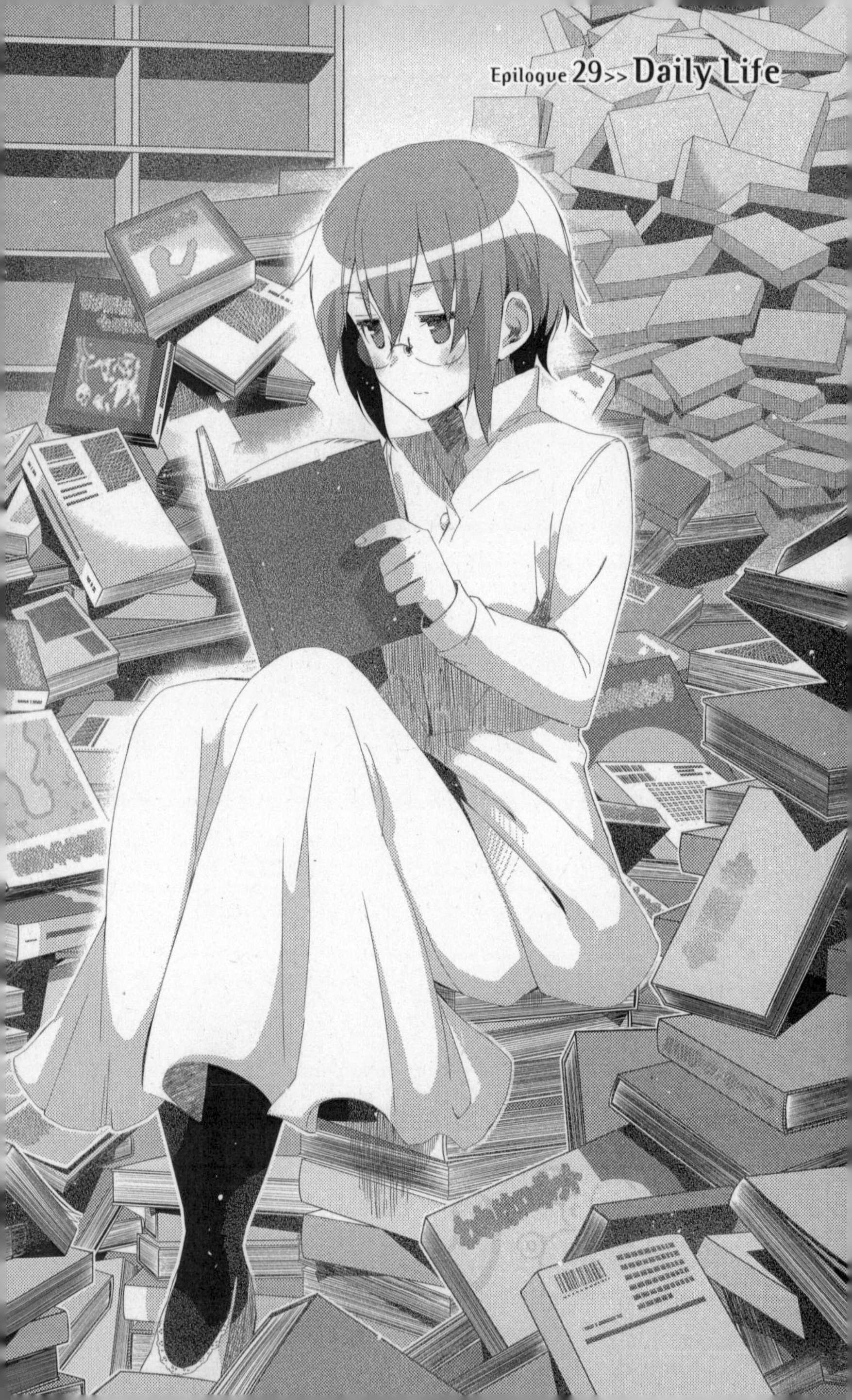
Epilogue 29>> Daily Life

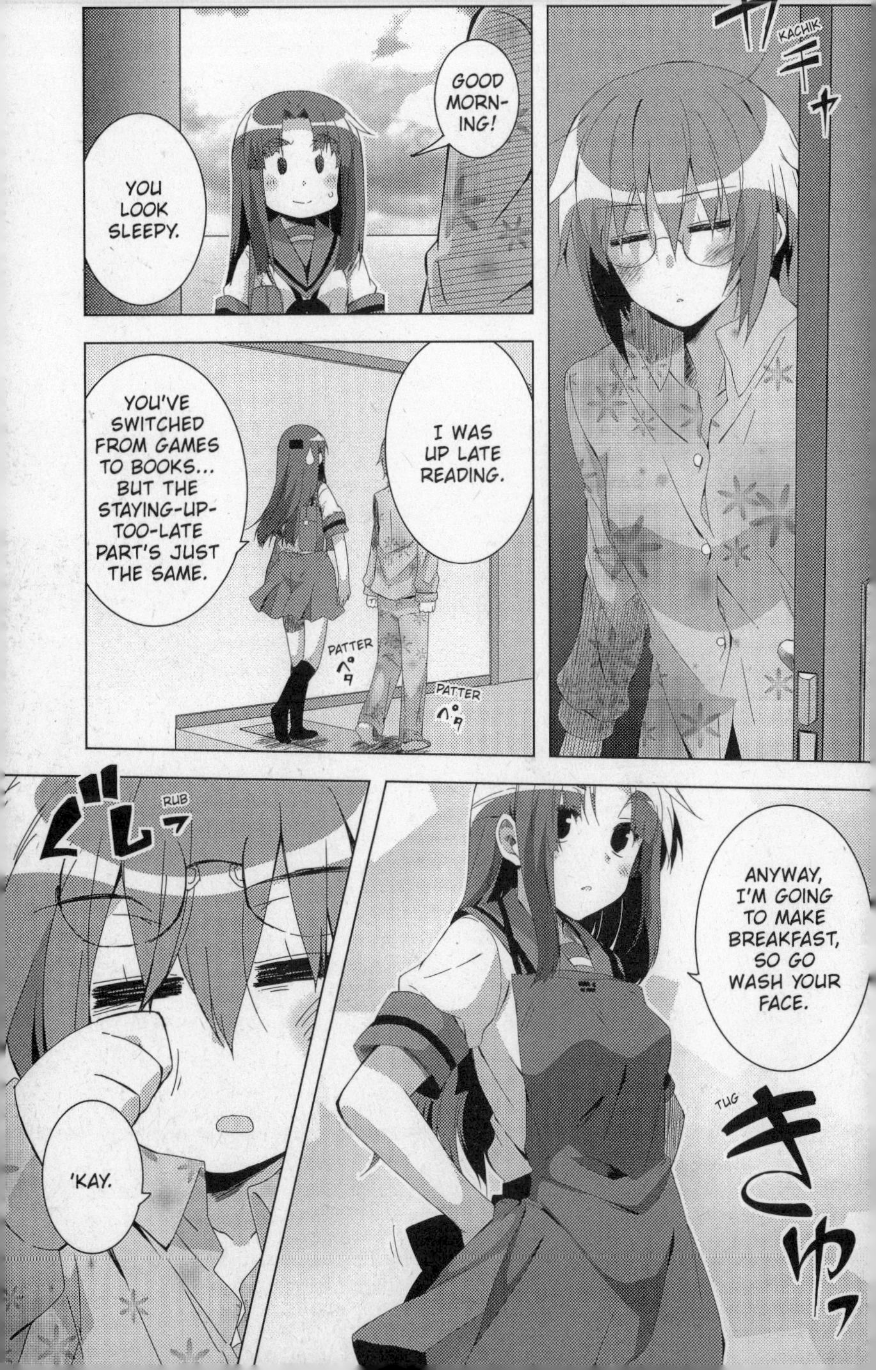
ガチャ
KACHIK
GOOD MORNING!
YOU LOOK SLEEPY.
I WAS UP LATE READING.
YOU'VE SWITCHED FROM GAMES TO BOOKS... BUT THE STAYING-UP-TOO-LATE PART'S JUST THE SAME.
PATTER
ペタ
PATTER
ペタ
ANYWAY, I'M GOING TO MAKE BREAKFAST, SO GO WASH YOUR FACE.
TUG
きゅっ
RUB
ぐしっ
'KAY.

TUNK
ガ ガ

JUST ONE.

HOW MANY SLICES OF TOAST DO YOU WANT?

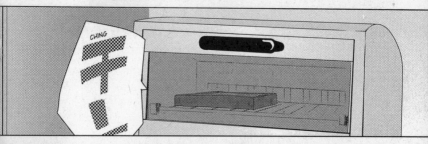

CHING
チー

THE WAY SHE EATS SURE HASN'T CHANGED.

?

ムシャ
NOM
ムシャ
NOM
NOM
NOM
モグ
NOM

STAAARE
じー

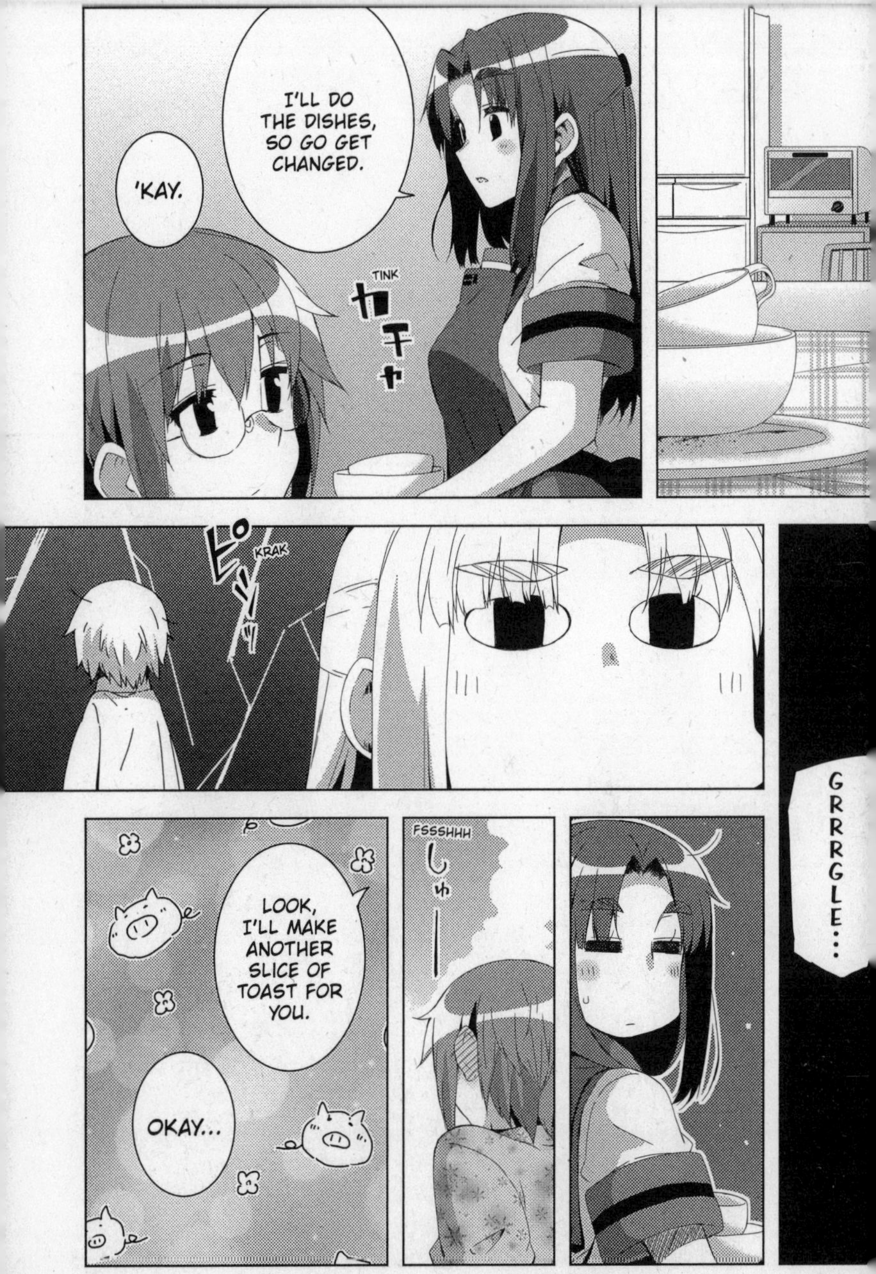
I'LL DO THE DISHES, SO GO GET CHANGED.
'KAY.
TINK
カチャ
GRRRGLE...
KRAK
ピシッ
FSSSHHH
しゅー
LOOK, I'LL MAKE ANOTHER SLICE OF TOAST FOR YOU.
OKAY...

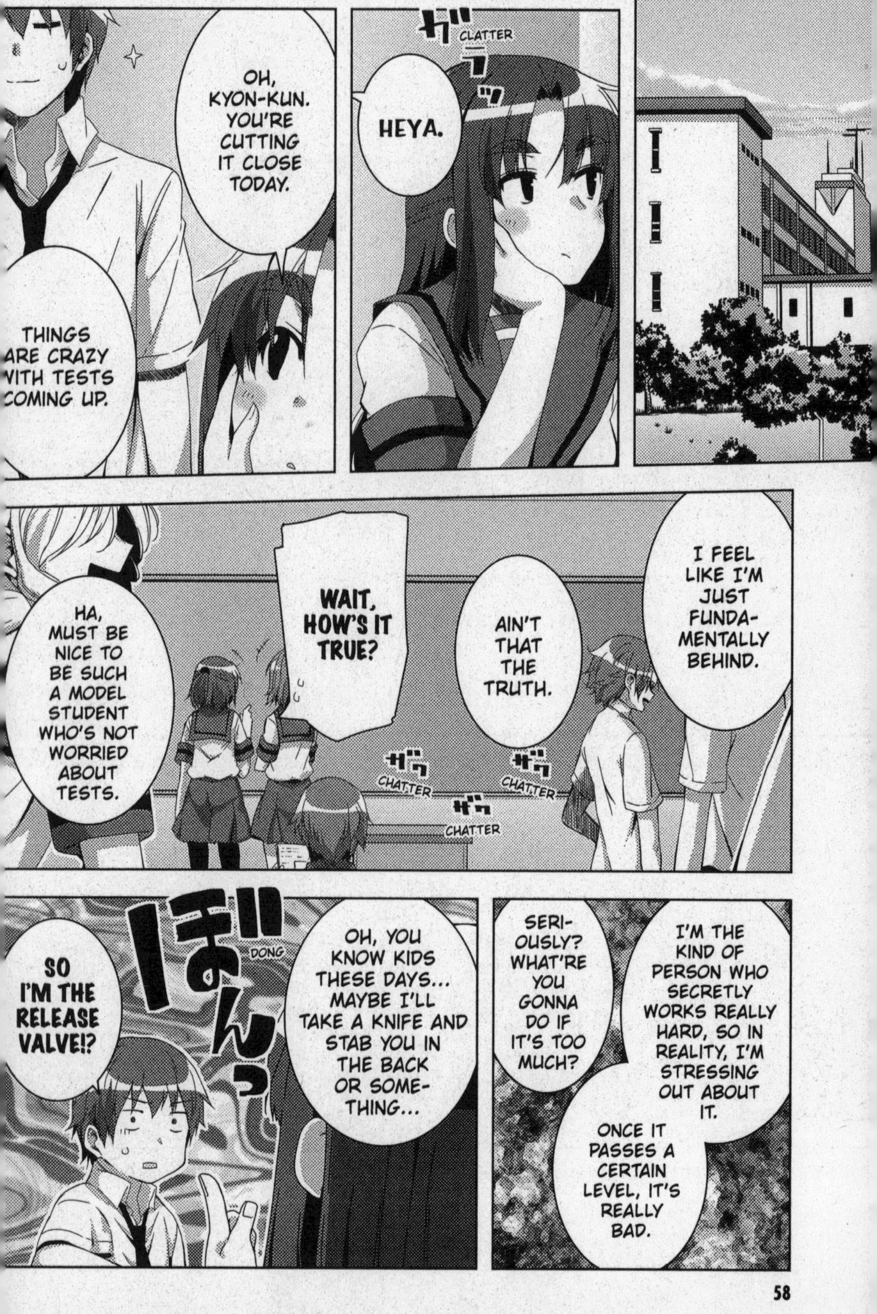
CLATTER
HEYA.
OH, KYON-KUN. YOU'RE CUTTING IT CLOSE TODAY.
THINGS ARE CRAZY WITH TESTS COMING UP.
I FEEL LIKE I'M JUST FUNDA-MENTALLY BEHIND.
AIN'T THAT THE TRUTH.
WAIT, HOW'S IT TRUE?
CHATTER
CHATTER
CHATTER
HA, MUST BE NICE TO BE SUCH A MODEL STUDENT WHO'S NOT WORRIED ABOUT TESTS.
I'M THE KIND OF PERSON WHO SECRETLY WORKS REALLY HARD, SO IN REALITY, I'M STRESSING OUT ABOUT IT.
SERI-OUSLY? WHAT'RE YOU GONNA DO IF IT'S TOO MUCH?
ONCE IT PASSES A CERTAIN LEVEL, IT'S REALLY BAD.
OH, YOU KNOW KIDS THESE DAYS... MAYBE I'LL TAKE A KNIFE AND STAB YOU IN THE BACK OR SOME-THING...
DONG
SO I'M THE RELEASE VALVE!?

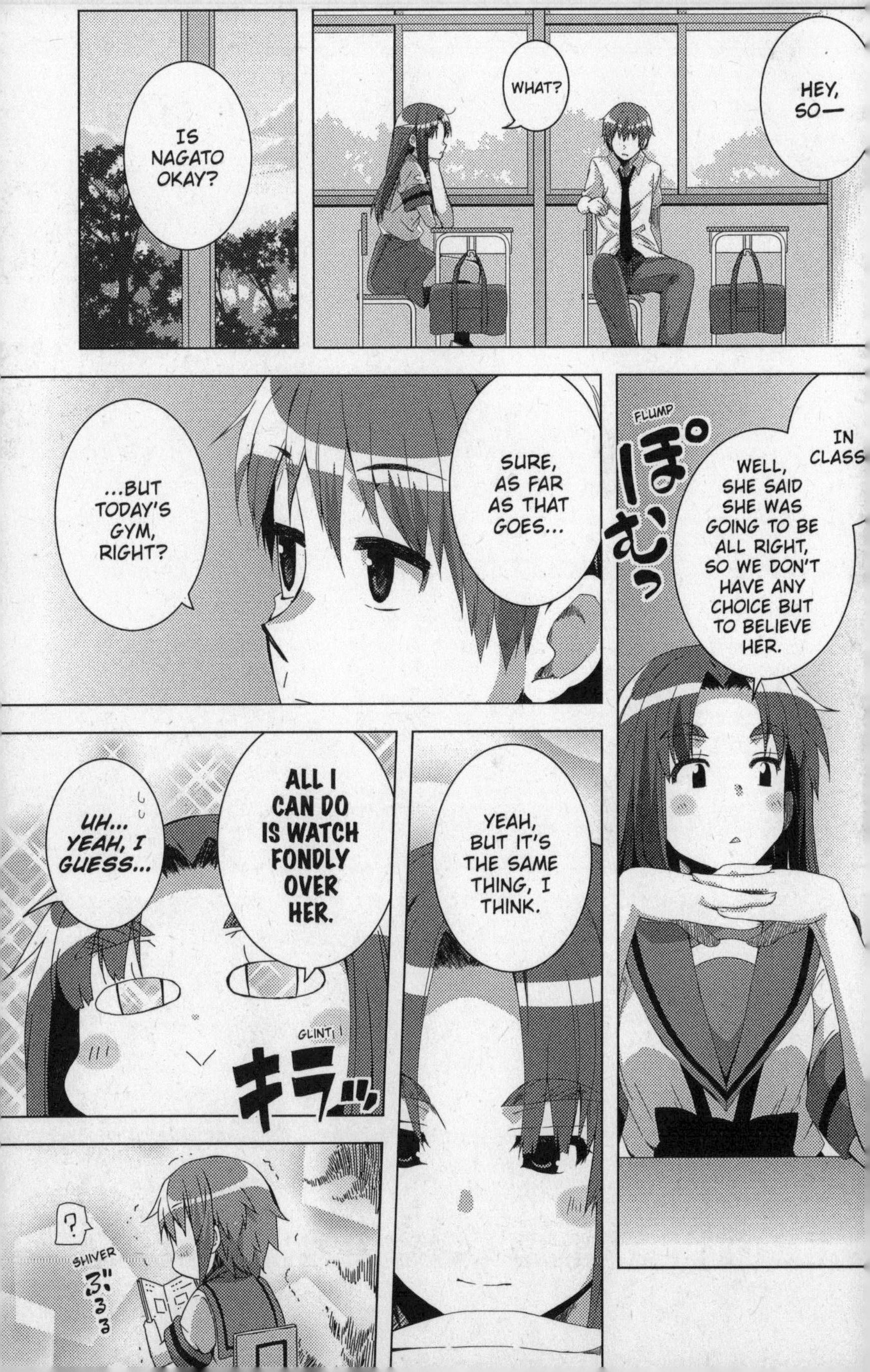
HEY, SO—
WHAT?
IS NAGATO OKAY?
IN CLASS
FLUMP
ぽむっ
WELL, SHE SAID SHE WAS GOING TO BE ALL RIGHT, SO WE DON'T HAVE ANY CHOICE BUT TO BELIEVE HER.
SURE, AS FAR AS THAT GOES...
...BUT TODAY'S GYM, RIGHT?
YEAH, BUT IT'S THE SAME THING, I THINK.
ALL I CAN DO IS WATCH FONDLY OVER HER.
UH... YEAH, I GUESS...
GLINT
キラッ
?
SHIVER
ぶるる

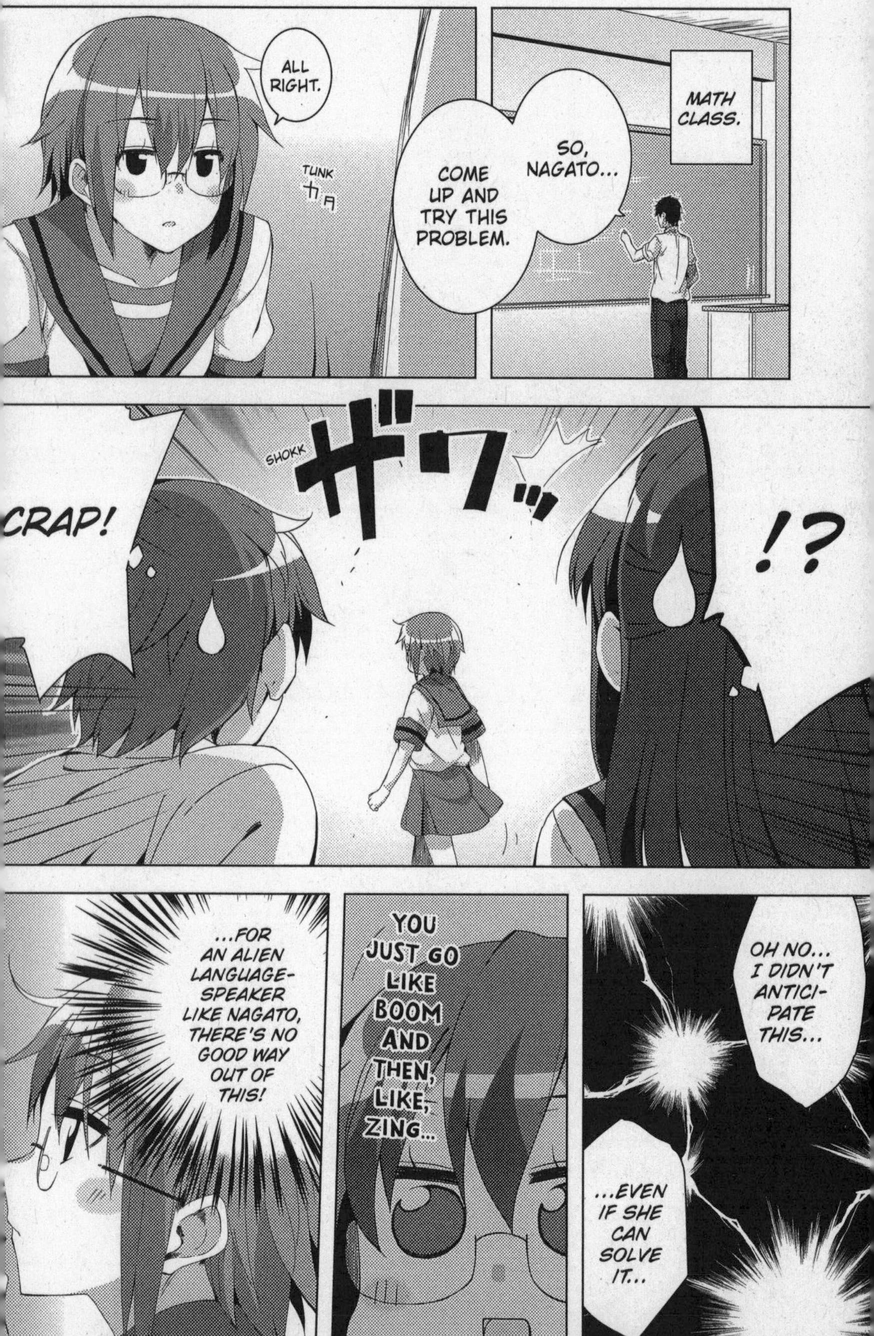
MATH CLASS.
SO, NAGATO...
COME UP AND TRY THIS PROBLEM.
ALL RIGHT.
TUNK
カタ
!?
ザワッ
SHOKK
CRAP!
OH NO... I DIDN'T ANTICI-PATE THIS...
...EVEN IF SHE CAN SOLVE IT...
YOU JUST GO LIKE BOOM AND THEN, LIKE, ZING...
...FOR AN ALIEN LANGUAGE-SPEAKER LIKE NAGATO, THERE'S NO GOOD WAY OUT OF THIS!

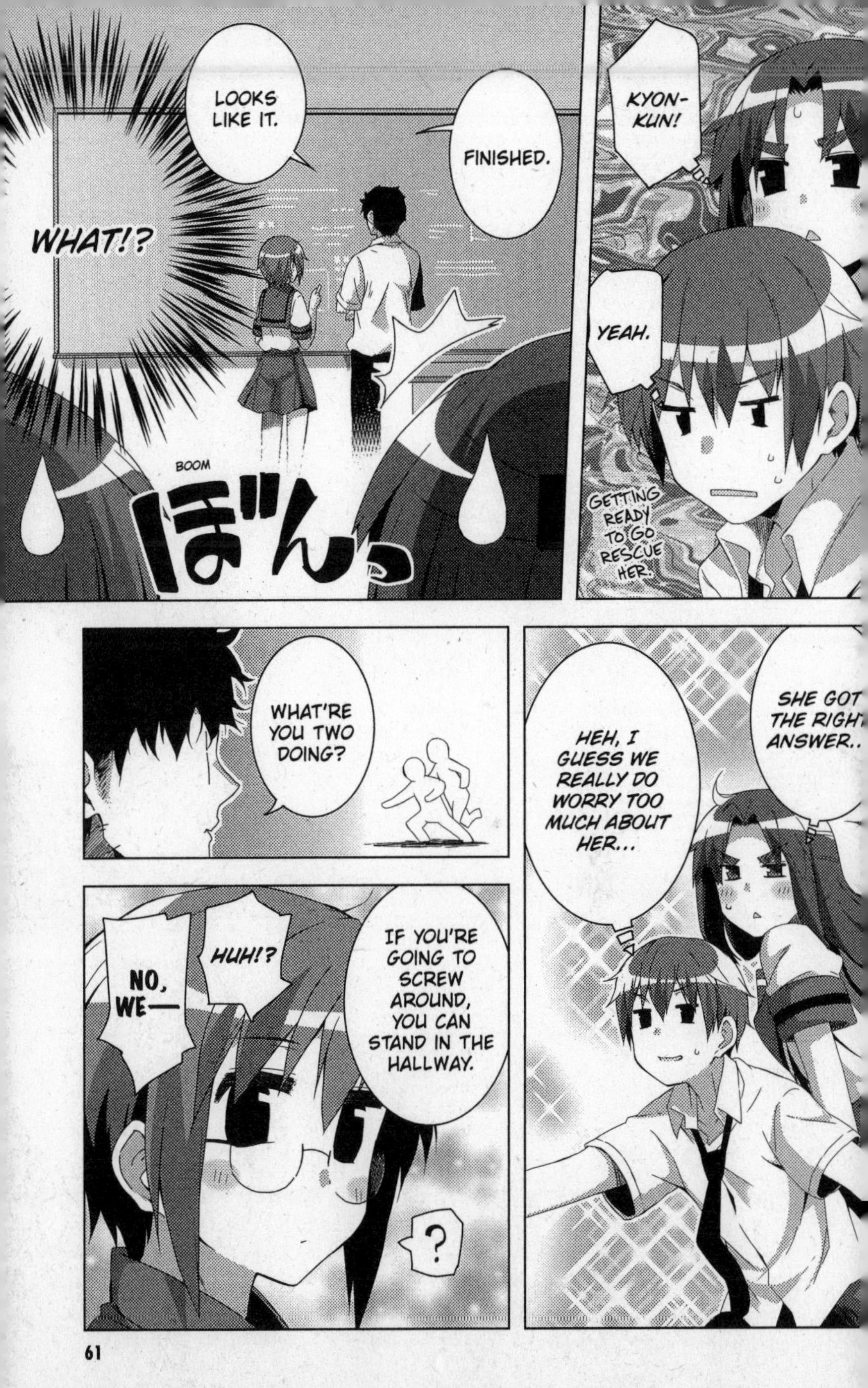
KYON-KUN!
YEAH.
GETTING READY TO GO RESCUE HER.
FINISHED.
LOOKS LIKE IT.
WHAT!?
BOOM
ぼんっ
SHE GOT THE RIGHT ANSWER..
HEH, I GUESS WE REALLY DO WORRY TOO MUCH ABOUT HER...
WHAT'RE YOU TWO DOING?
IF YOU'RE GOING TO SCREW AROUND, YOU CAN STAND IN THE HALLWAY.
HUH!?
NO, WE—
?

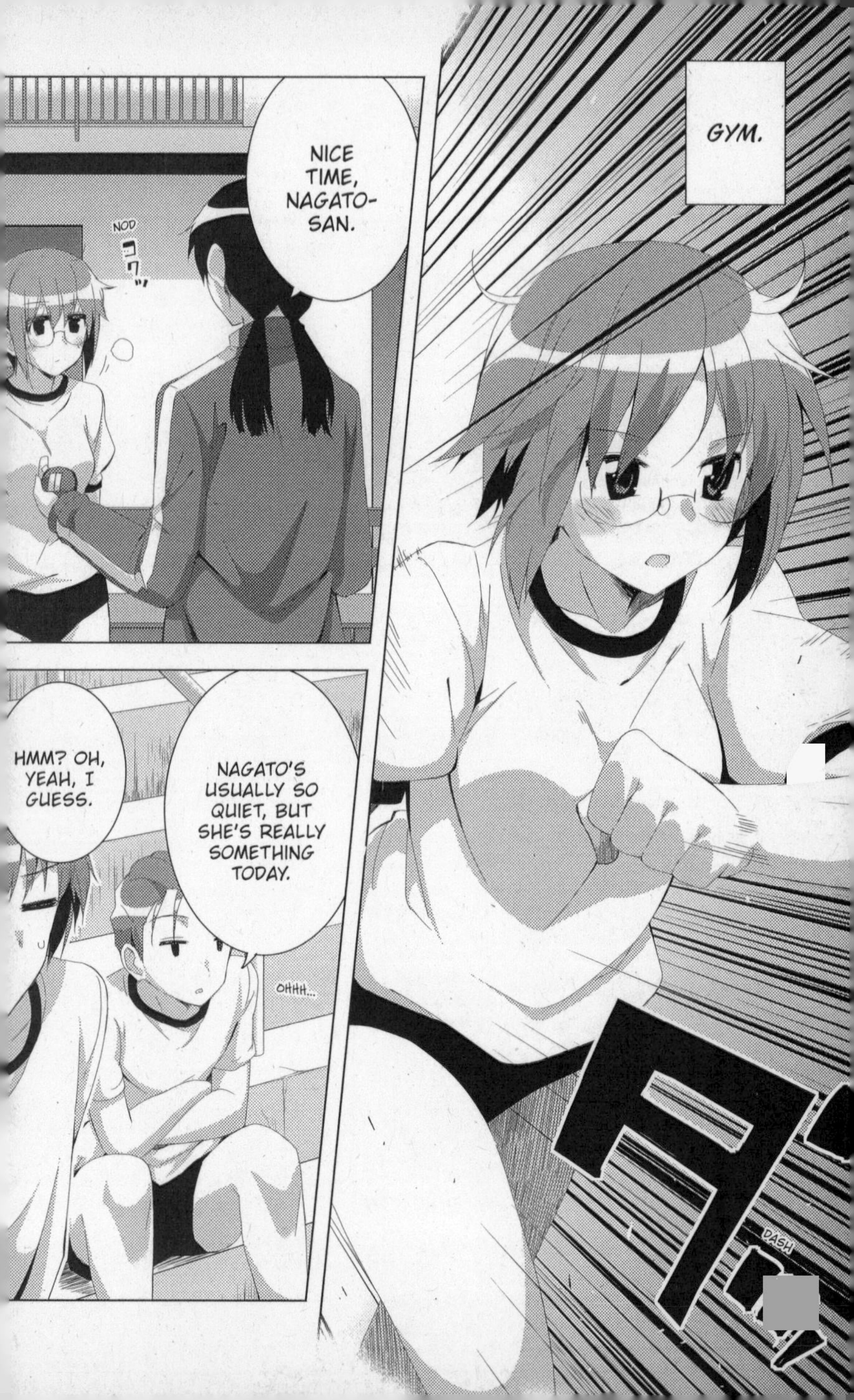
GYM.
DASH
NICE TIME, NAGATO-SAN.
NOD
NAGATO'S USUALLY SO QUIET, BUT SHE'S REALLY SOMETHING TODAY.
HMM? OH, YEAH, I GUESS.
OHHH...

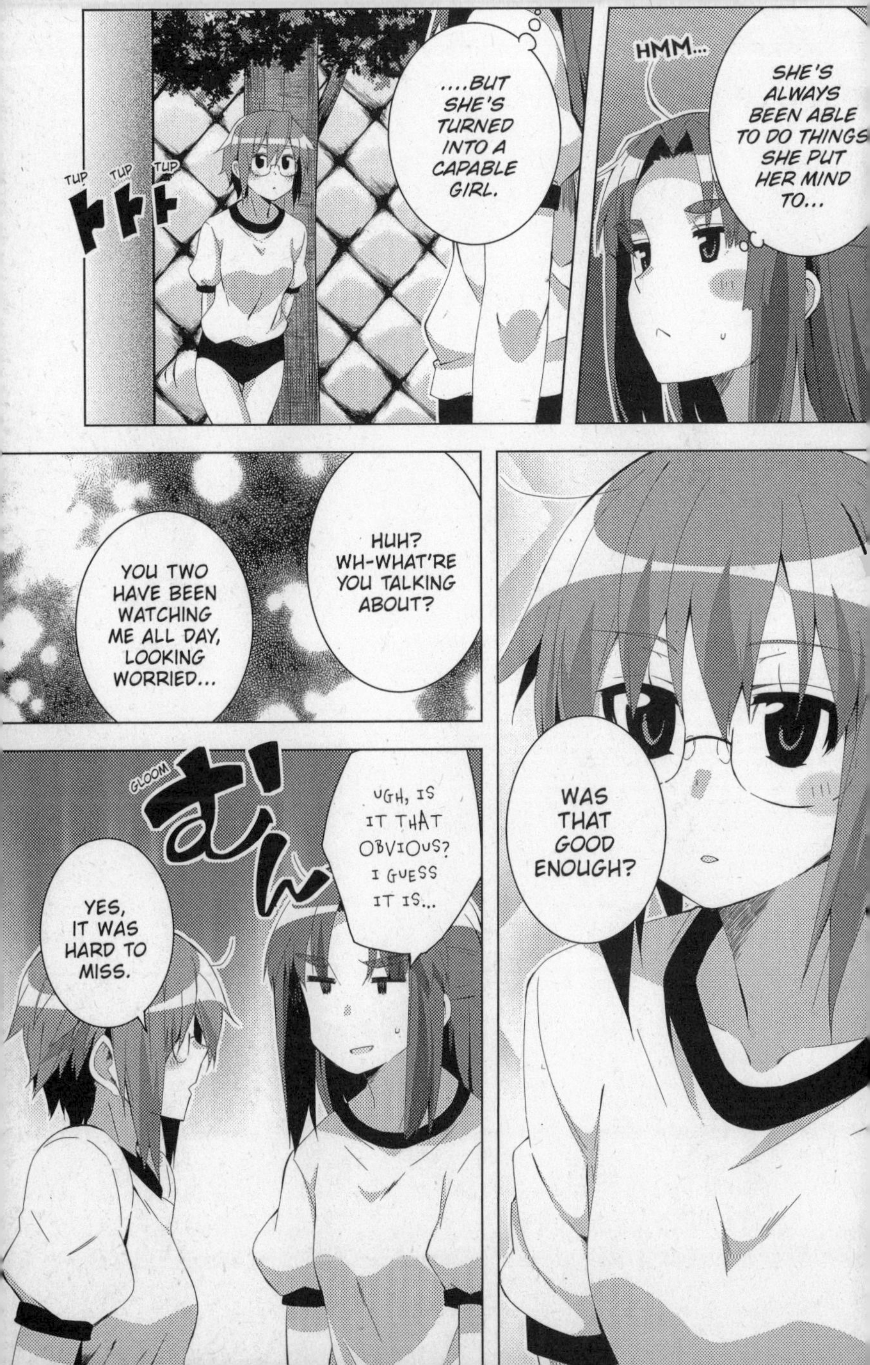
HMM...
SHE'S ALWAYS BEEN ABLE TO DO THINGS SHE PUT HER MIND TO...
....BUT SHE'S TURNED INTO A CAPABLE GIRL.
TUP TUP TUP
トトト
WAS THAT GOOD ENOUGH?
HUH? WH-WHAT'RE YOU TALKING ABOUT?
YOU TWO HAVE BEEN WATCHING ME ALL DAY, LOOKING WORRIED...
GLOOM
むん
UGH, IS IT THAT OBVIOUS? I GUESS IT IS...
YES, IT WAS HARD TO MISS.

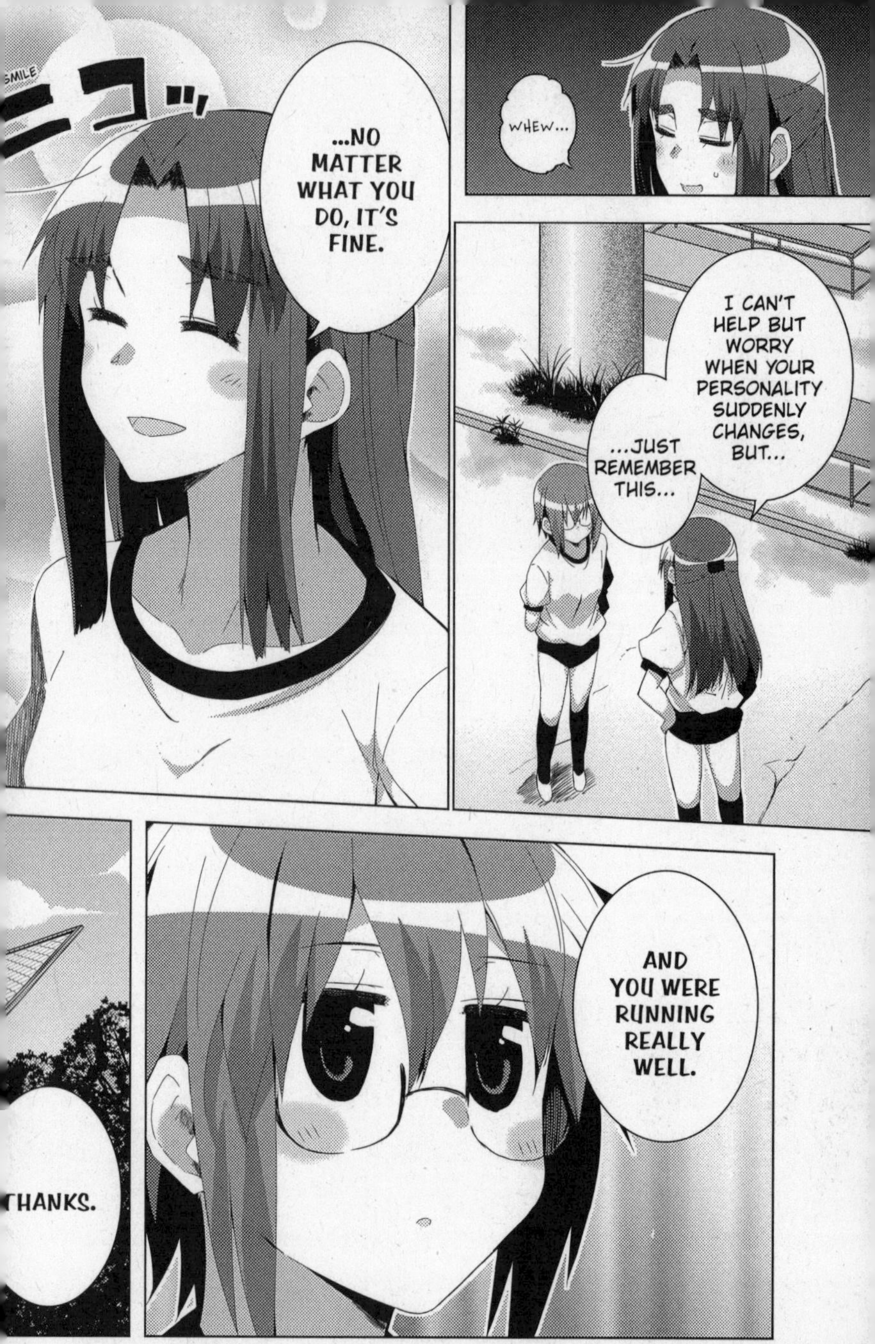
WHEW...
I CAN'T HELP BUT WORRY WHEN YOUR PERSONALITY SUDDENLY CHANGES, BUT...
...JUST REMEMBER THIS...
SMILE
...NO MATTER WHAT YOU DO, IT'S FINE.
AND YOU WERE RUNNING REALLY WELL.
THANKS.

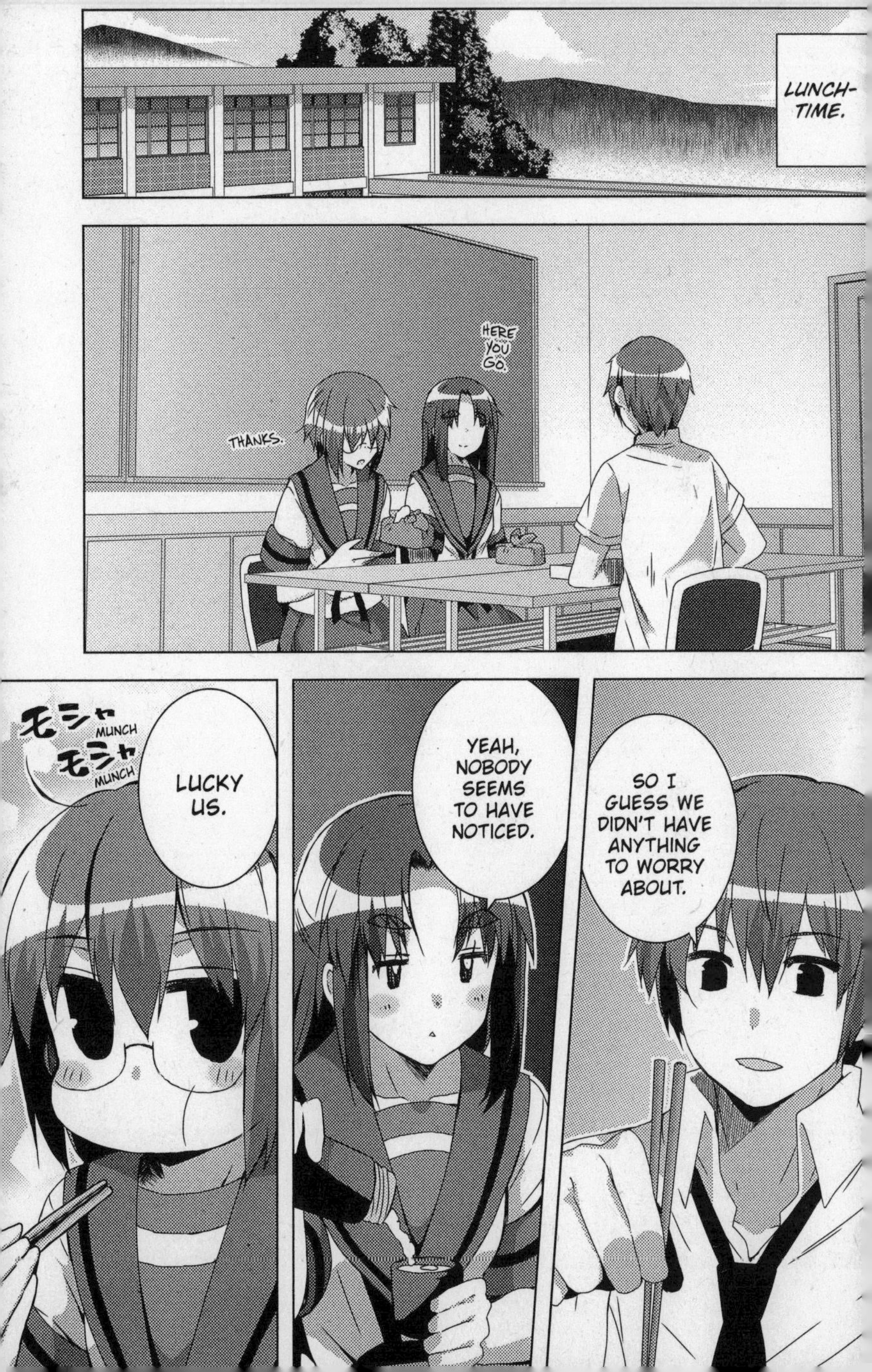
LUNCH-TIME.
HERE YOU GO.
THANKS.
SO I GUESS WE DIDN'T HAVE ANYTHING TO WORRY ABOUT.
YEAH, NOBODY SEEMS TO HAVE NOTICED.
LUCKY US.
モシャ MUNCH
モシャ MUNCH

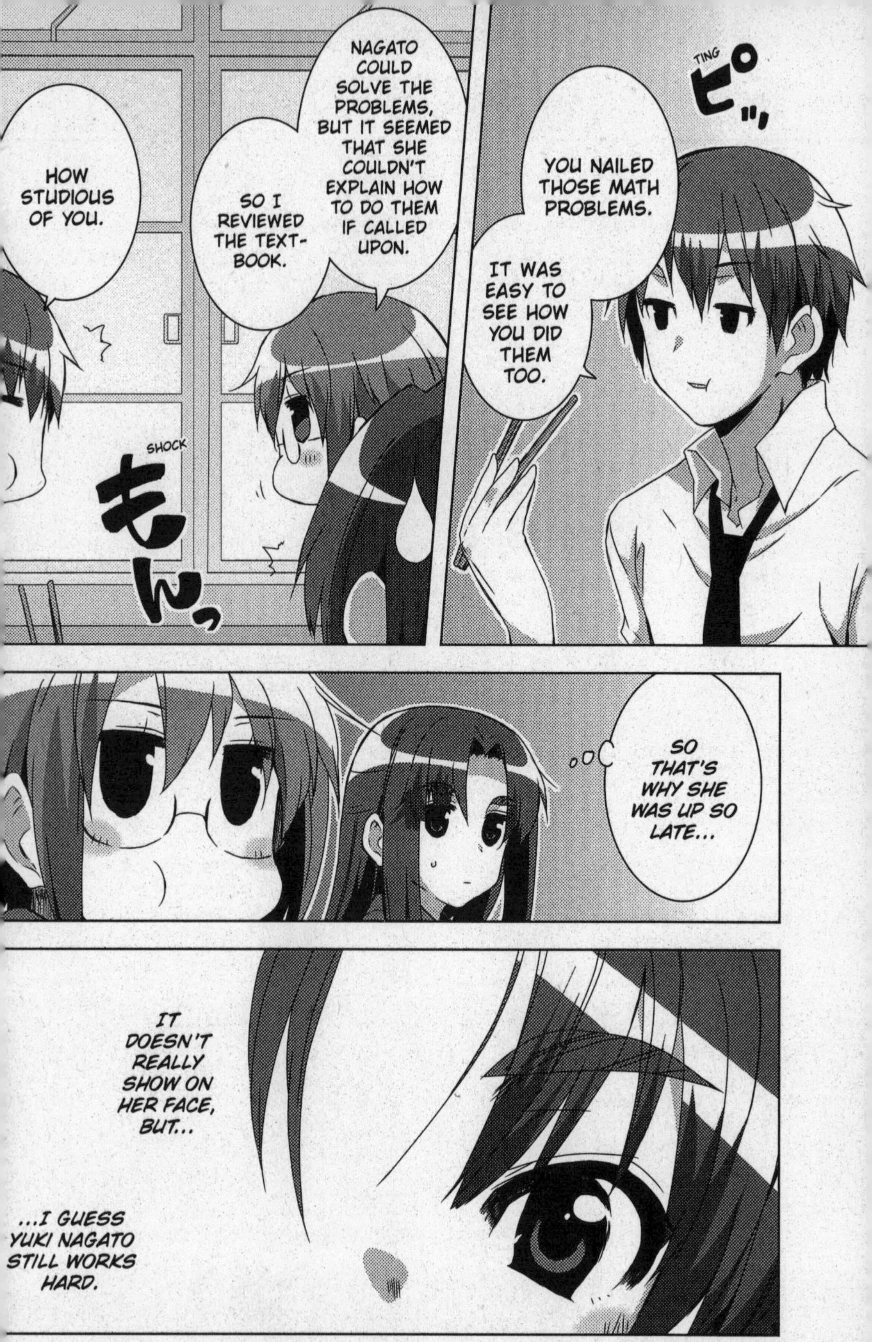
TING
ピッ
YOU NAILED THOSE MATH PROBLEMS.
IT WAS EASY TO SEE HOW YOU DID THEM TOO.
NAGATO COULD SOLVE THE PROBLEMS, BUT IT SEEMED THAT SHE COULDN'T EXPLAIN HOW TO DO THEM IF CALLED UPON.
SO I REVIEWED THE TEXT-BOOK.
HOW STUDIOUS OF YOU.
SHOCK
もんっ
SO THAT'S WHY SHE WAS UP SO LATE...
IT DOESN'T REALLY SHOW ON HER FACE, BUT...
...I GUESS YUKI NAGATO STILL WORKS HARD.

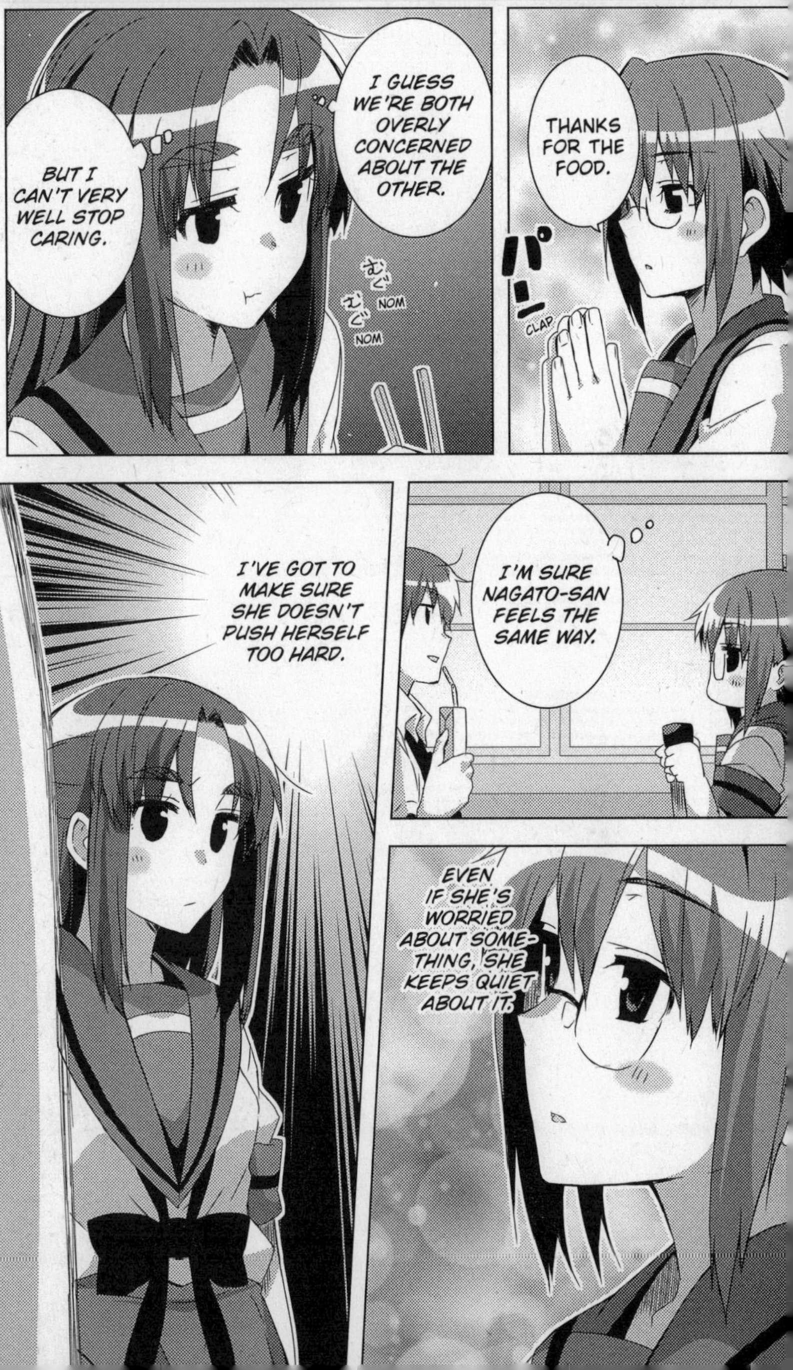
THANKS FOR THE FOOD.
パン
CLAP
I GUESS WE'RE BOTH OVERLY CONCERNED ABOUT THE OTHER.
むぐ NOM
むぐ NOM
BUT I CAN'T VERY WELL STOP CARING.
I'M SURE NAGATO-SAN FEELS THE SAME WAY.
EVEN IF SHE'S WORRIED ABOUT SOME-THING, SHE KEEPS QUIET ABOUT IT.
I'VE GOT TO MAKE SURE SHE DOESN'T PUSH HERSELF TOO HARD.

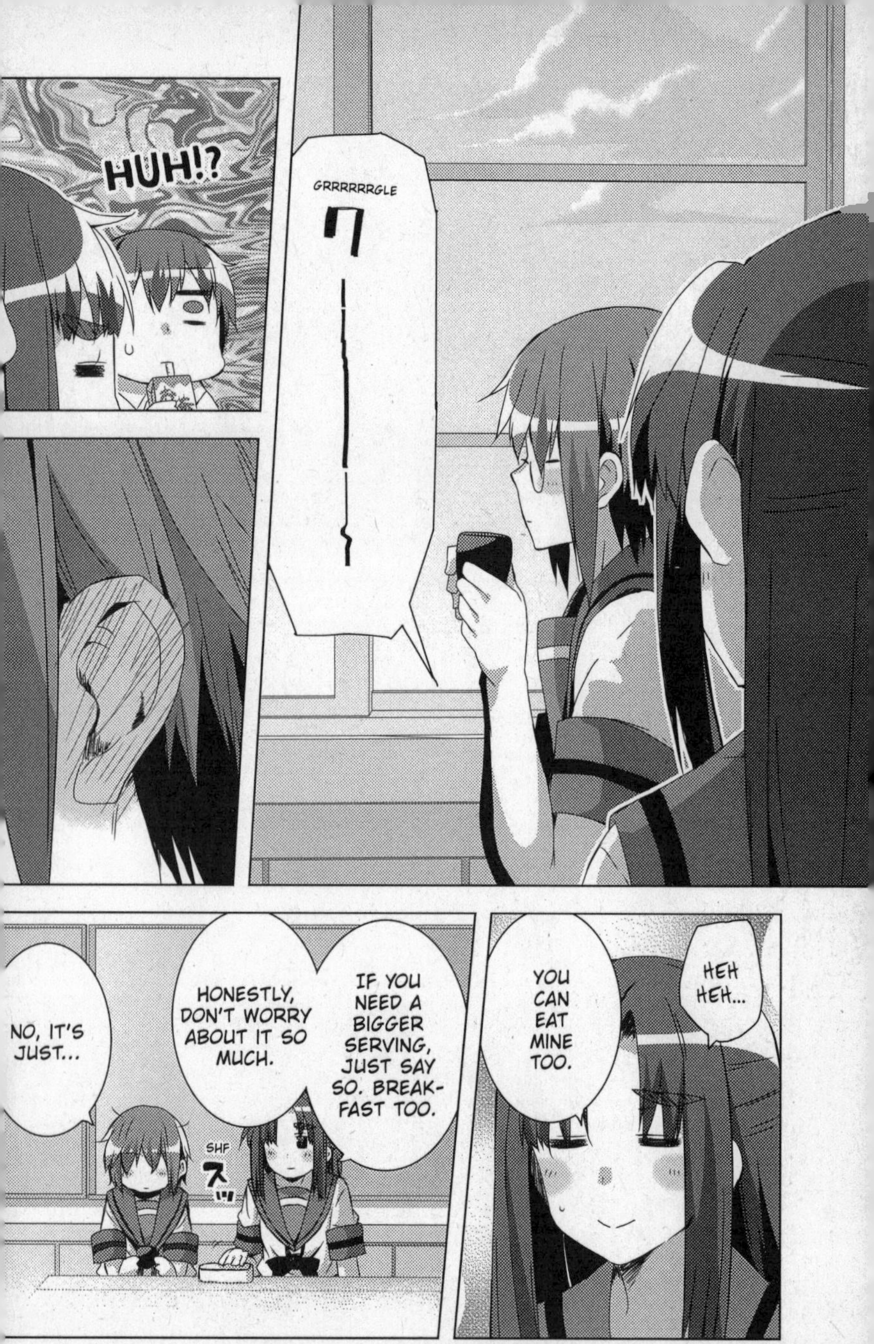
GRRRRRRGLE
HUH!?
HEH HEH...
YOU CAN EAT MINE TOO.
IF YOU NEED A BIGGER SERVING, JUST SAY SO. BREAK-FAST TOO.
HONESTLY, DON'T WORRY ABOUT IT SO MUCH.
SHF
NO, IT'S JUST...

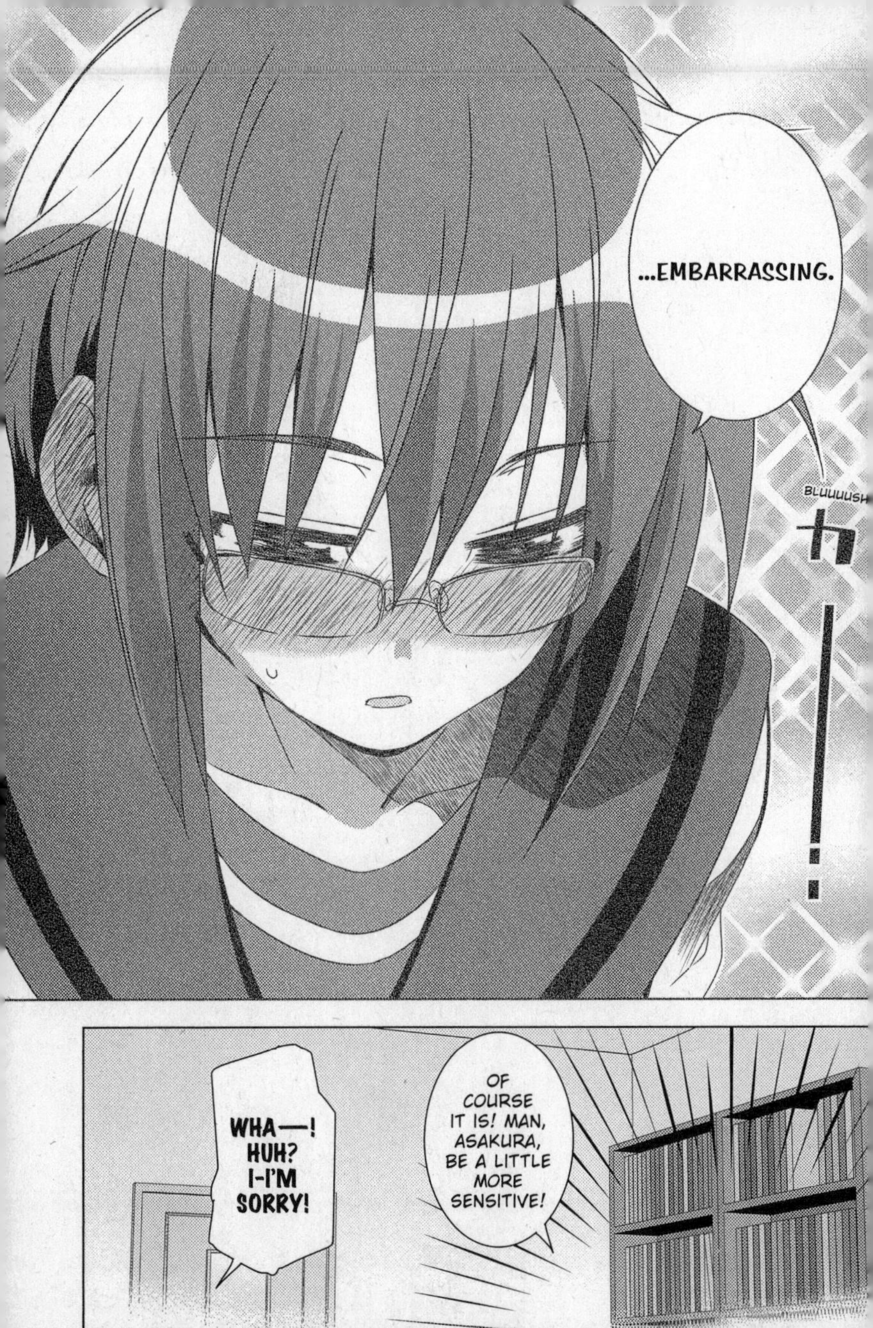
...EMBARRASSING.
BLUUUUSH
カー!!
OF COURSE IT IS! MAN, ASAKURA, BE A LITTLE MORE SENSITIVE!
WHA—! HUH? I-I'M SORRY!

AFTER SCHOOL.

HMM? HMM.

HMMMM.

IT'S NO GOOD. I DON'T UNDER-STAND THIS AT ALL.

WHAT'S WRONG?

GUH

HMMMM.

MMMMM

む む む...

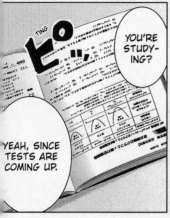

TING

ピッ

YOU'RE STUDY-ING?

YEAH, SINCE TESTS ARE COMING UP.

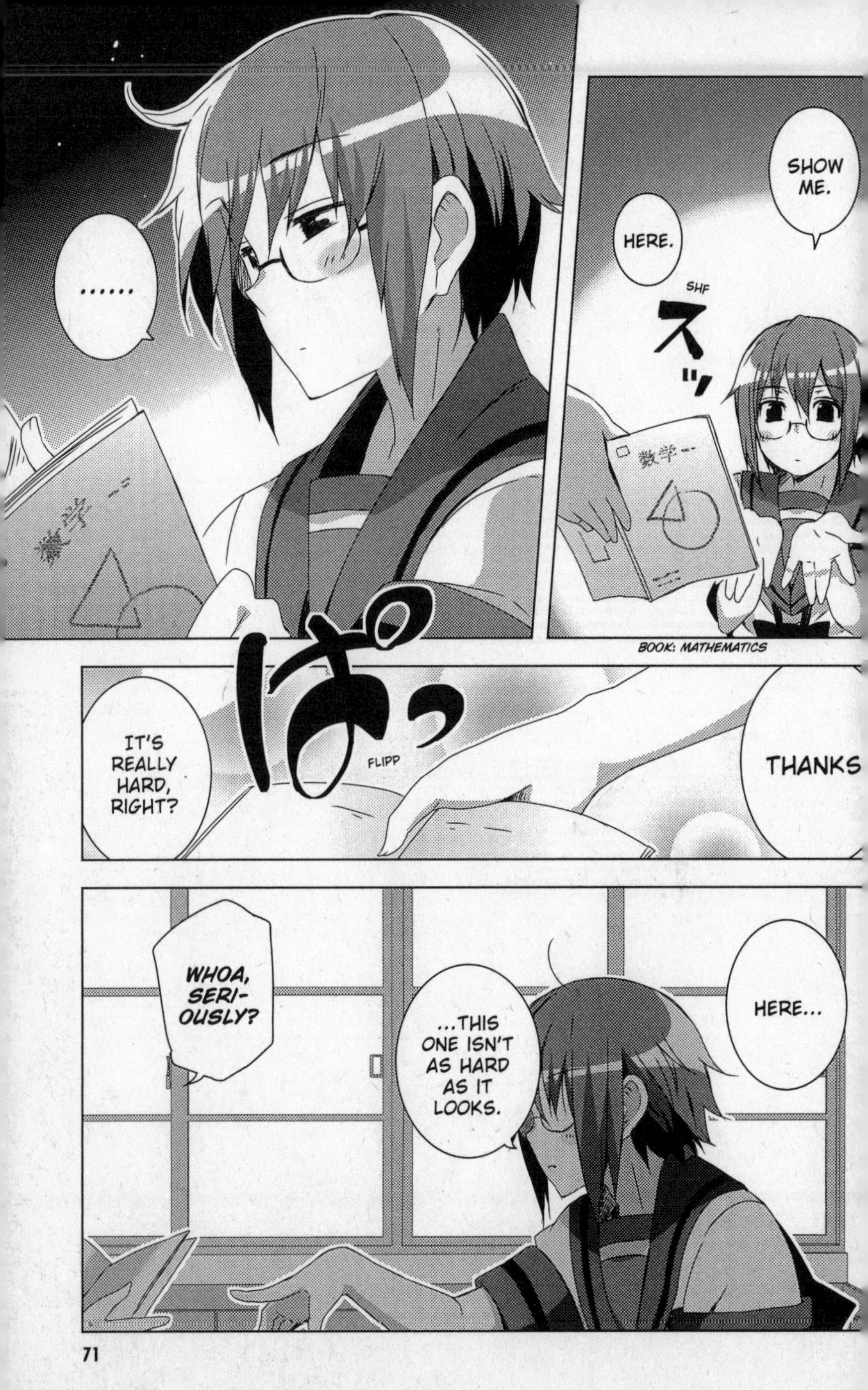
SHOW ME.
HERE.
SHF
スッ
数学
BOOK: MATHEMATICS
......
THANKS
ぱっ
FLIPP
IT'S REALLY HARD, RIGHT?
HERE...
...THIS ONE ISN'T AS HARD AS IT LOOKS.
WHOA, SERI-OUSLY?

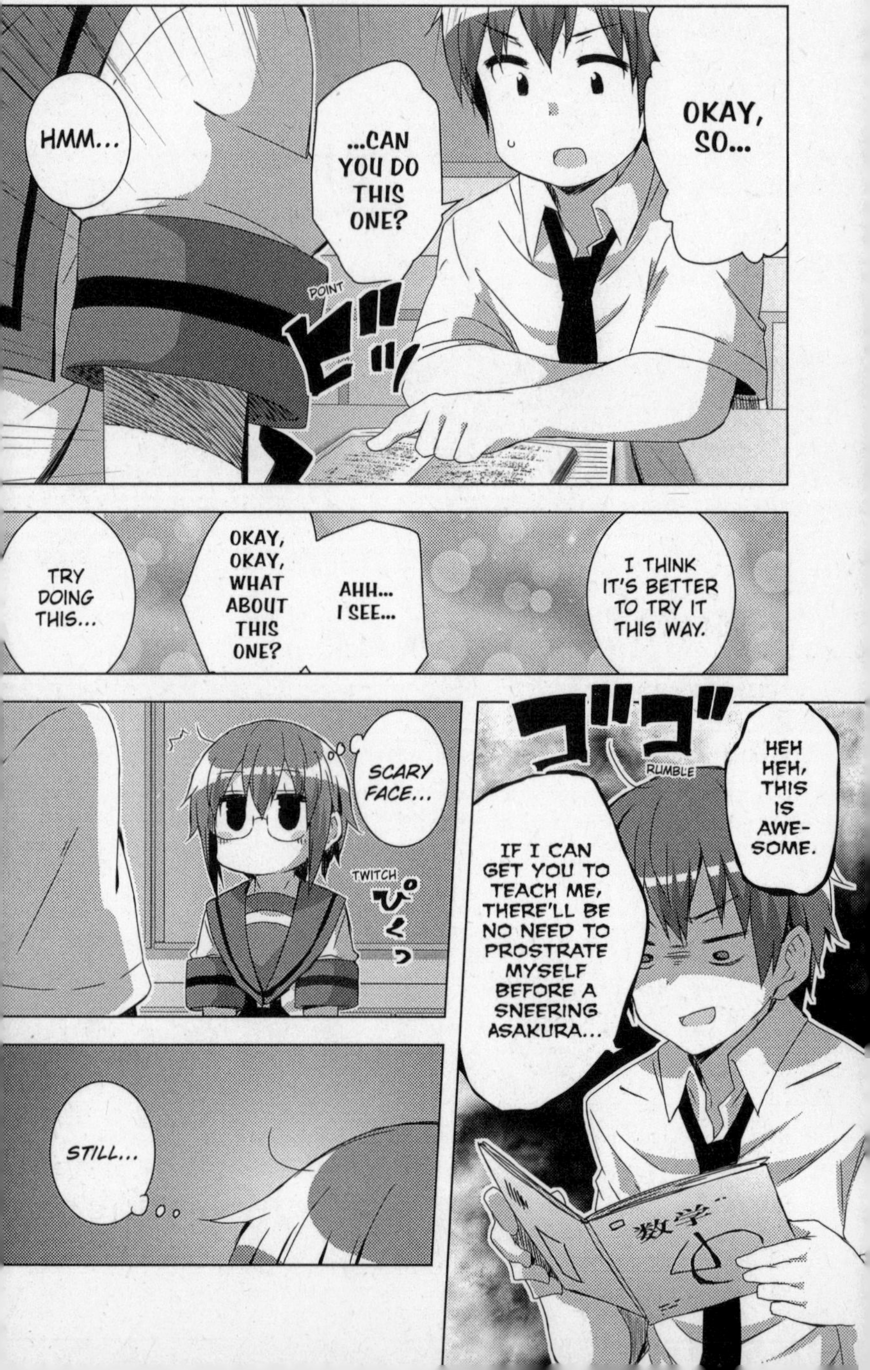
OKAY, SO...
...CAN YOU DO THIS ONE?
POINT
ビッ
HMM...
I THINK IT'S BETTER TO TRY IT THIS WAY.
AHH... I SEE...
OKAY, OKAY, WHAT ABOUT THIS ONE?
TRY DOING THIS...
ゴゴ
RUMBLE
HEH HEH, THIS IS AWESOME.
IF I CAN GET YOU TO TEACH ME, THERE'LL BE NO NEED TO PROSTRATE MYSELF BEFORE A SNEERING ASAKURA...
数学
SCARY FACE...
TWITCH
ぴくっ
STILL...

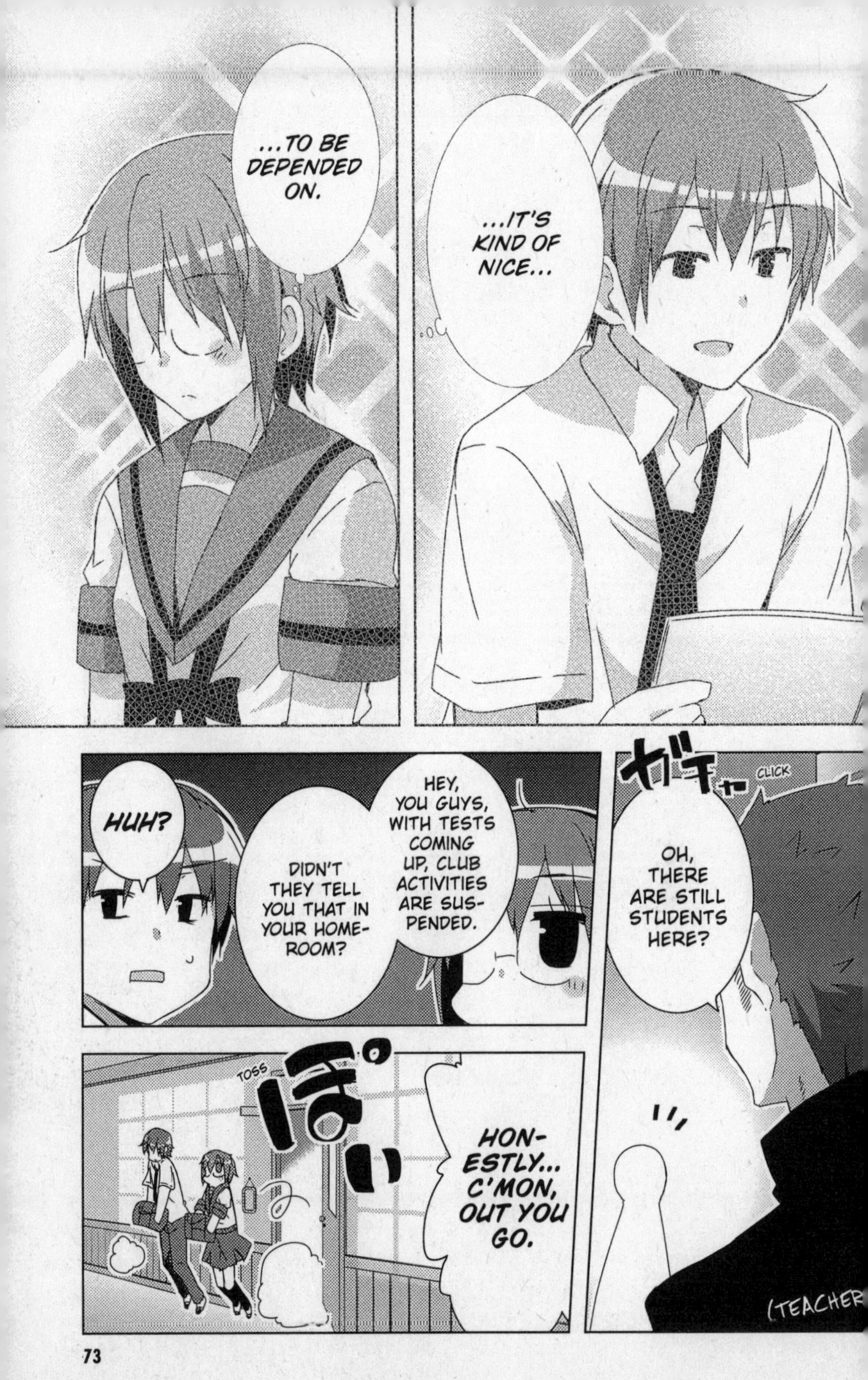
...IT'S KIND OF NICE...
...TO BE DEPENDED ON.
ガチャ
CLICK
OH, THERE ARE STILL STUDENTS HERE?
(TEACHER
HEY, YOU GUYS, WITH TESTS COMING UP, CLUB ACTIVITIES ARE SUS-PENDED.
DIDN'T THEY TELL YOU THAT IN YOUR HOME-ROOM?
HUH?
HON-ESTLY... C'MON, OUT YOU GO.
ぽい
TOSS

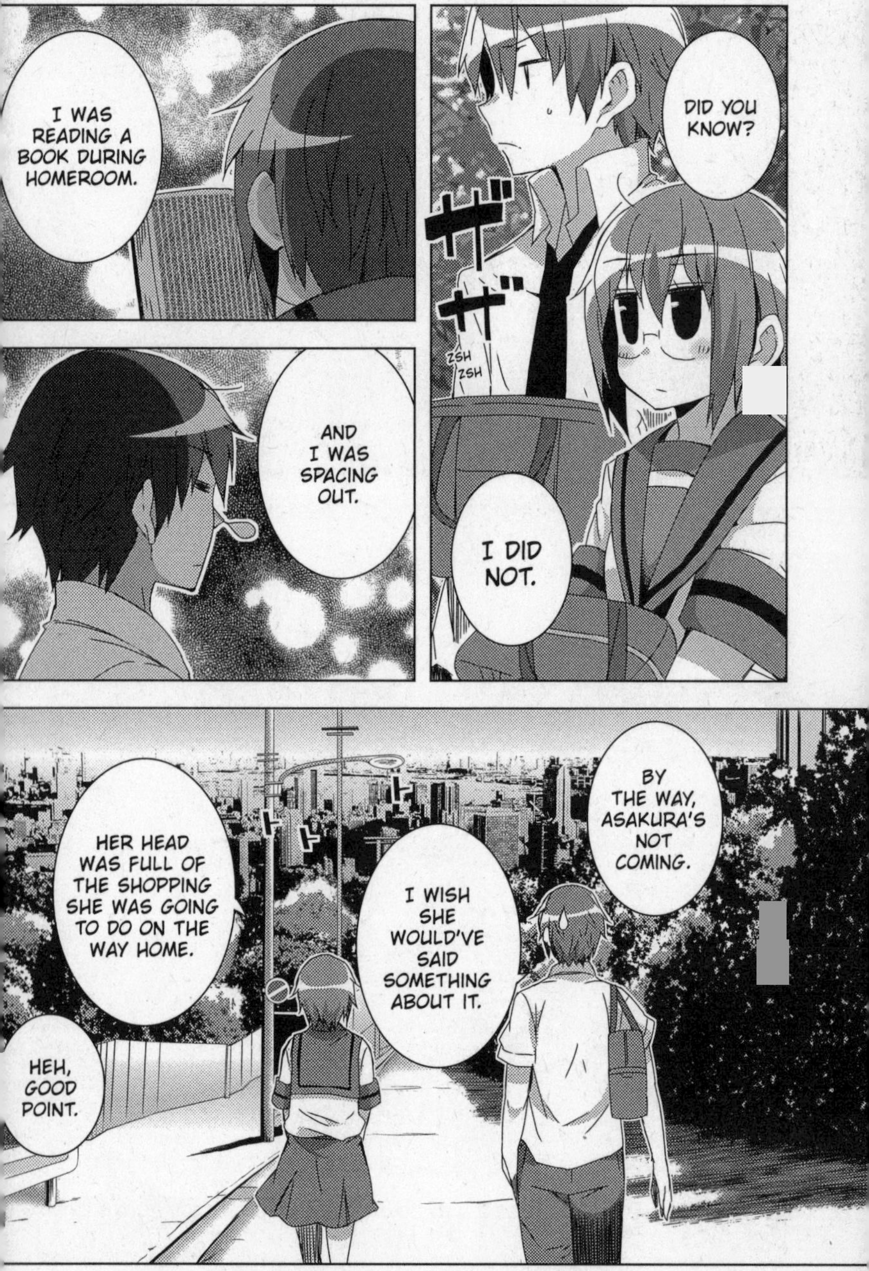
DID YOU KNOW?
ZSH ZSH
I DID NOT.
I WAS READING A BOOK DURING HOMEROOM.
AND I WAS SPACING OUT.
BY THE WAY, ASAKURA'S NOT COMING.
I WISH SHE WOULD'VE SAID SOMETHING ABOUT IT.
HER HEAD WAS FULL OF THE SHOPPING SHE WAS GOING TO DO ON THE WAY HOME.
HEH, GOOD POINT.

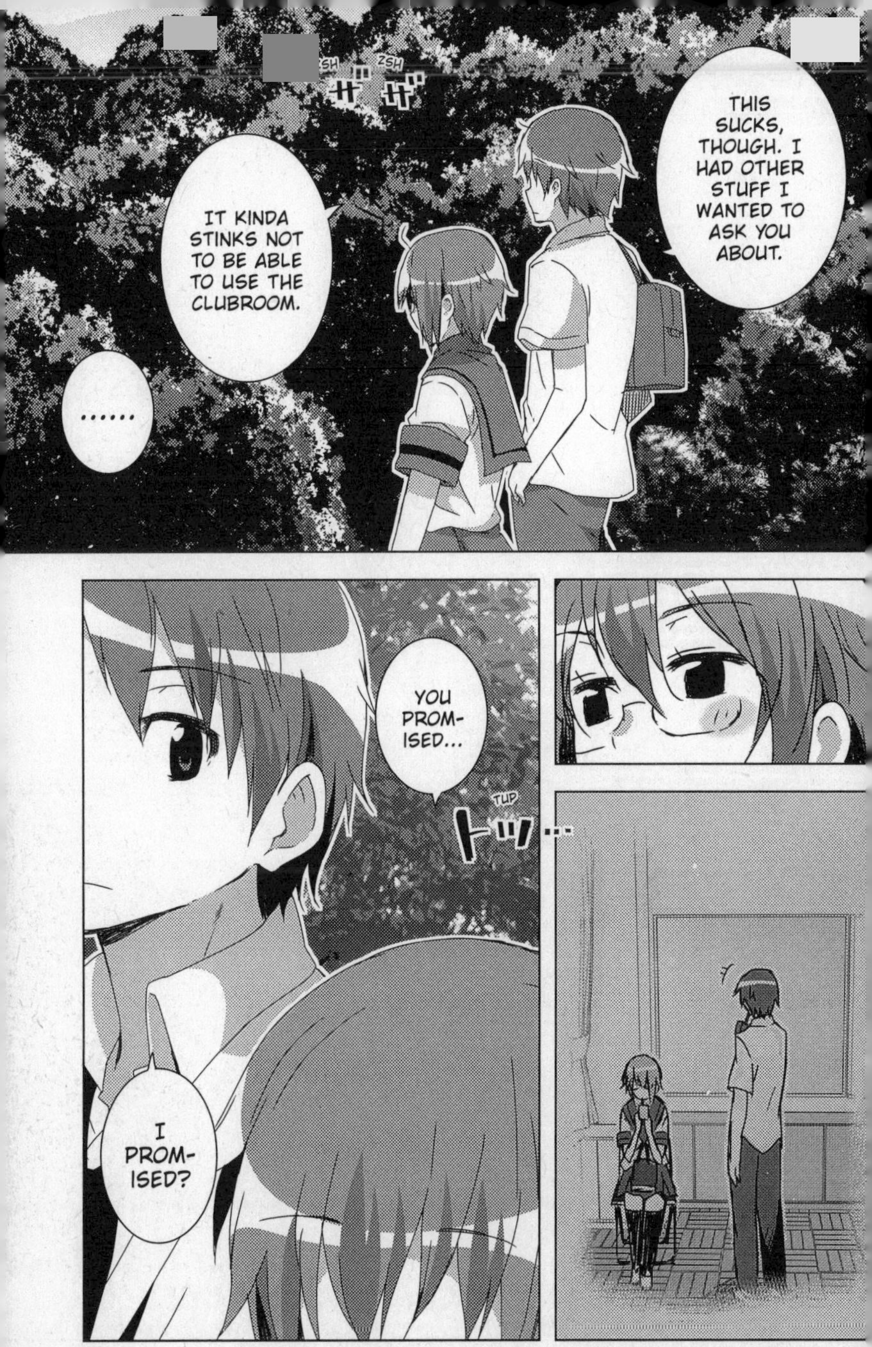
ZSH ZSH
THIS SUCKS, THOUGH. I HAD OTHER STUFF I WANTED TO ASK YOU ABOUT.
IT KINDA STINKS NOT TO BE ABLE TO USE THE CLUBROOM.
......
YOU PROMISED...
TUP
I PROMISED?

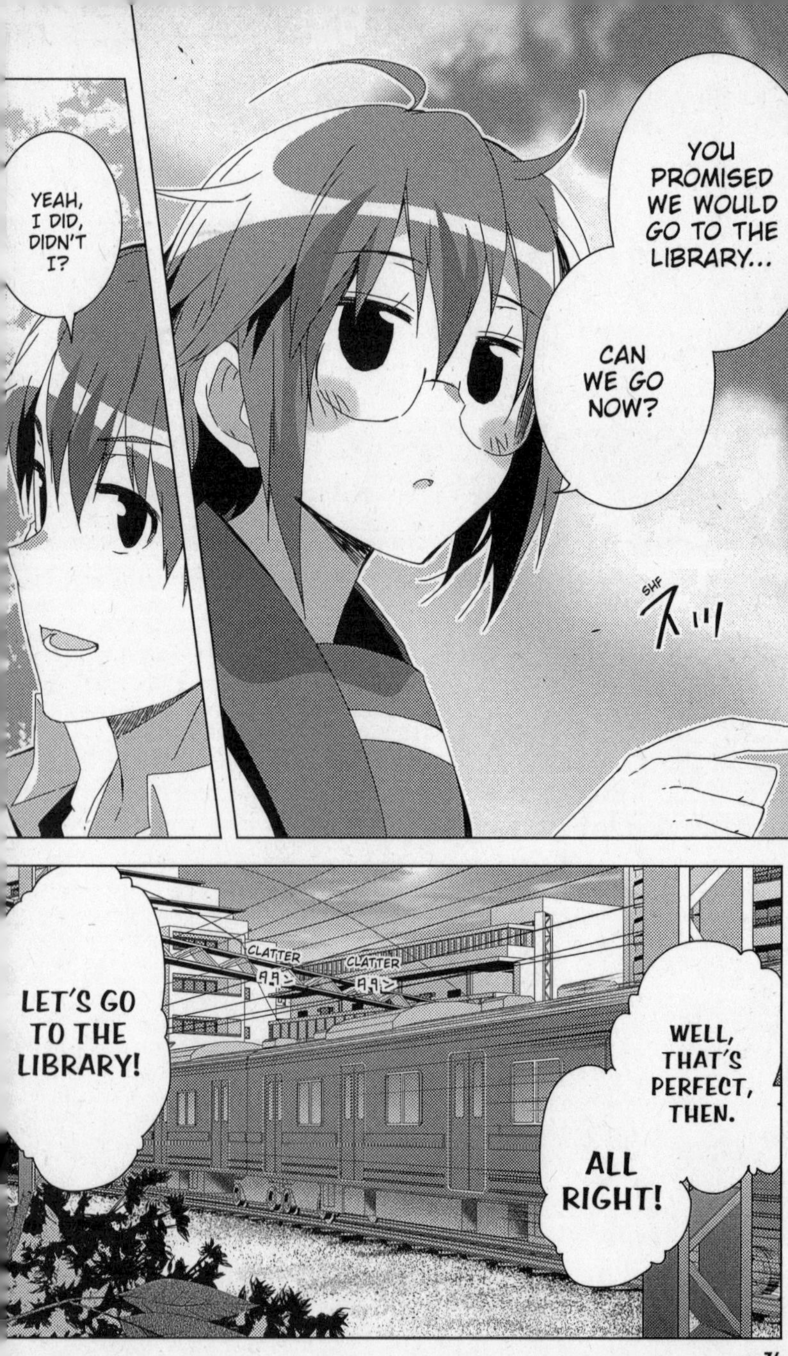
YOU PROMISED WE WOULD GO TO THE LIBRARY...
CAN WE GO NOW?
SHF
スッ
YEAH, I DID, DIDN'T I?
WELL, THAT'S PERFECT, THEN.
ALL RIGHT!
CLATTER
CLATTER
LET'S GO TO THE LIBRARY!

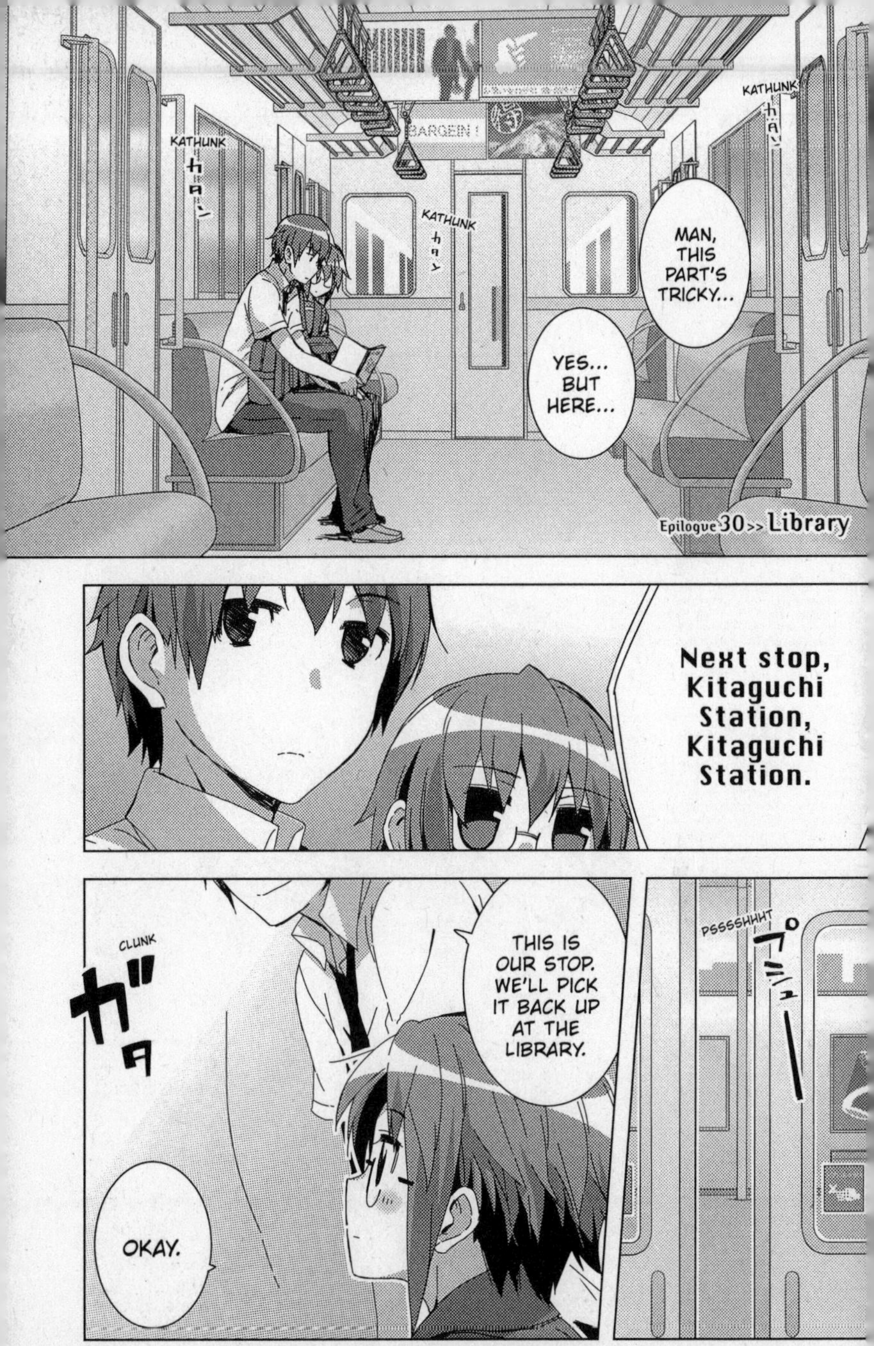
KATHUNK
MAN, THIS PART'S TRICKY...
YES... BUT HERE...
KATHUNK
KATHUNK
Epilogue 30>> Library
Next stop, Kitaguchi Station, Kitaguchi Station.
PSSSSHHHT
THIS IS OUR STOP. WE'LL PICK IT BACK UP AT THE LIBRARY.
CLUNK
OKAY.

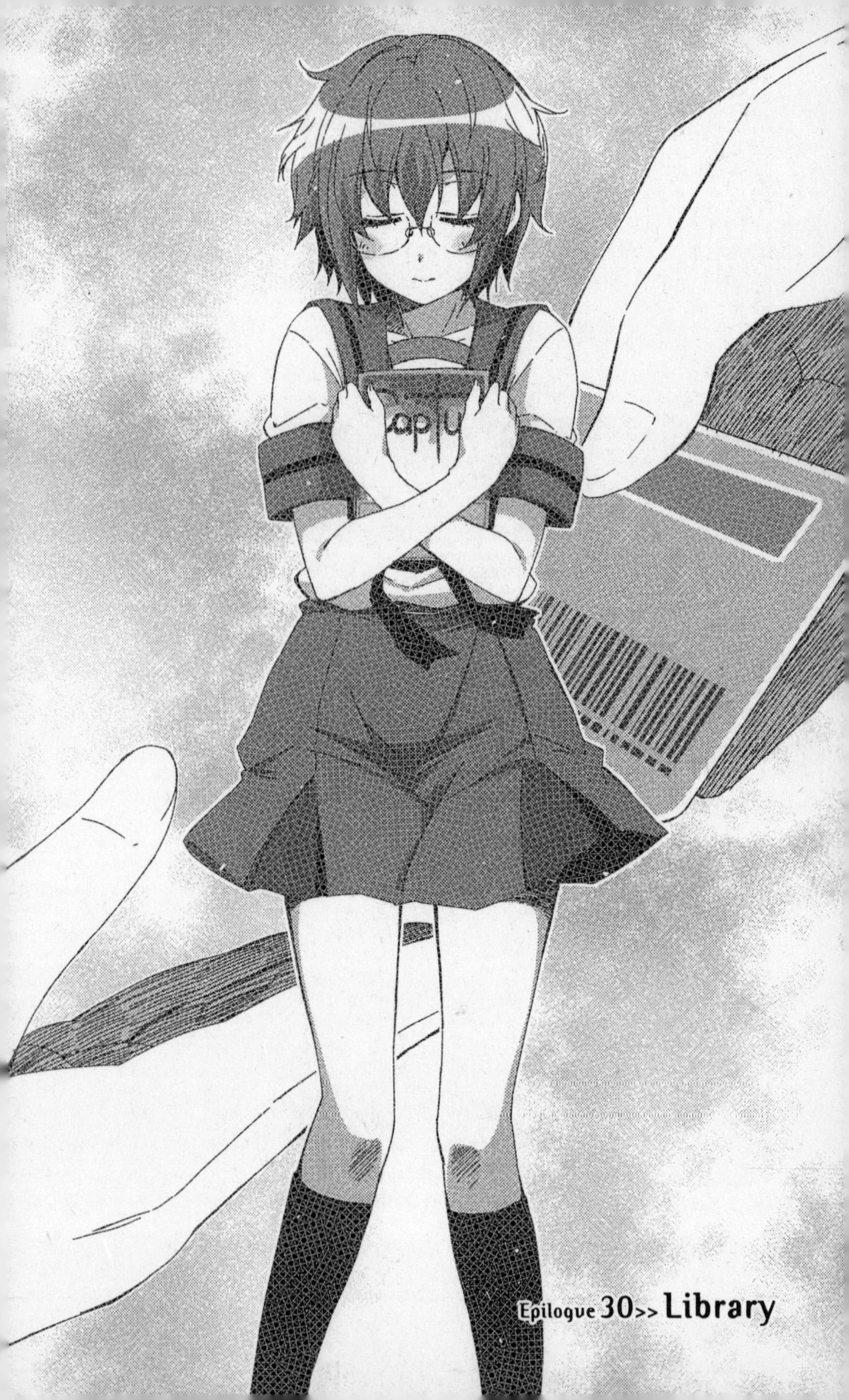

Epilogue 30>> Library

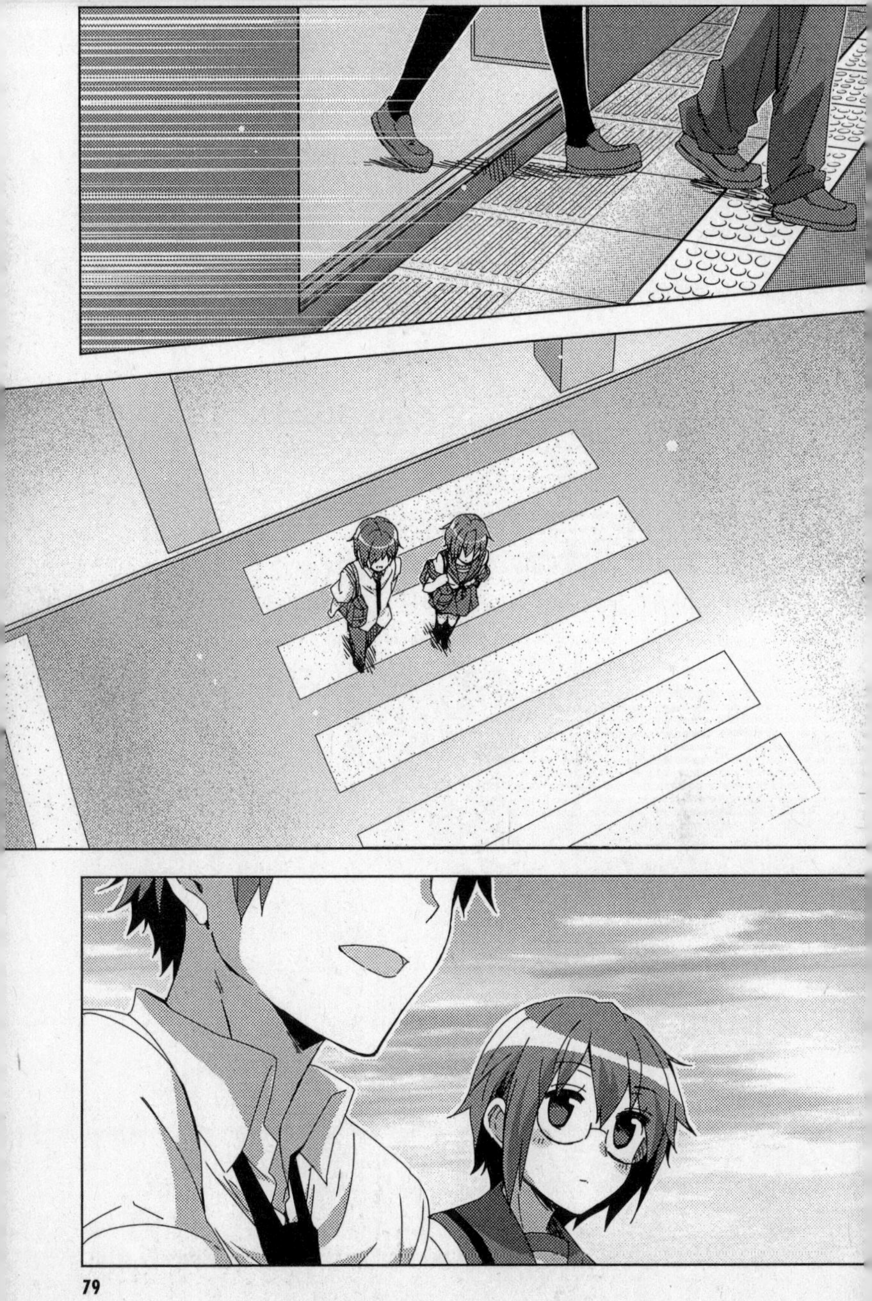

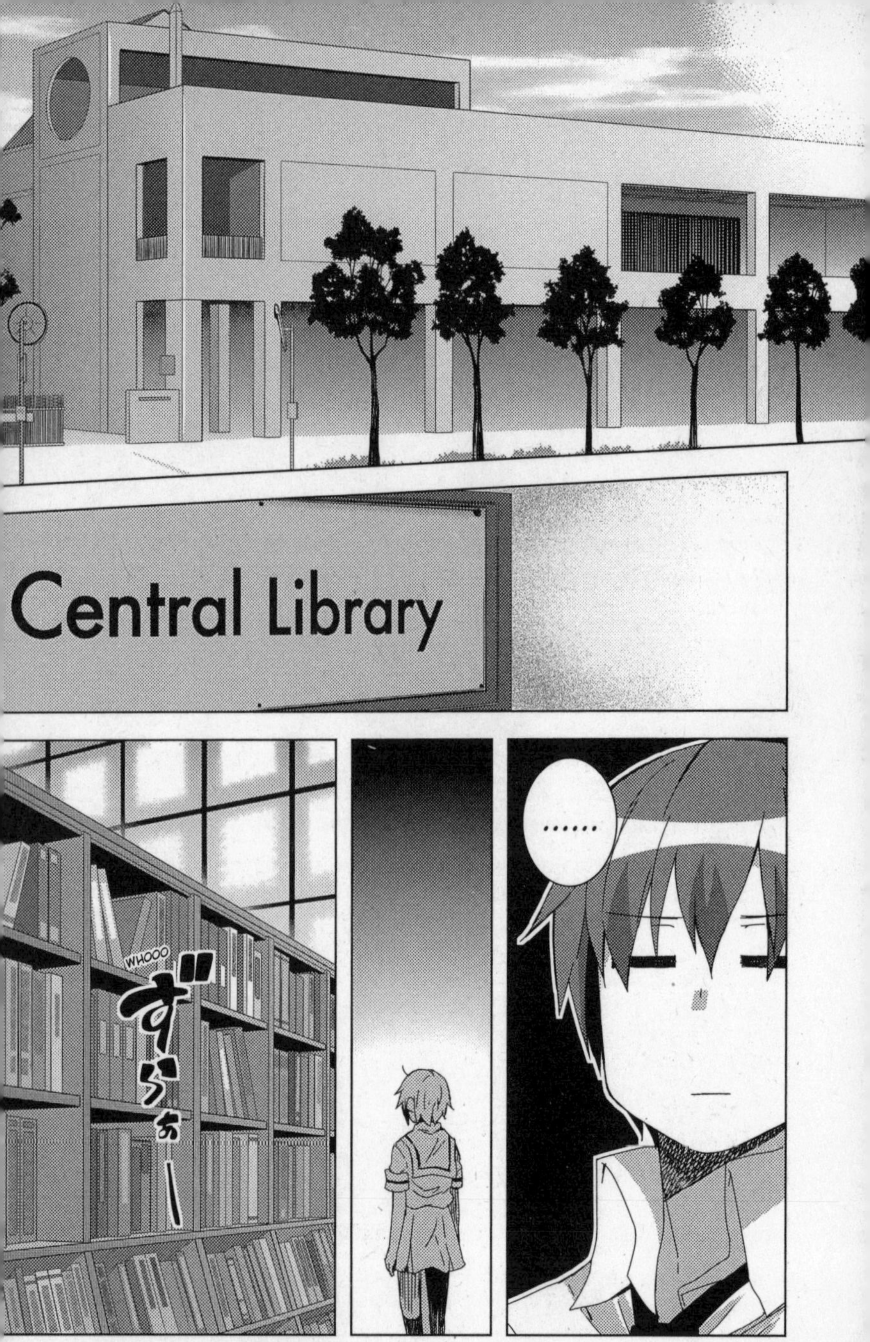
Central Library
......
WHOOO
ずらぁー

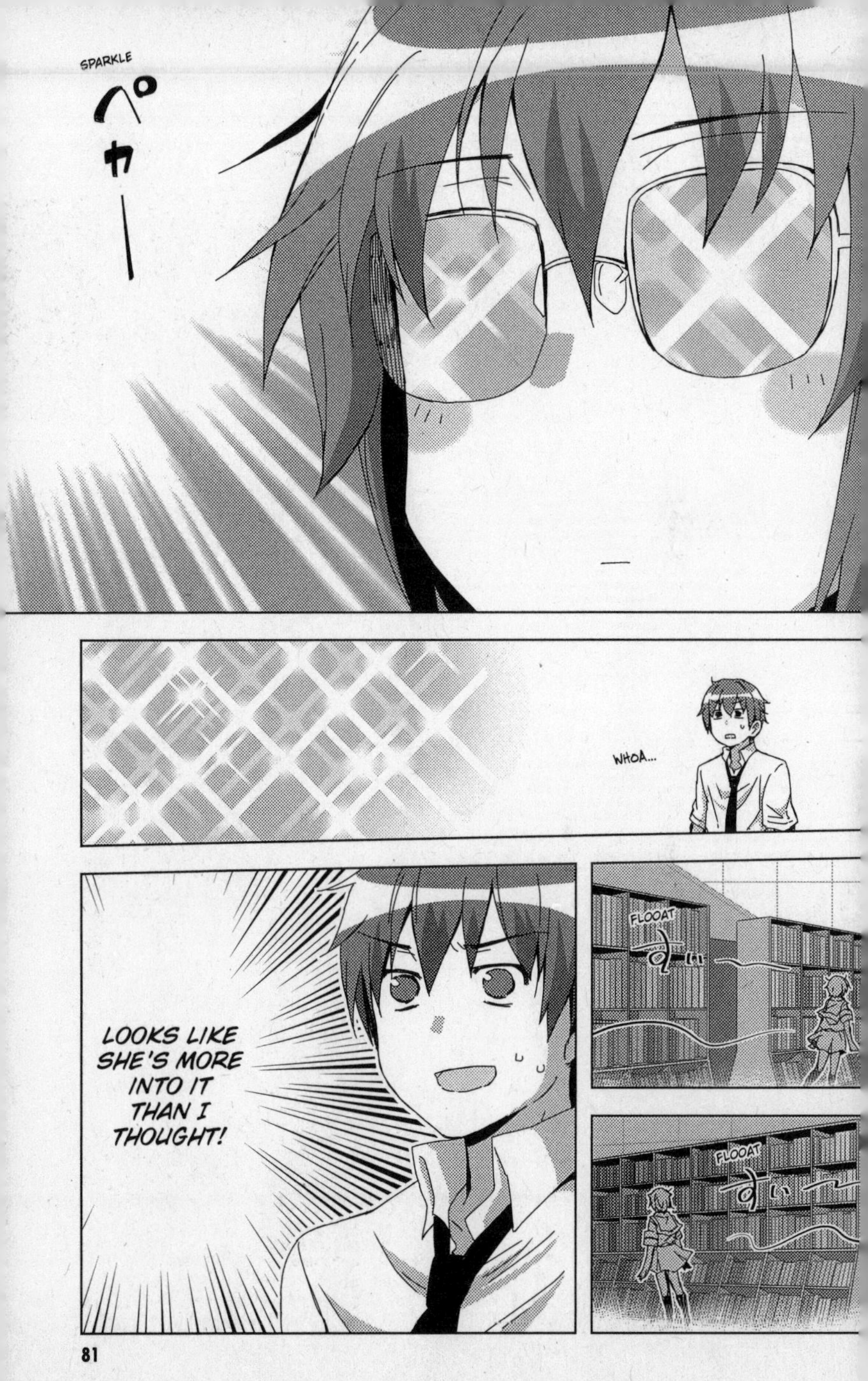
SPARKLE
ペカー
WHOA...
FLOOAT
FLOOAT
LOOKS LIKE SHE'S MORE INTO IT THAN I THOUGHT!

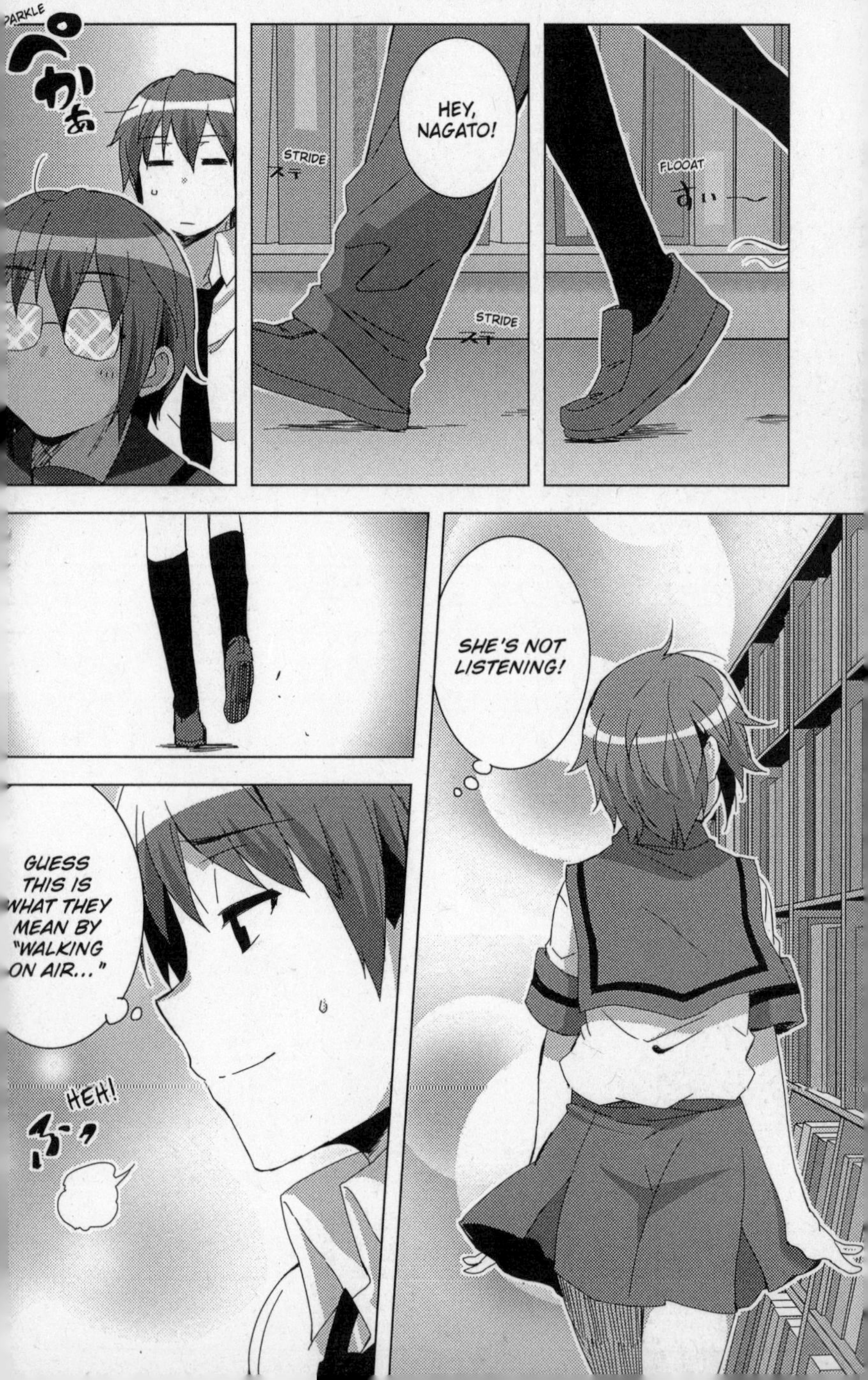
FLOOAT
すぃ〜
HEY, NAGATO!
STRIDE
ステ
STRIDE
ステ
PARKLE
ぺかぁ
SHE'S NOT LISTENING!
GUESS THIS IS WHAT THEY MEAN BY "WALKING ON AIR..."
HEH!
ふっ

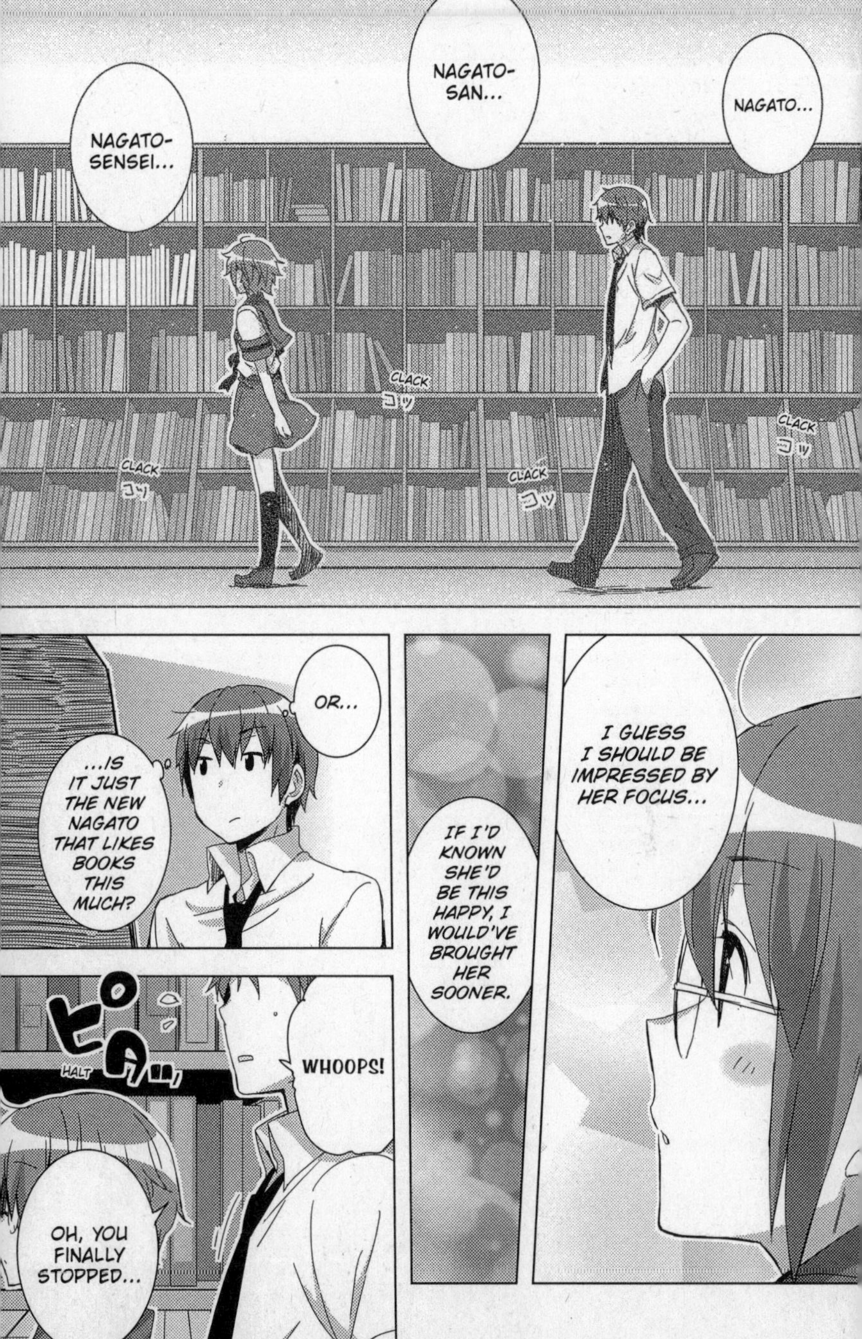
NAGATO...
NAGATO-SAN...
NAGATO-SENSEI...
CLACK コツ
CLACK コツ
CLACK コツ
CLACK コツ
I GUESS I SHOULD BE IMPRESSED BY HER FOCUS...
IF I'D KNOWN SHE'D BE THIS HAPPY, I WOULD'VE BROUGHT HER SOONER.
OR...
...IS IT JUST THE NEW NAGATO THAT LIKES BOOKS THIS MUCH?
WHOOPS!
HALT ピタ
OH, YOU FINALLY STOPPED...

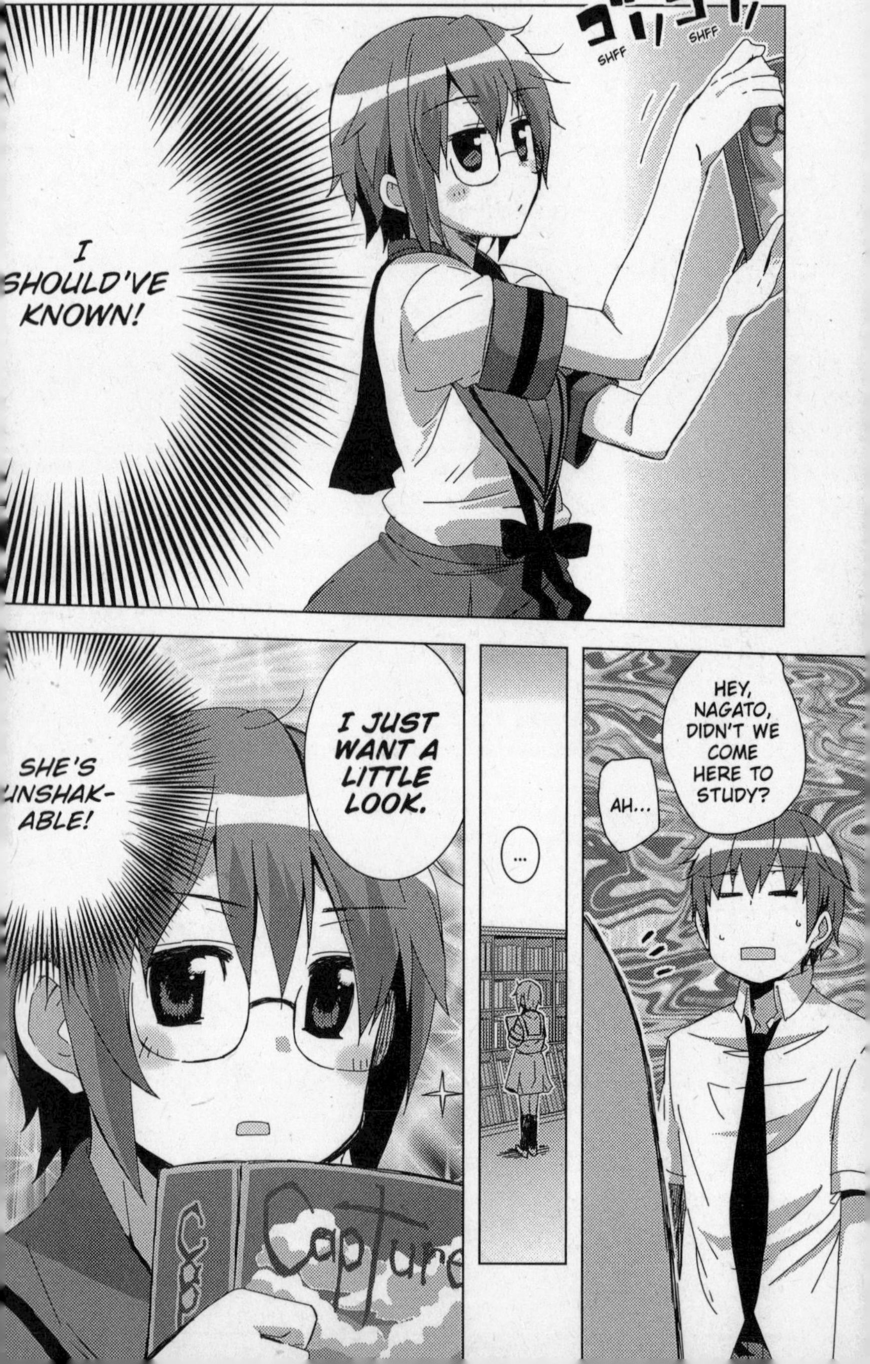
ゴソゴソ
SHFF SHFF
I SHOULD'VE KNOWN!
HEY, NAGATO, DIDN'T WE COME HERE TO STUDY?
AH...
...
I JUST WANT A LITTLE LOOK.
SHE'S UNSHAK-ABLE!
Capture

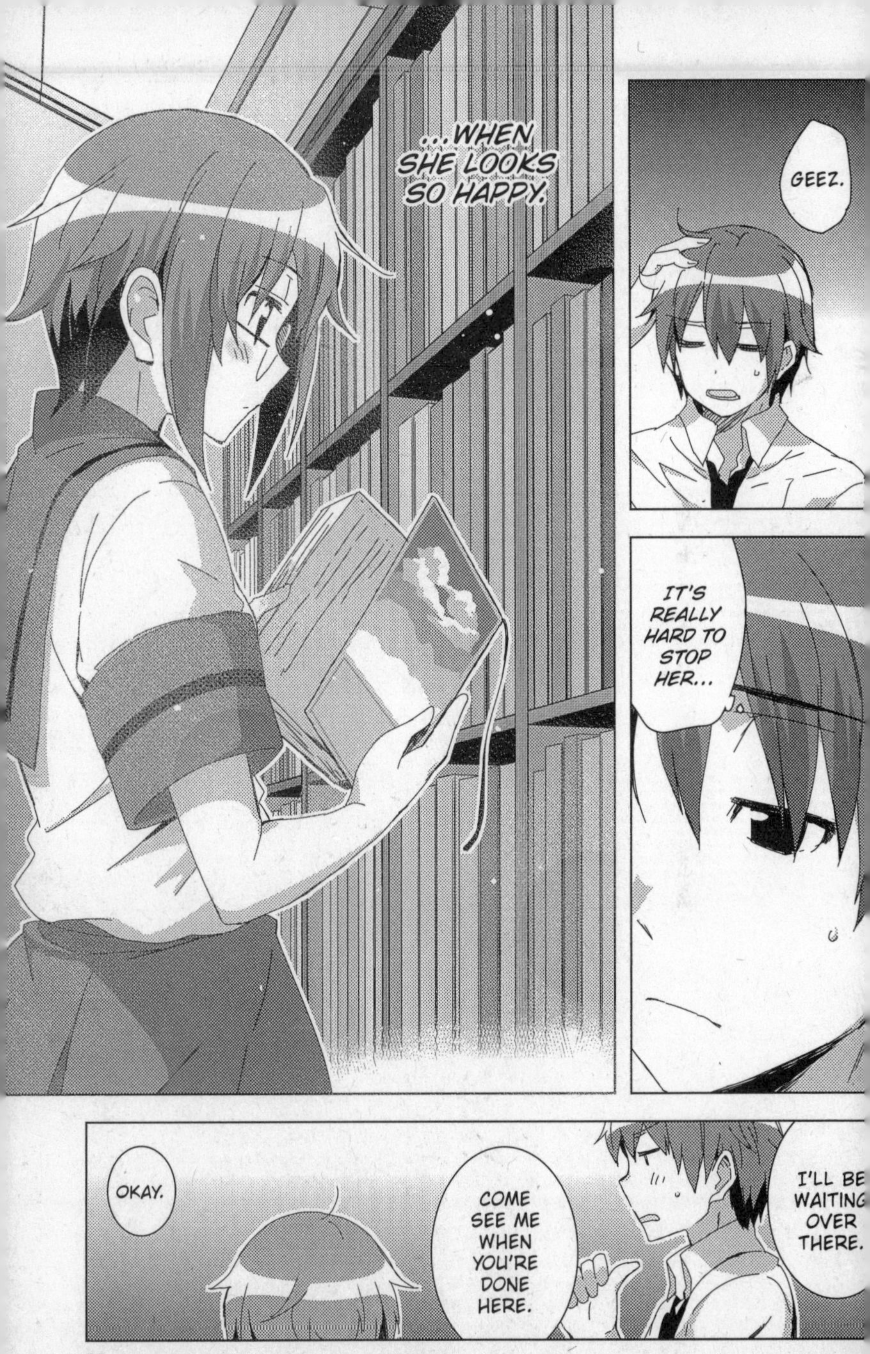
GEEZ.
IT'S REALLY HARD TO STOP HER...
...WHEN SHE LOOKS SO HAPPY.
I'LL BE WAITING OVER THERE.
COME SEE ME WHEN YOU'RE DONE HERE.
OKAY.

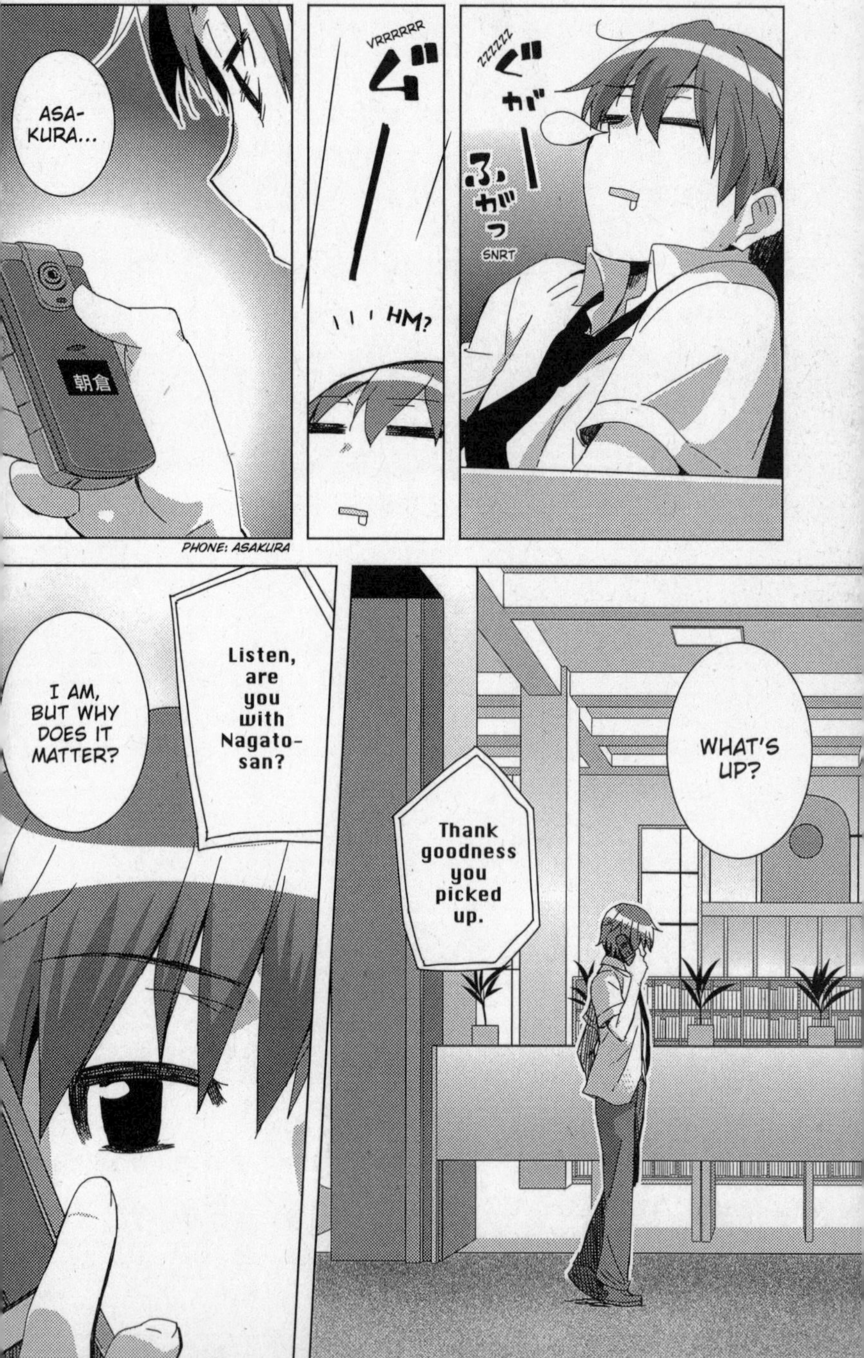
ZZZZZZ
ぐがー
ふがっ
SNRT
VRRRRRR
ヴー
HM?
ASA-KURA...
朝倉
PHONE: ASAKURA
WHAT'S UP?
Thank goodness you picked up.
Listen, are you with Nagato-san?
I AM, BUT WHY DOES IT MATTER?

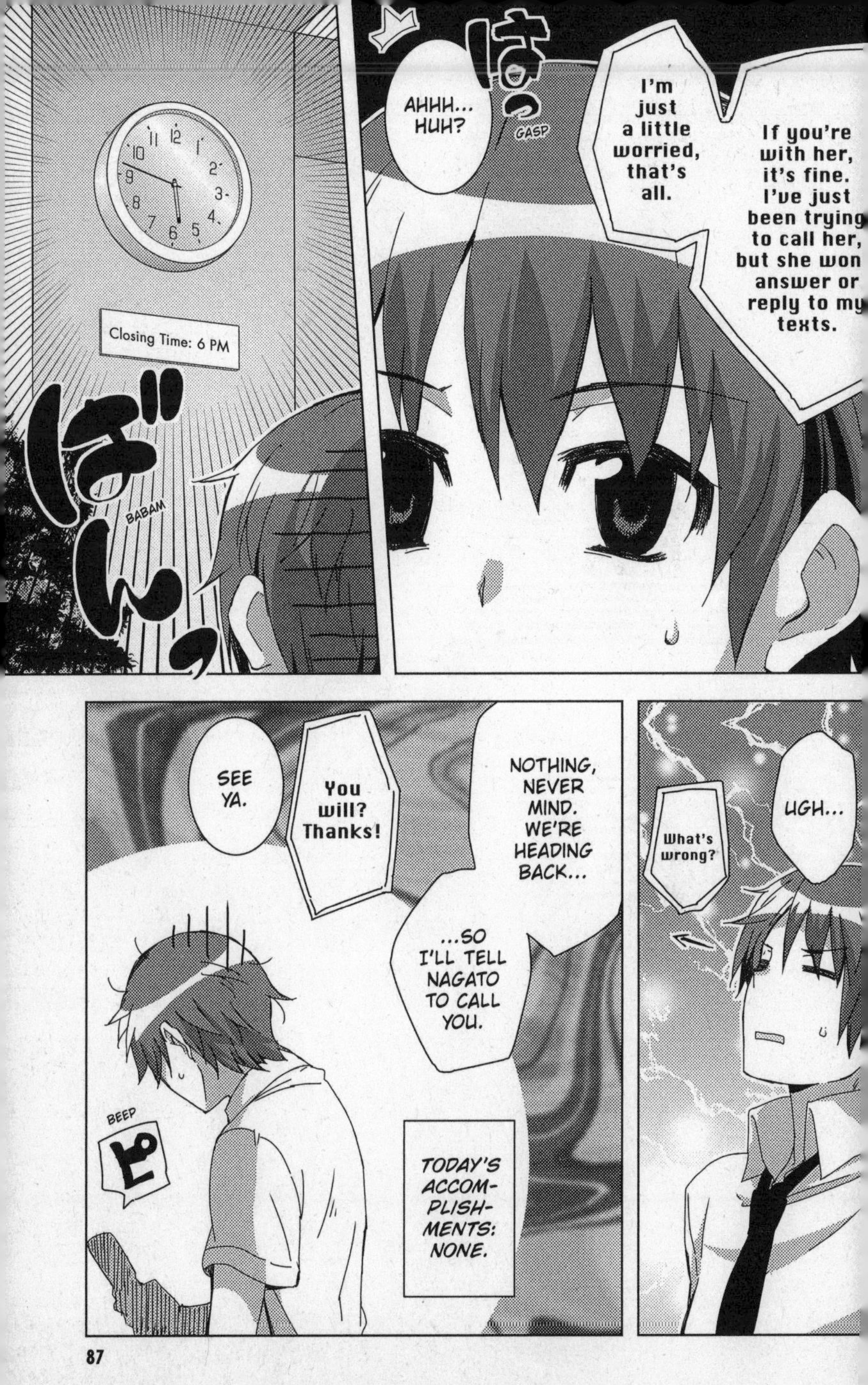

If you're with her, it's fine. I've just been trying to call her, but she won answer or reply to my texts.
I'm just a little worried, that's all.
はっ
GASP
AHHH... HUH?
Closing Time: 6 PM
ばんっ
BABAM
UGH...
What's wrong?
NOTHING, NEVER MIND. WE'RE HEADING BACK...
...SO I'LL TELL NAGATO TO CALL YOU.
You will? Thanks!
SEE YA.
TODAY'S ACCOM-PLISH-MENTS: NONE.
ピ
BEEP

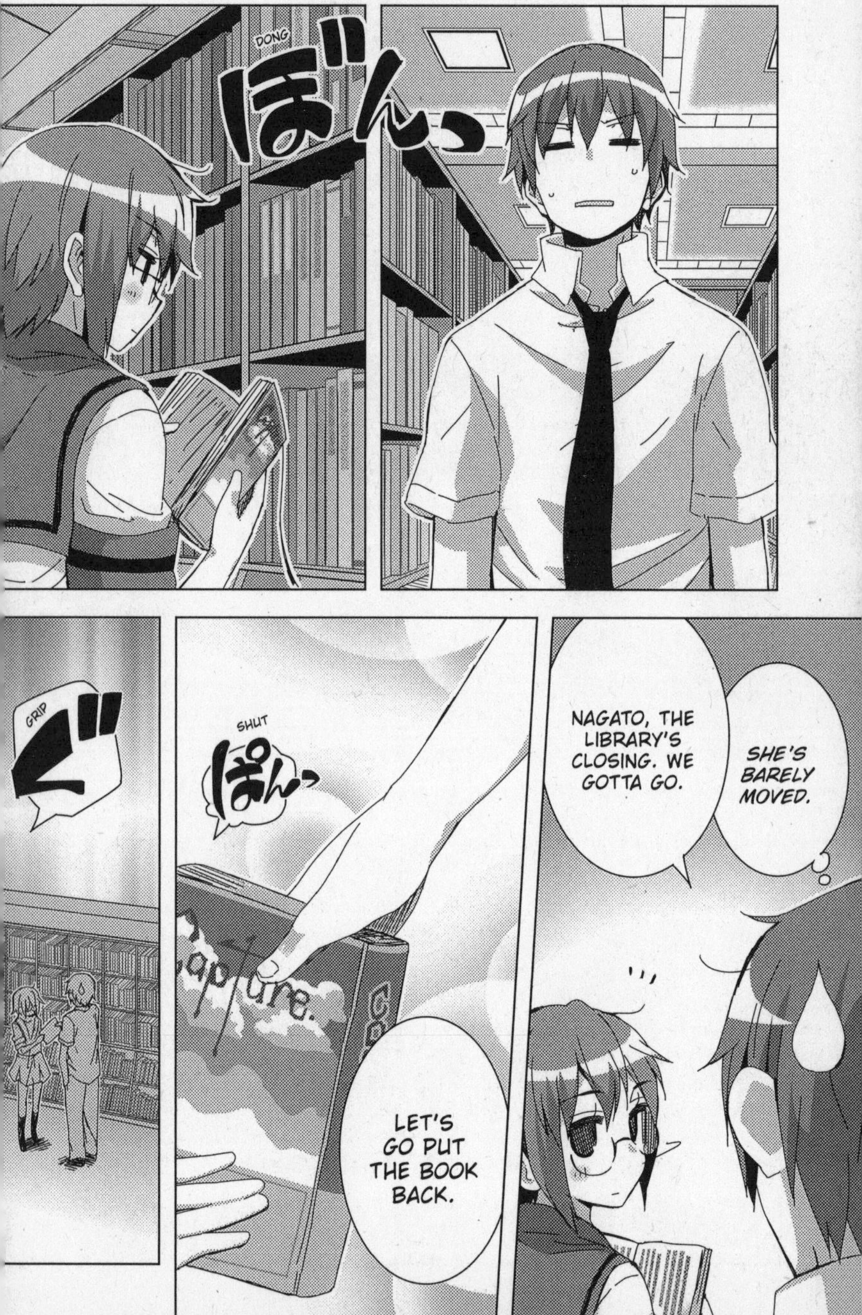
DONG
ぼんっ
SHE'S BARELY MOVED.
NAGATO, THE LIBRARY'S CLOSING. WE GOTTA GO.
...
LET'S GO PUT THE BOOK BACK.
SHUT
ぱんっ
GRIP
ぐ

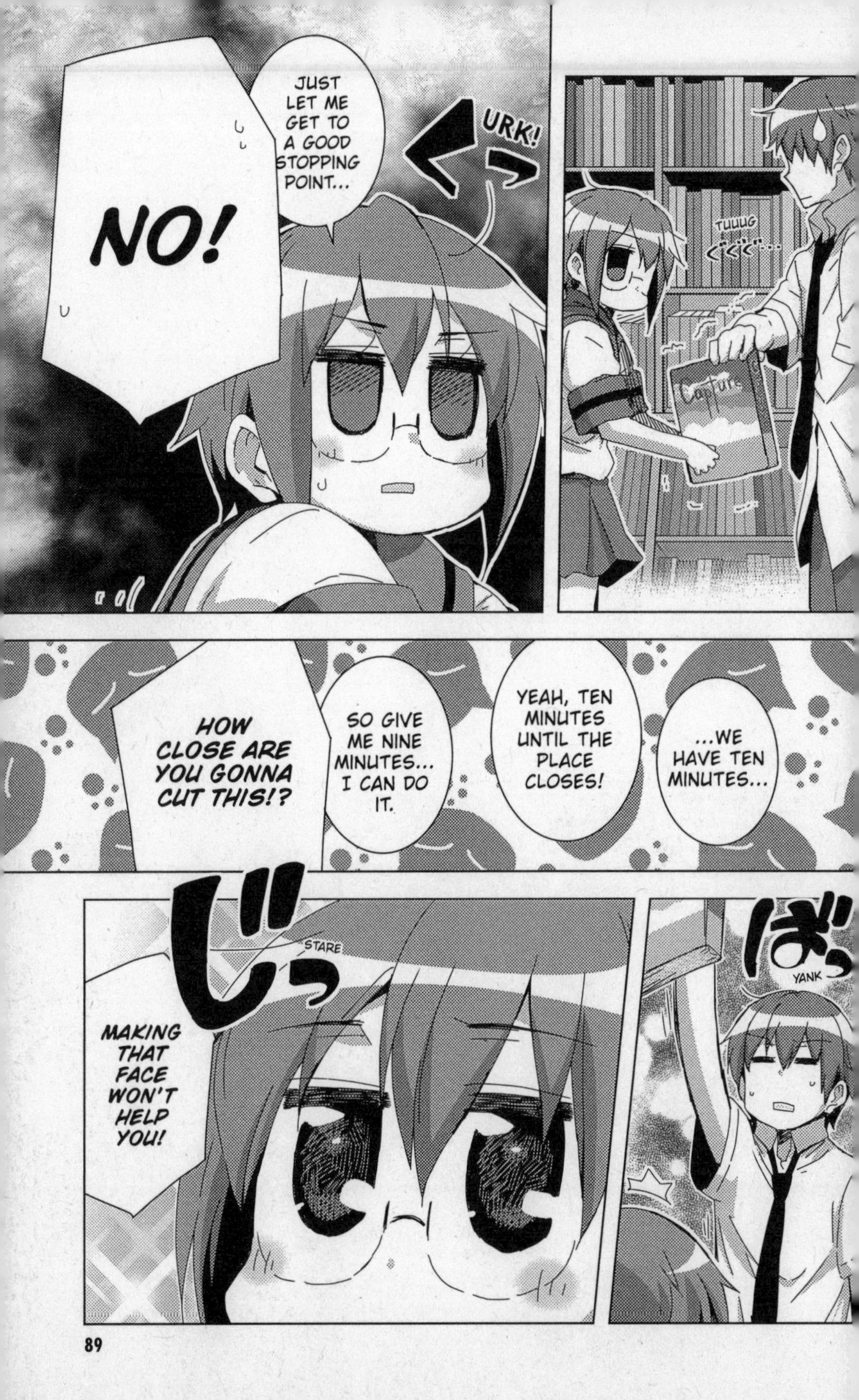
TUUUG
ぐぐぐ…
URK!
JUST LET ME GET TO A GOOD STOPPING POINT...
NO!
...WE HAVE TEN MINUTES...
YEAH, TEN MINUTES UNTIL THE PLACE CLOSES!
SO GIVE ME NINE MINUTES... I CAN DO IT.
HOW CLOSE ARE YOU GONNA CUT THIS!?
ばっ
YANK
じっ
STARE
MAKING THAT FACE WON'T HELP YOU!

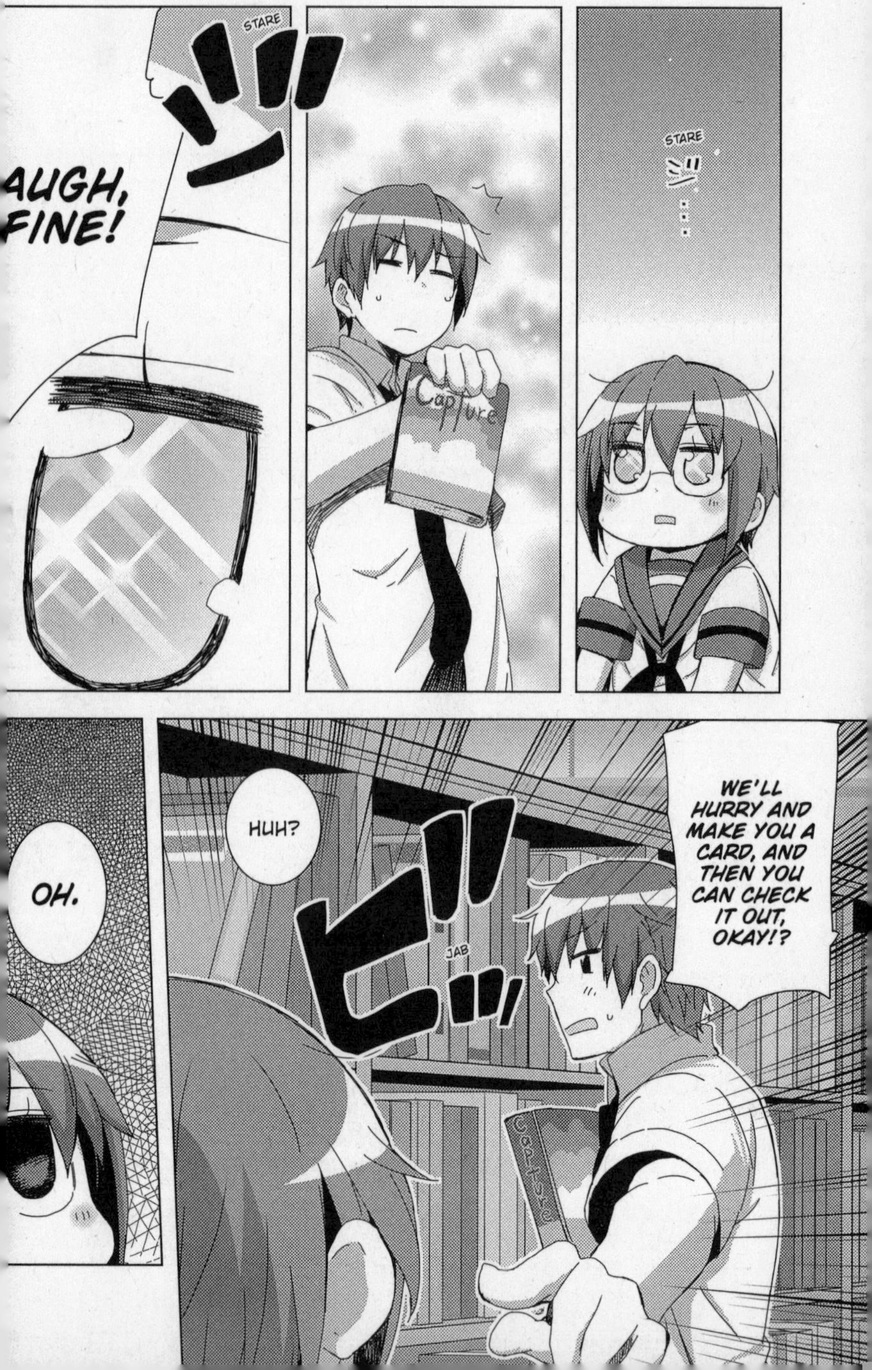
STARE
Capture
STARE
AUGH, FINE!
WE'LL HURRY AND MAKE YOU A CARD, AND THEN YOU CAN CHECK IT OUT, OKAY!?
HUH?
JAB
Capture
OH.

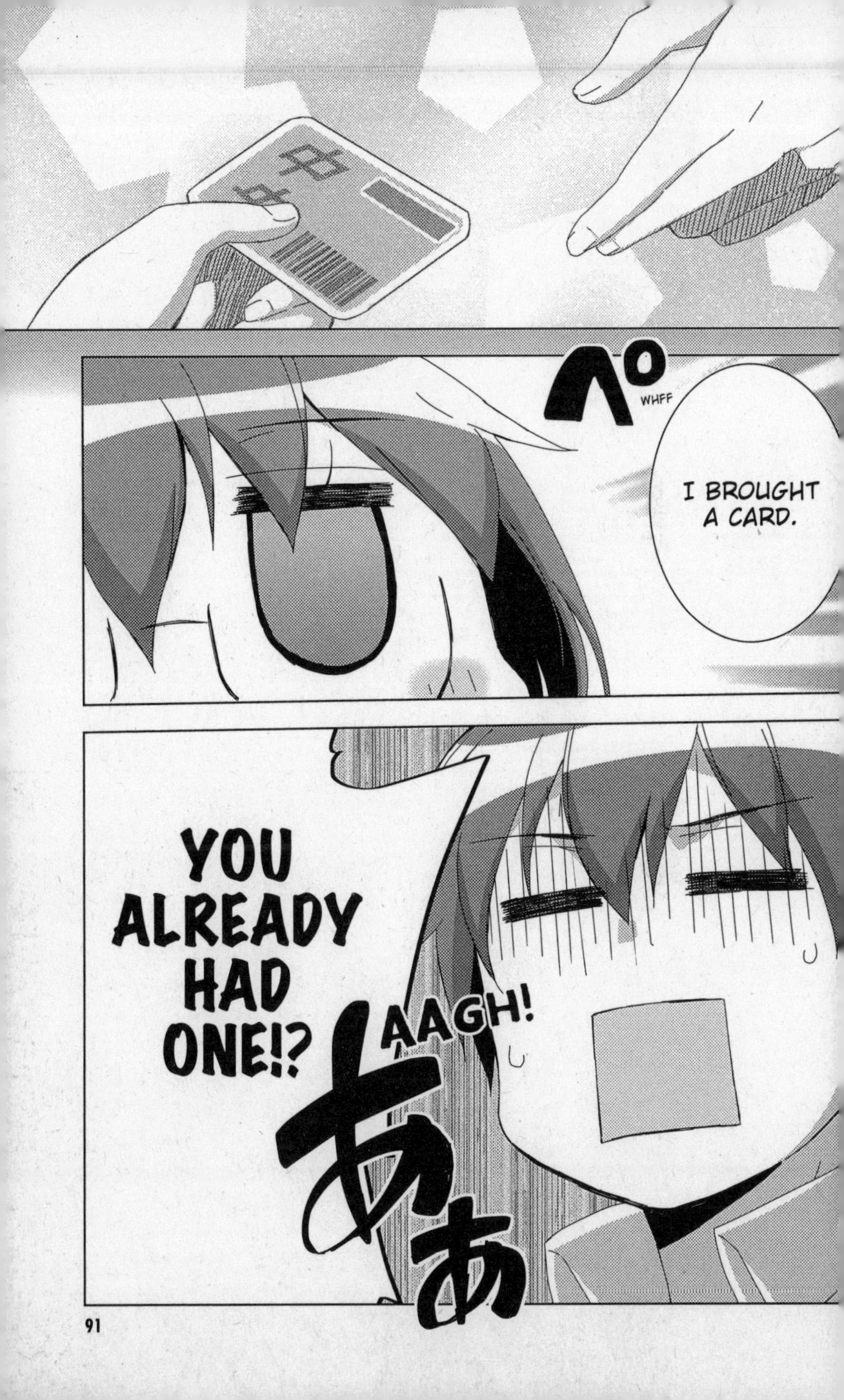
WHFF
I BROUGHT A CARD.
YOU ALREADY HAD ONE!?
AAGH!

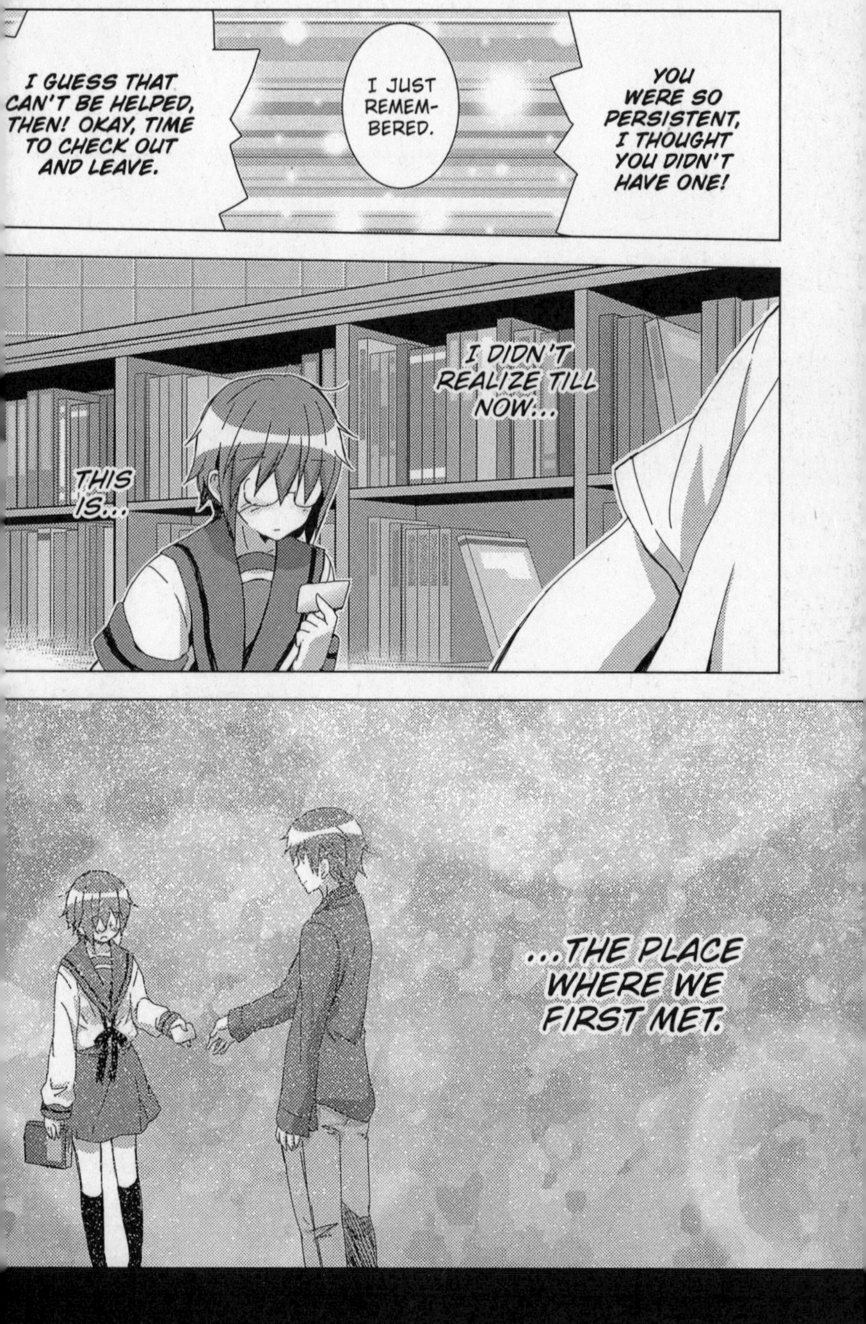
YOU WERE SO PERSISTENT, I THOUGHT YOU DIDN'T HAVE ONE!
I JUST REMEMBERED.
I GUESS THAT CAN'T BE HELPED, THEN! OKAY, TIME TO CHECK OUT AND LEAVE.
I DIDN'T REALIZE TILL NOW...
THIS IS...
...THE PLACE WHERE WE FIRST MET.

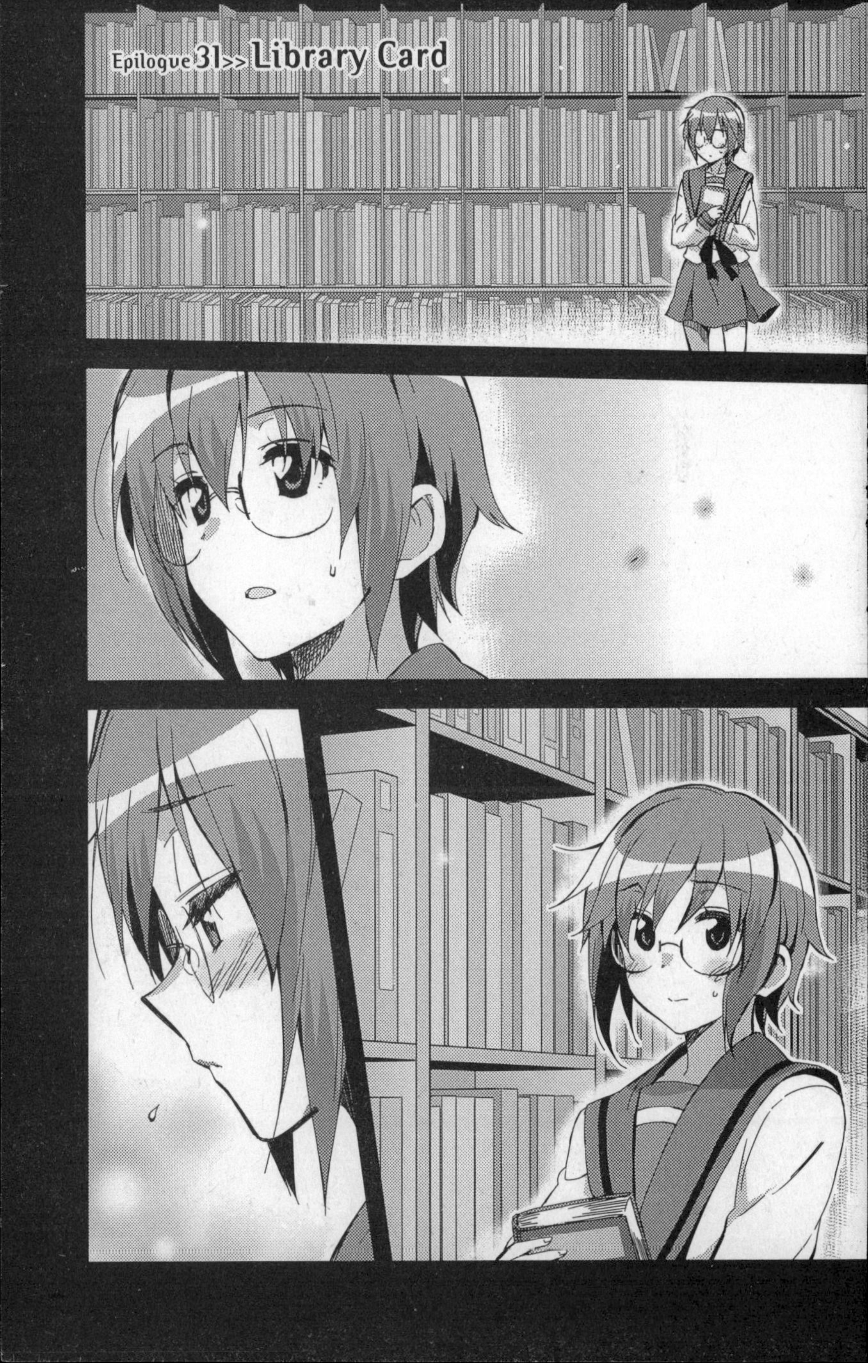
Epilogue 31>> Library Card

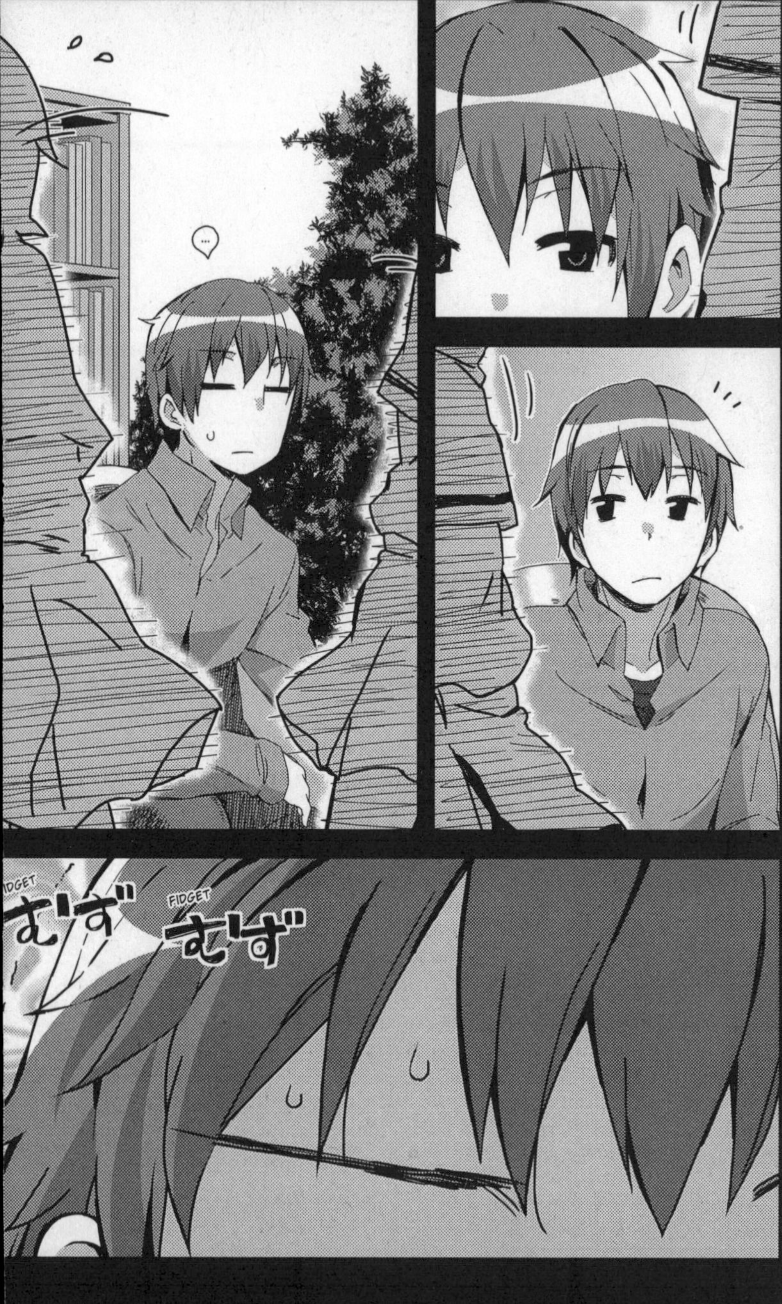
...
FIDGET
むず
IDGET
むず

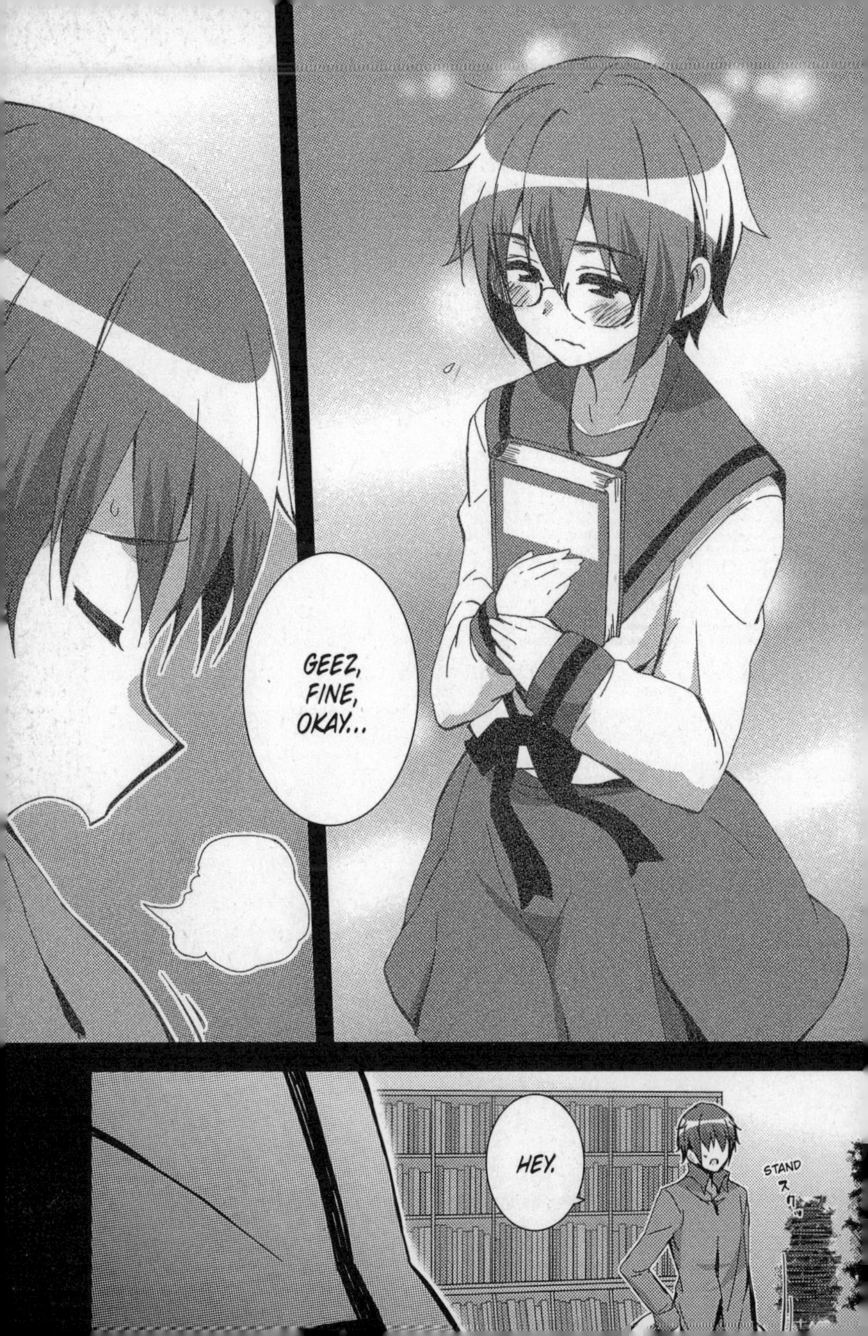
GEEZ, FINE, OKAY...
STAND
スクッ
HEY.

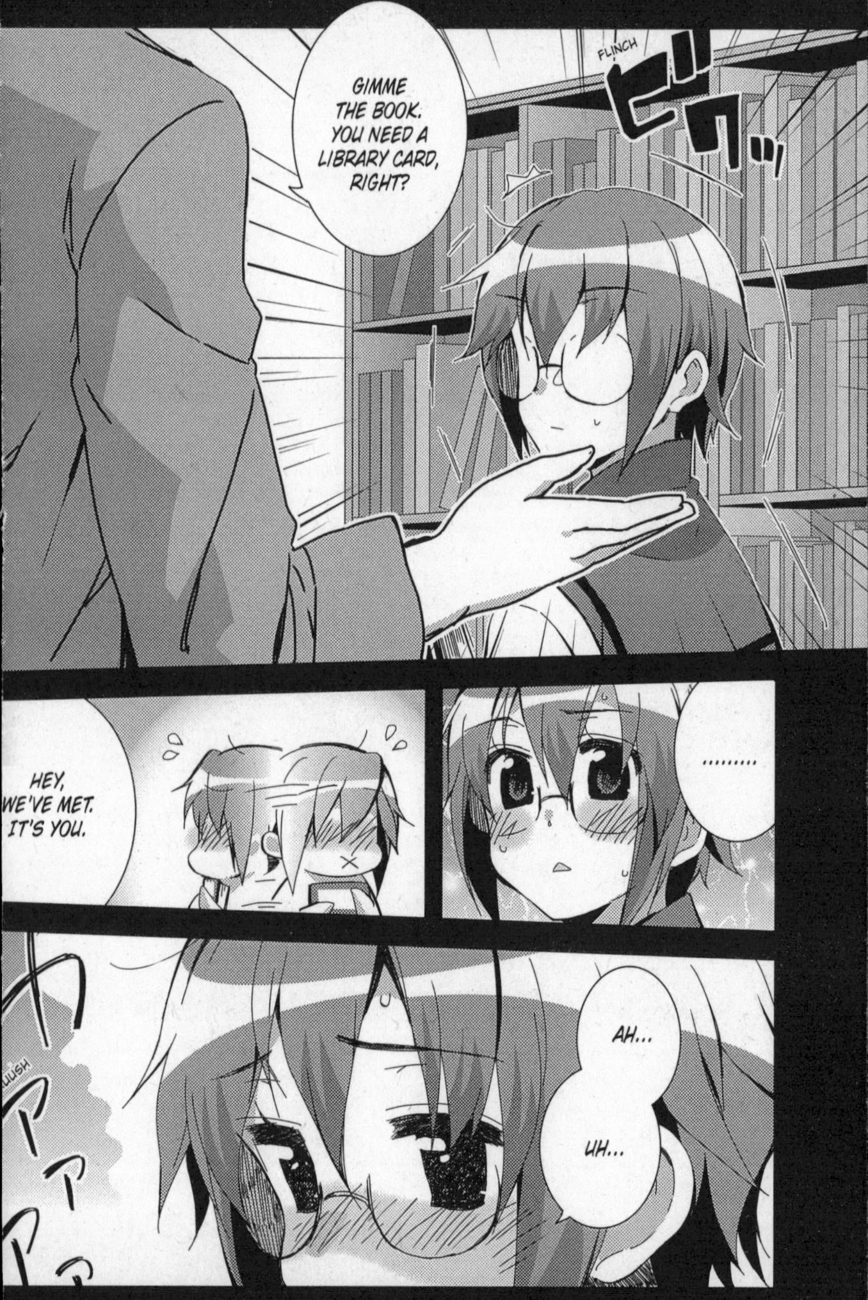
FLINCH
GIMME THE BOOK. YOU NEED A LIBRARY CARD, RIGHT?
....
HEY, WE'VE MET. IT'S YOU.
AH...
UH...

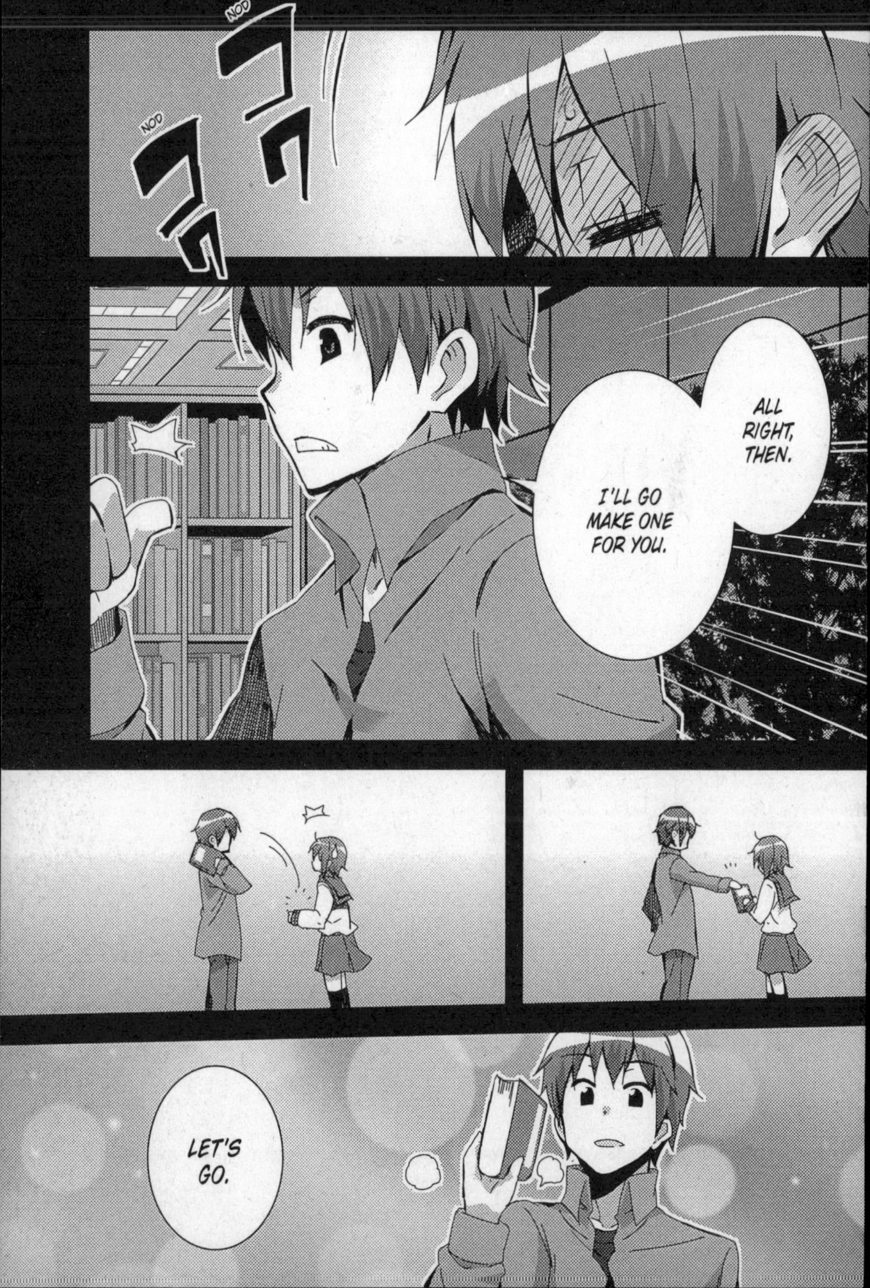
NOD
NOD
ALL RIGHT, THEN.
I'LL GO MAKE ONE FOR YOU.
LET'S GO.

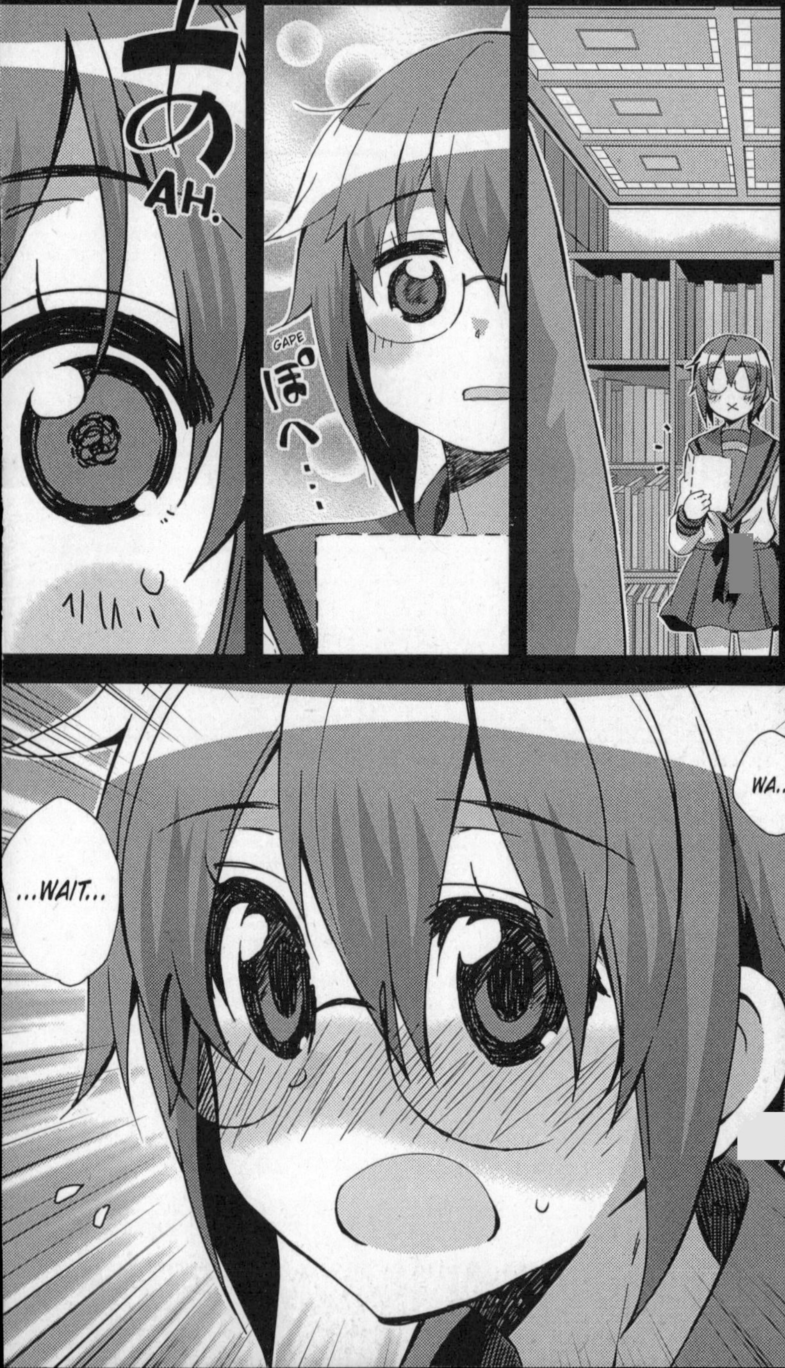
GAPE
ぽへ...
あ
AH.
WA...
...WAIT...

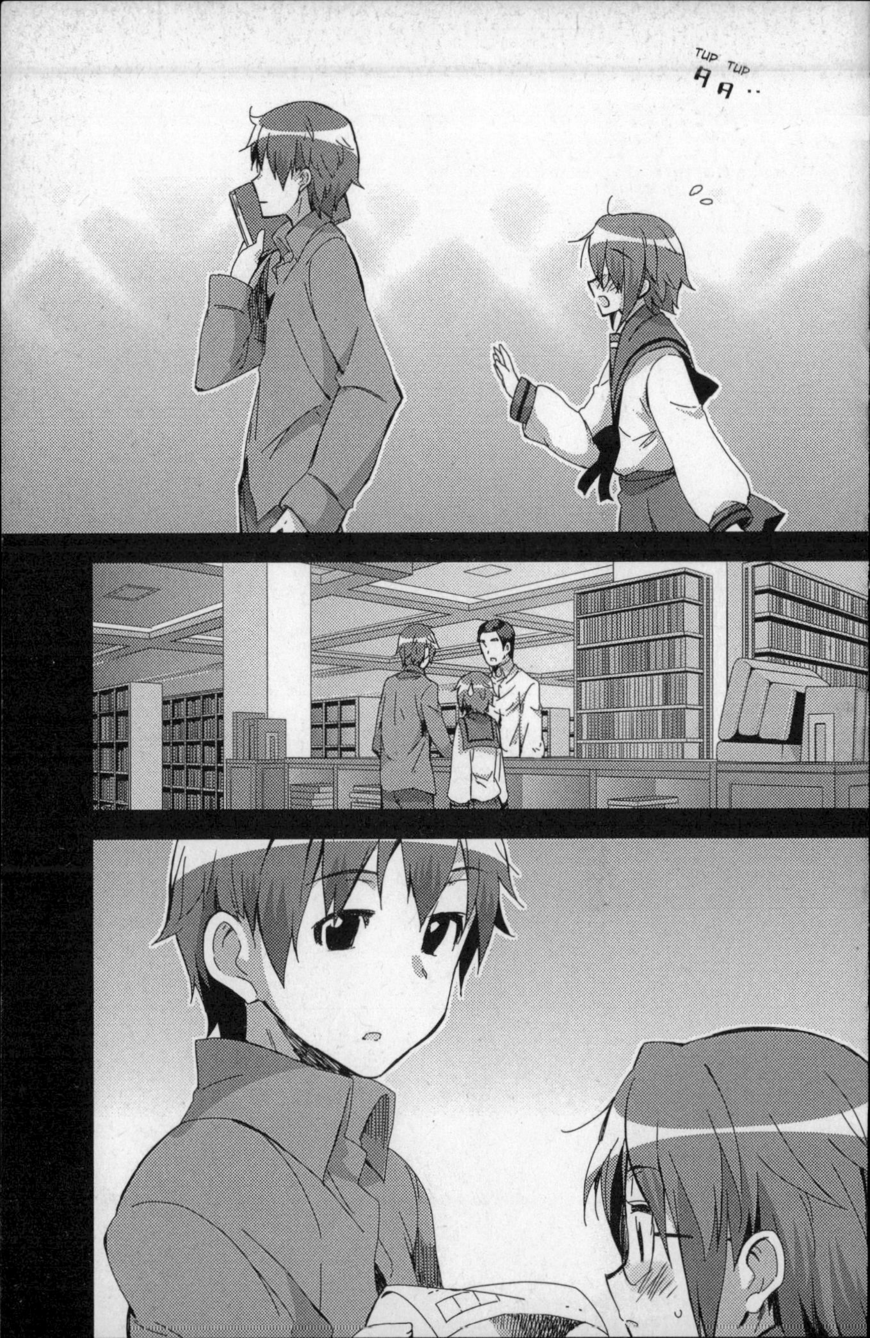
TUP TUP
タタ..

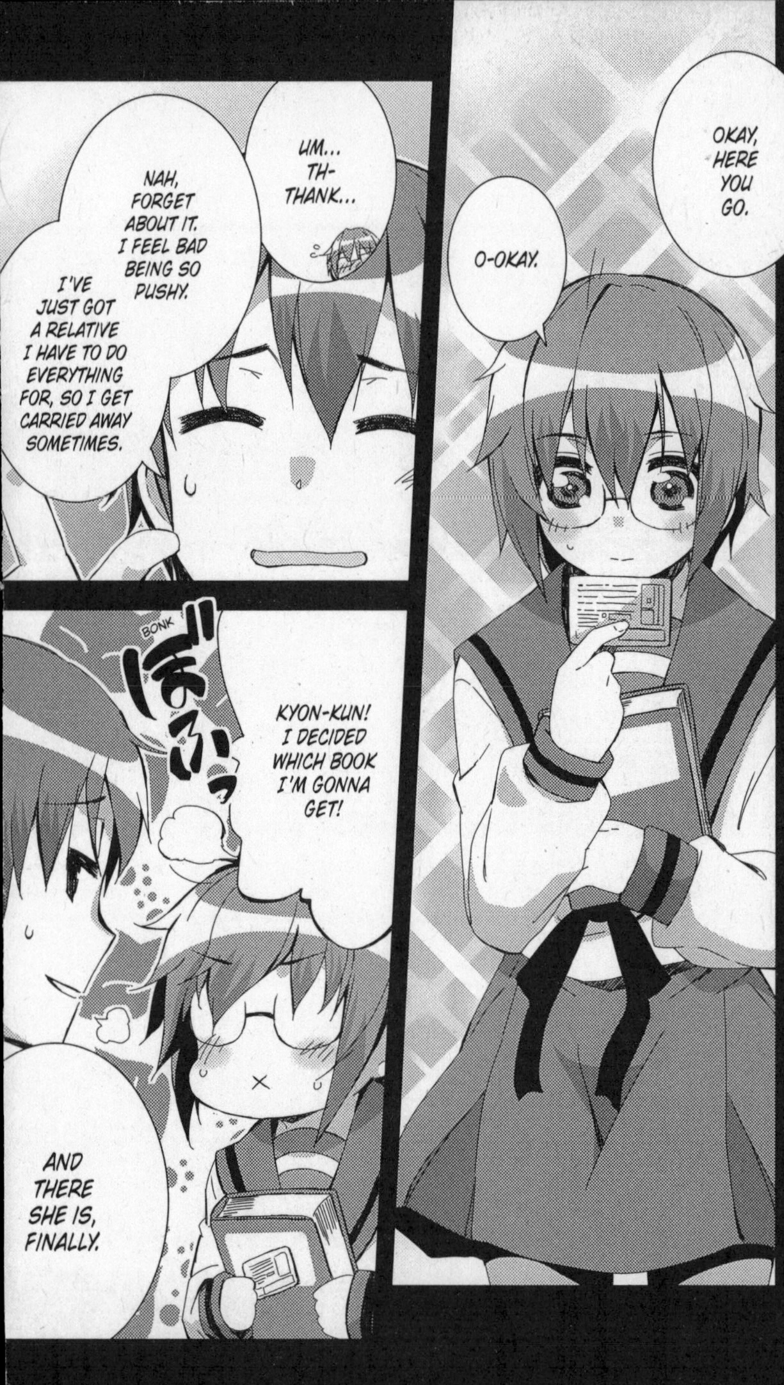
OKAY, HERE YOU GO.
O-OKAY.
UM... TH-THANK...
NAH, FORGET ABOUT IT. I FEEL BAD BEING SO PUSHY.
I'VE JUST GOT A RELATIVE I HAVE TO DO EVERYTHING FOR, SO I GET CARRIED AWAY SOMETIMES.
BONK
KYON-KUN! I DECIDED WHICH BOOK I'M GONNA GET!
AND THERE SHE IS, FINALLY.

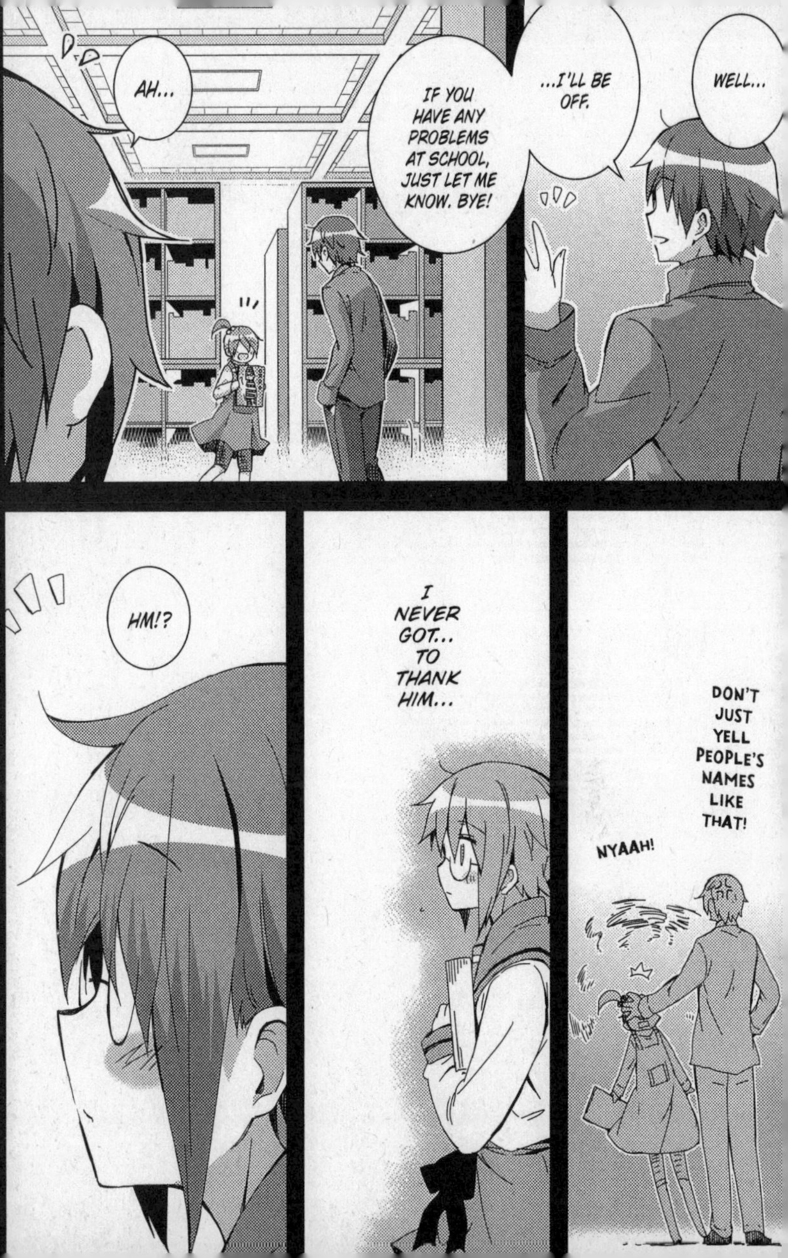
WELL...
...I'LL BE OFF.
IF YOU HAVE ANY PROBLEMS AT SCHOOL, JUST LET ME KNOW. BYE!
AH...
DON'T JUST YELL PEOPLE'S NAMES LIKE THAT!
NYAAH!
I NEVER GOT... TO THANK HIM...
HM!?

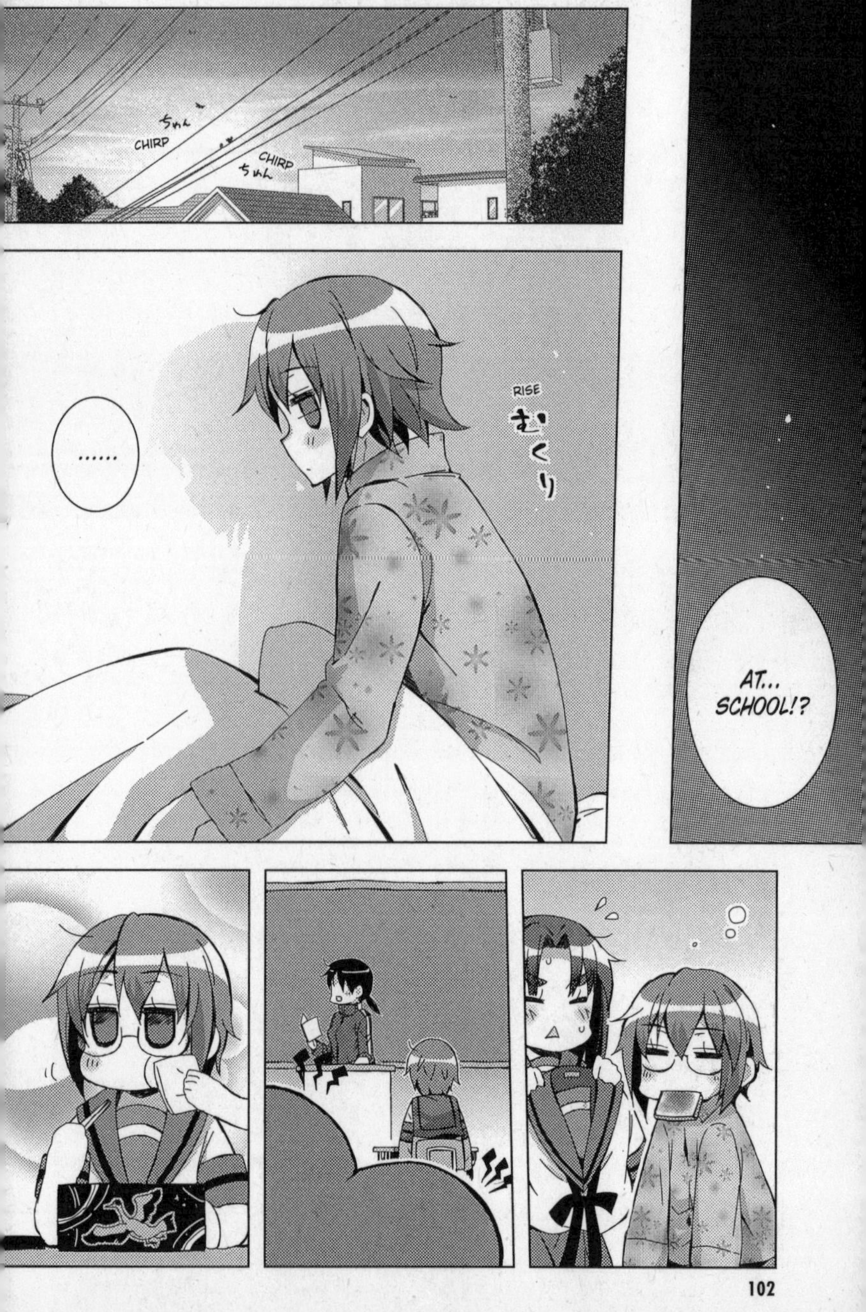
AT... SCHOOL!?
ちゅん
CHIRP
CHIRP
ちゅん
RISE
むくり
......

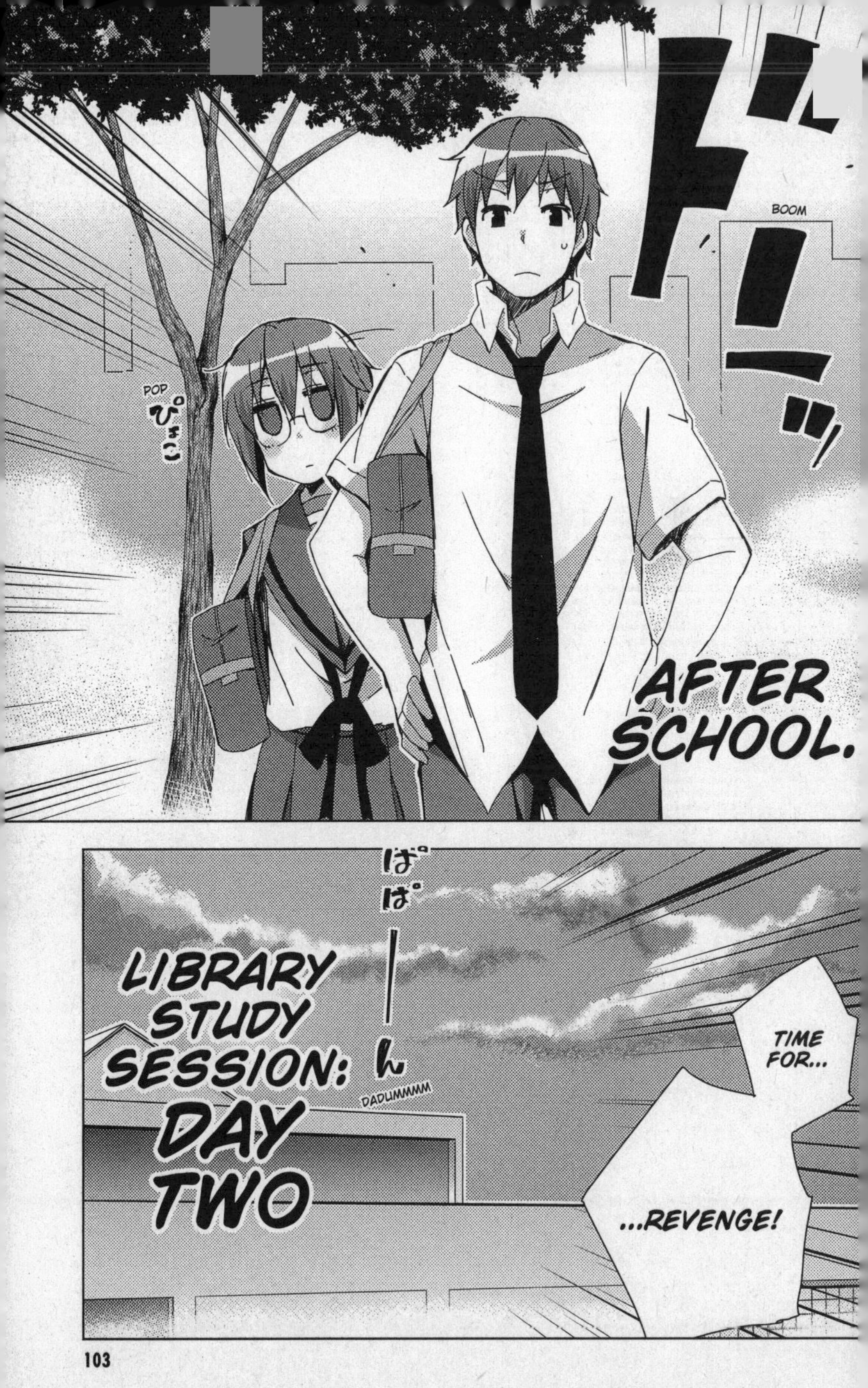

ドドーッ
BOOM
ぴょこ
POP
AFTER SCHOOL.
TIME FOR...
...REVENGE!
ぱぱーん
DADUMMMM
LIBRARY STUDY SESSION: DAY TWO

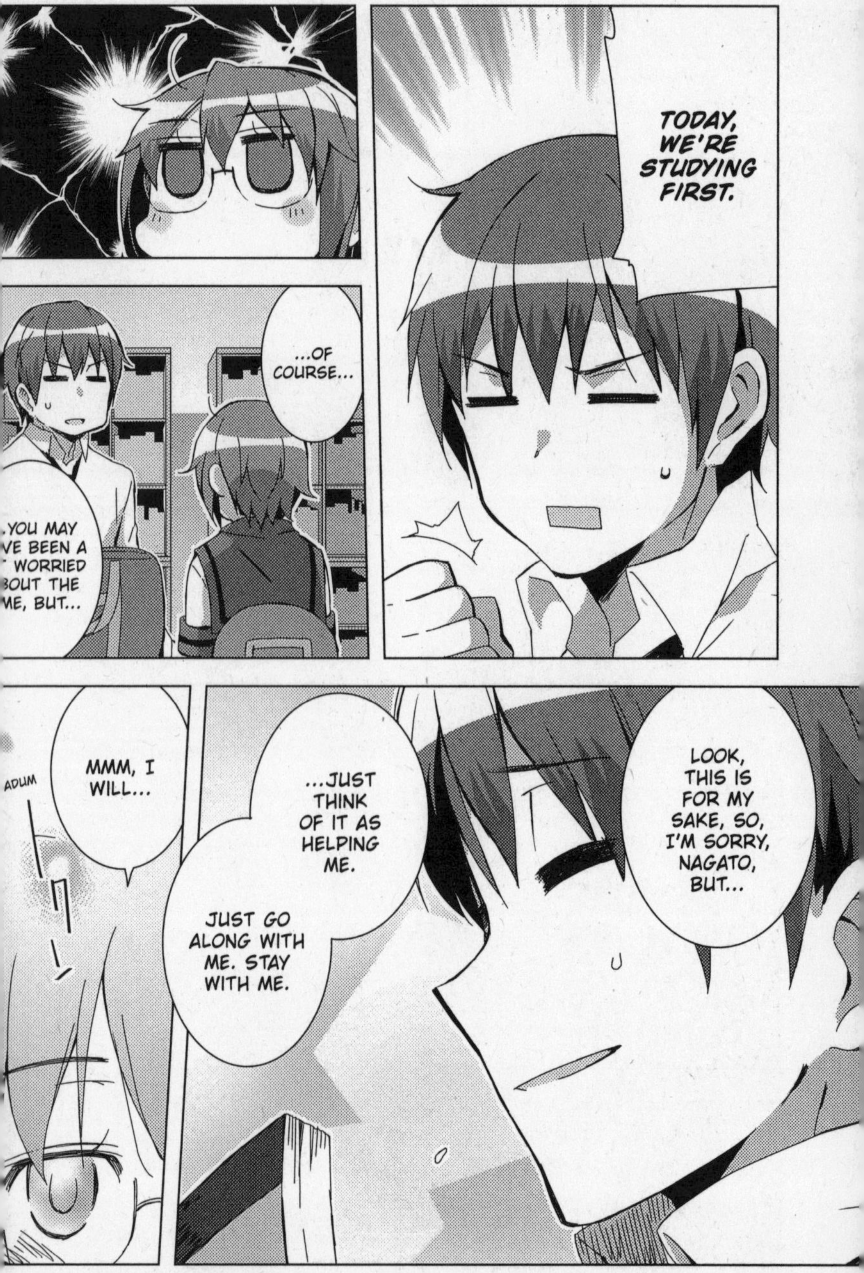
TODAY, WE'RE STUDYING FIRST.
...OF COURSE...
.YOU MAY VE BEEN A WORRIED BOUT THE ME, BUT...
LOOK, THIS IS FOR MY SAKE, SO, I'M SORRY, NAGATO, BUT...
...JUST THINK OF IT AS HELPING ME.
JUST GO ALONG WITH ME. STAY WITH ME.
MMM, I WILL...
ADUM

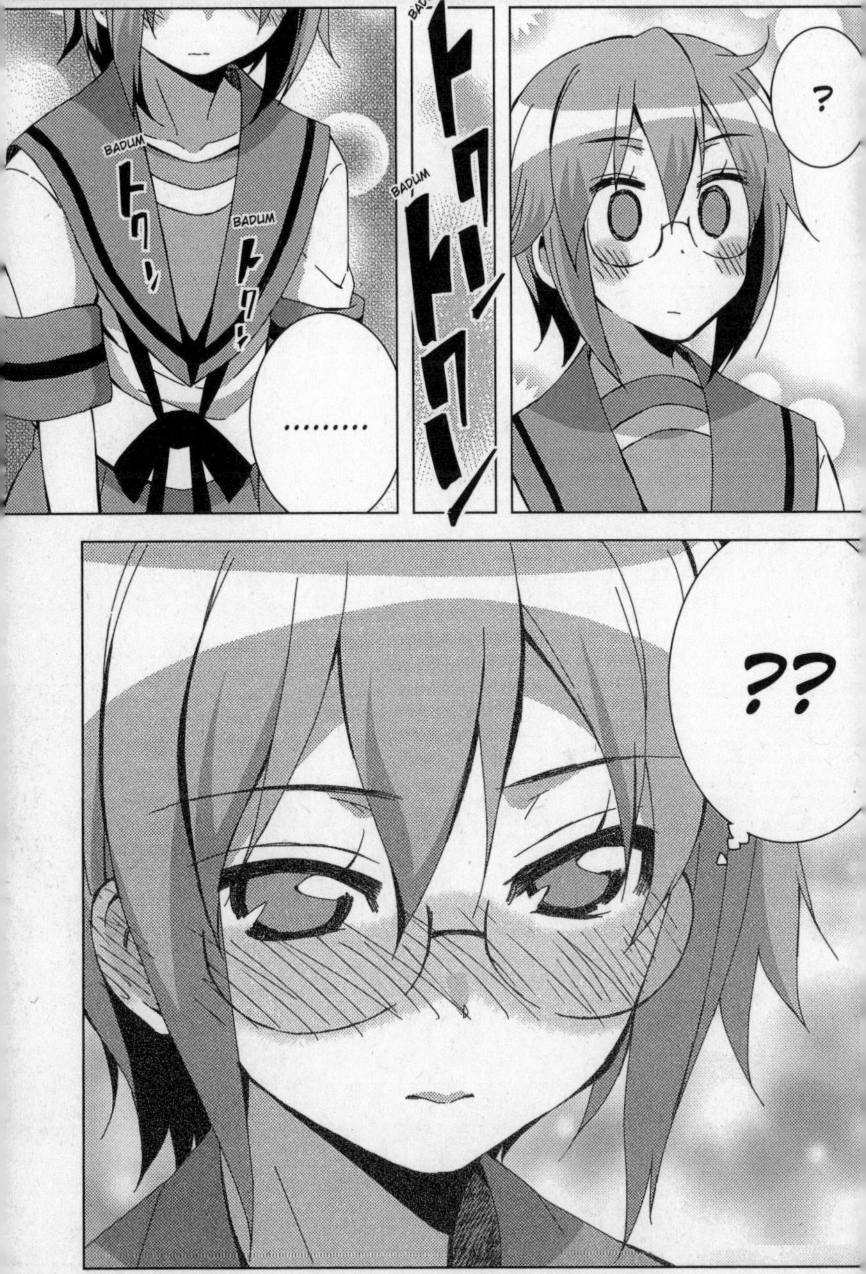
?
BADUM
トクン
BADUM
トクン
BADUM
トクン
BADUM
トクン
....
??

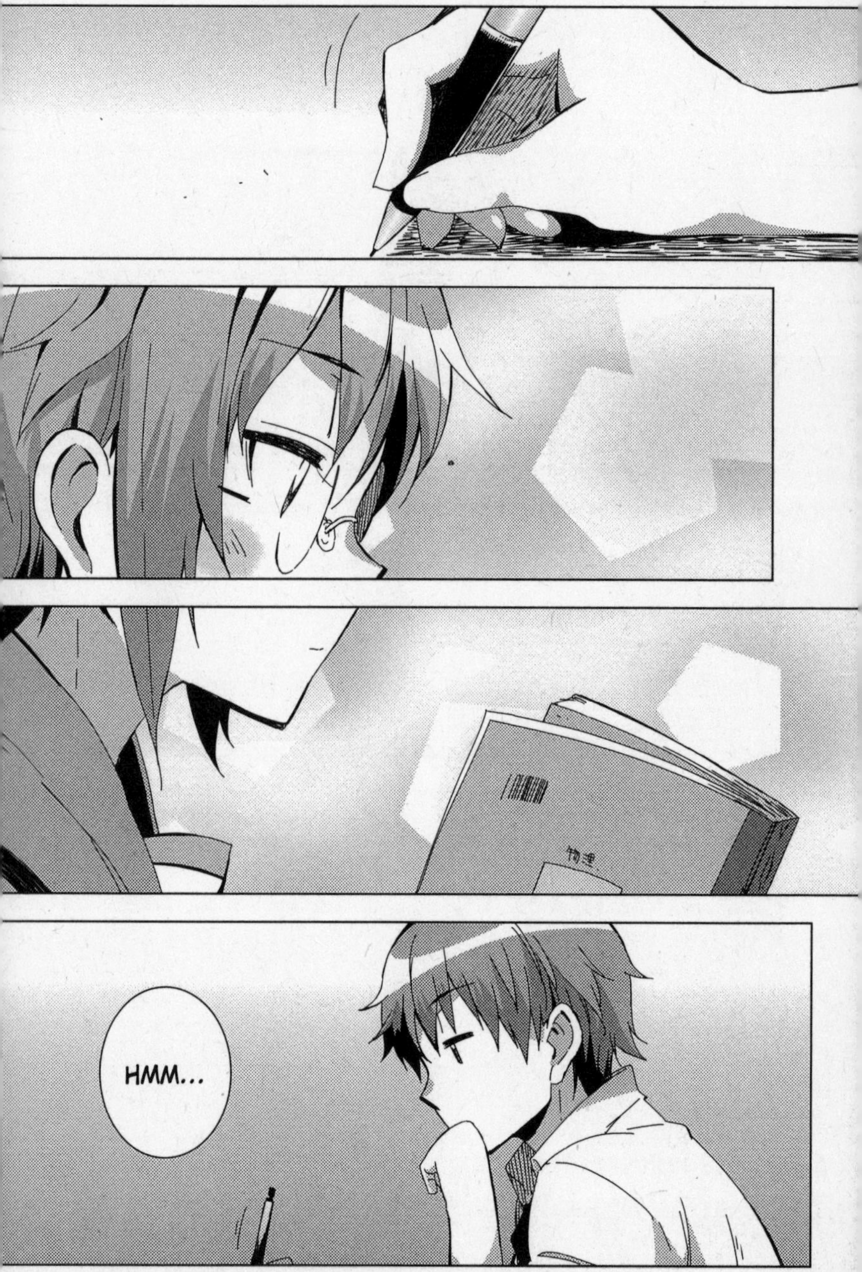
HMM...

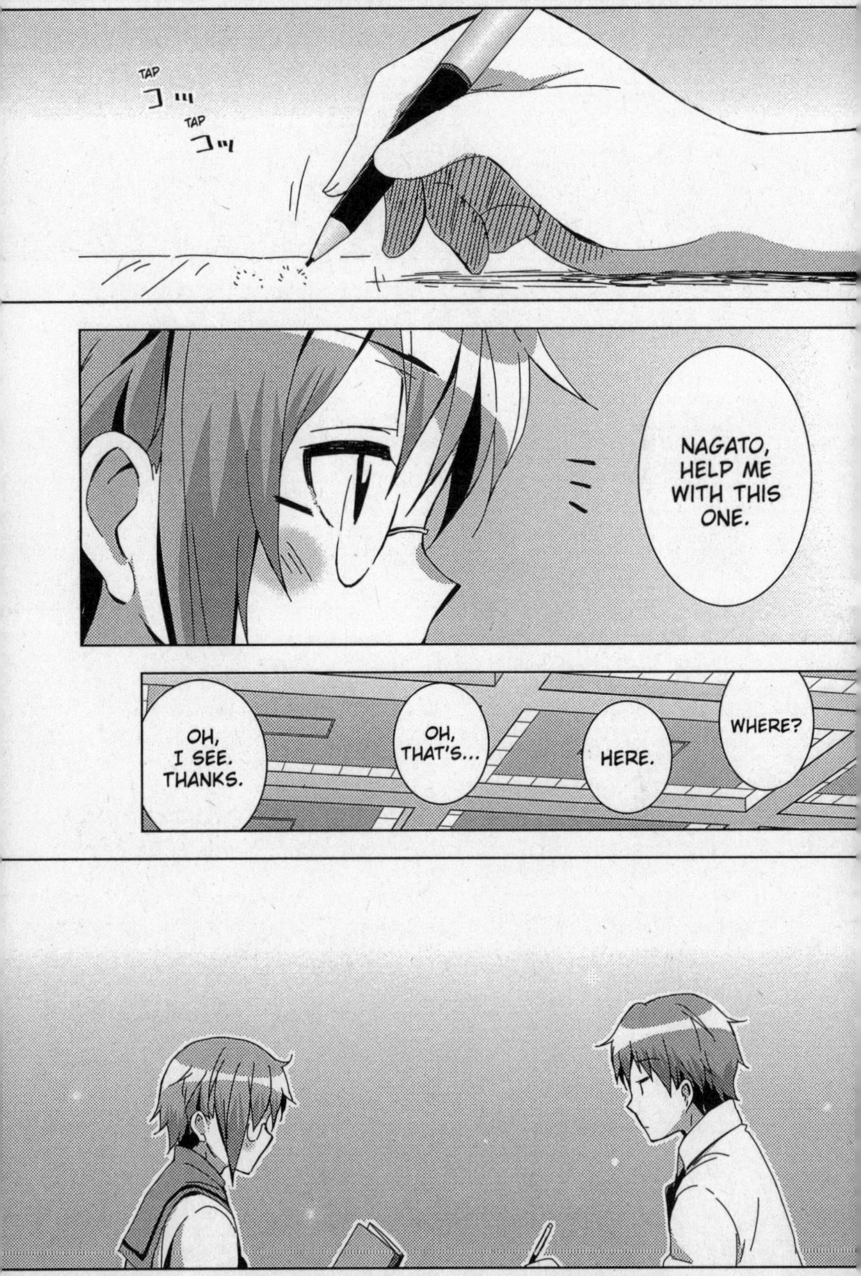
TAP
コッ
TAP
コッ
NAGATO, HELP ME WITH THIS ONE.
WHERE?
HERE.
OH, THAT'S...
OH, I SEE. THANKS.

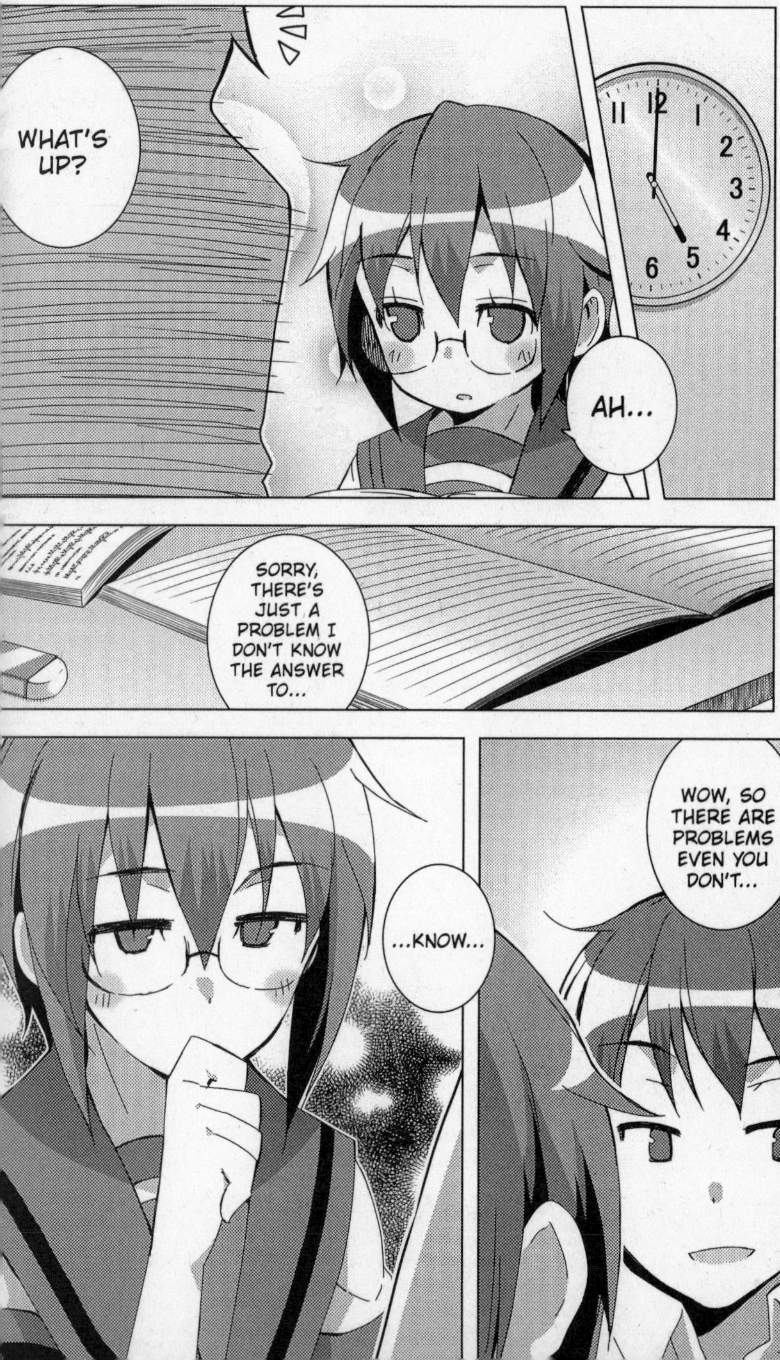
AH...
WHAT'S UP?
SORRY, THERE'S JUST A PROBLEM I DON'T KNOW THE ANSWER TO...
WOW, SO THERE ARE PROBLEMS EVEN YOU DON'T...
...KNOW...

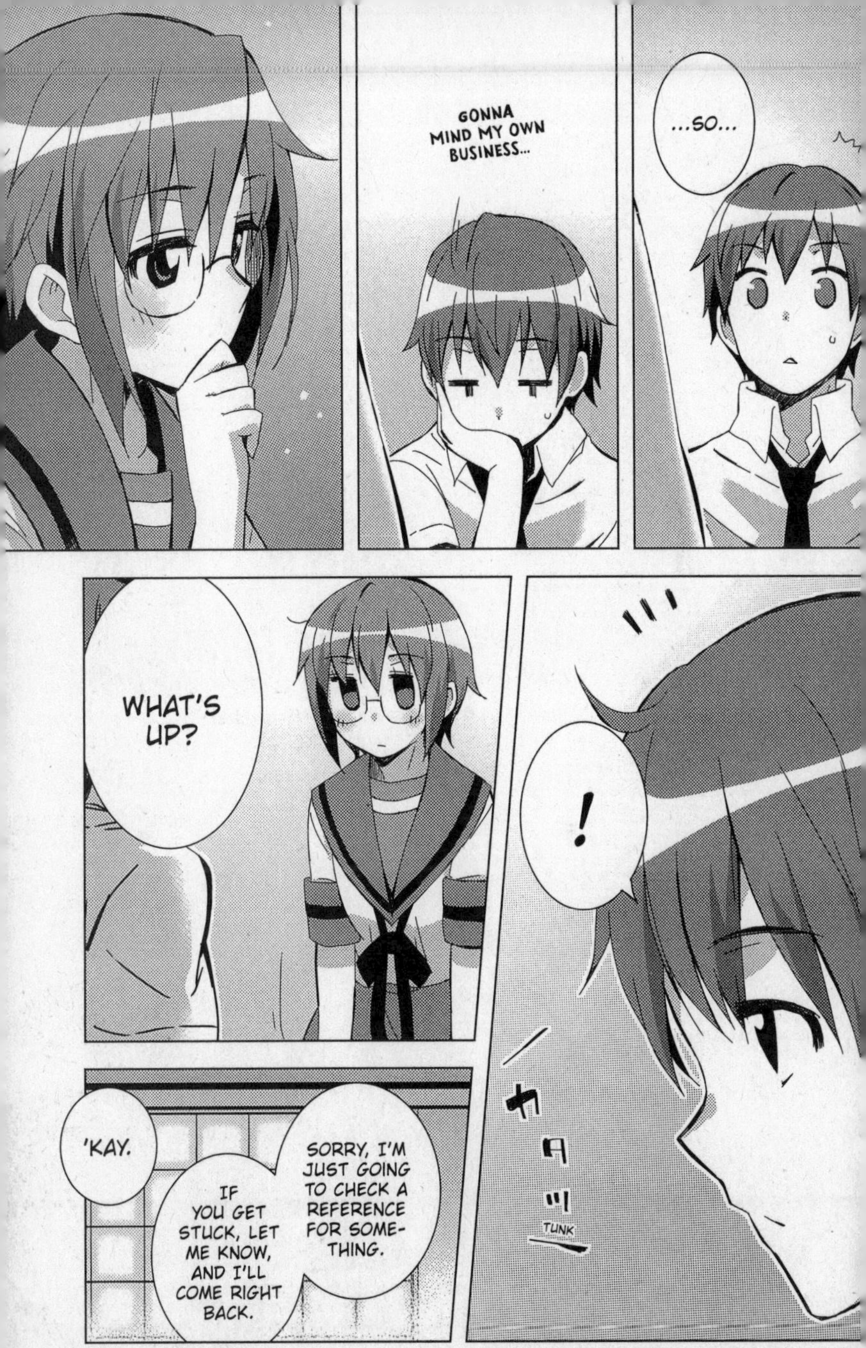
...SO...
GONNA MIND MY OWN BUSINESS...
!
TUNK
WHAT'S UP?
SORRY, I'M JUST GOING TO CHECK A REFERENCE FOR SOME-THING.
IF YOU GET STUCK, LET ME KNOW, AND I'LL COME RIGHT BACK.
'KAY.

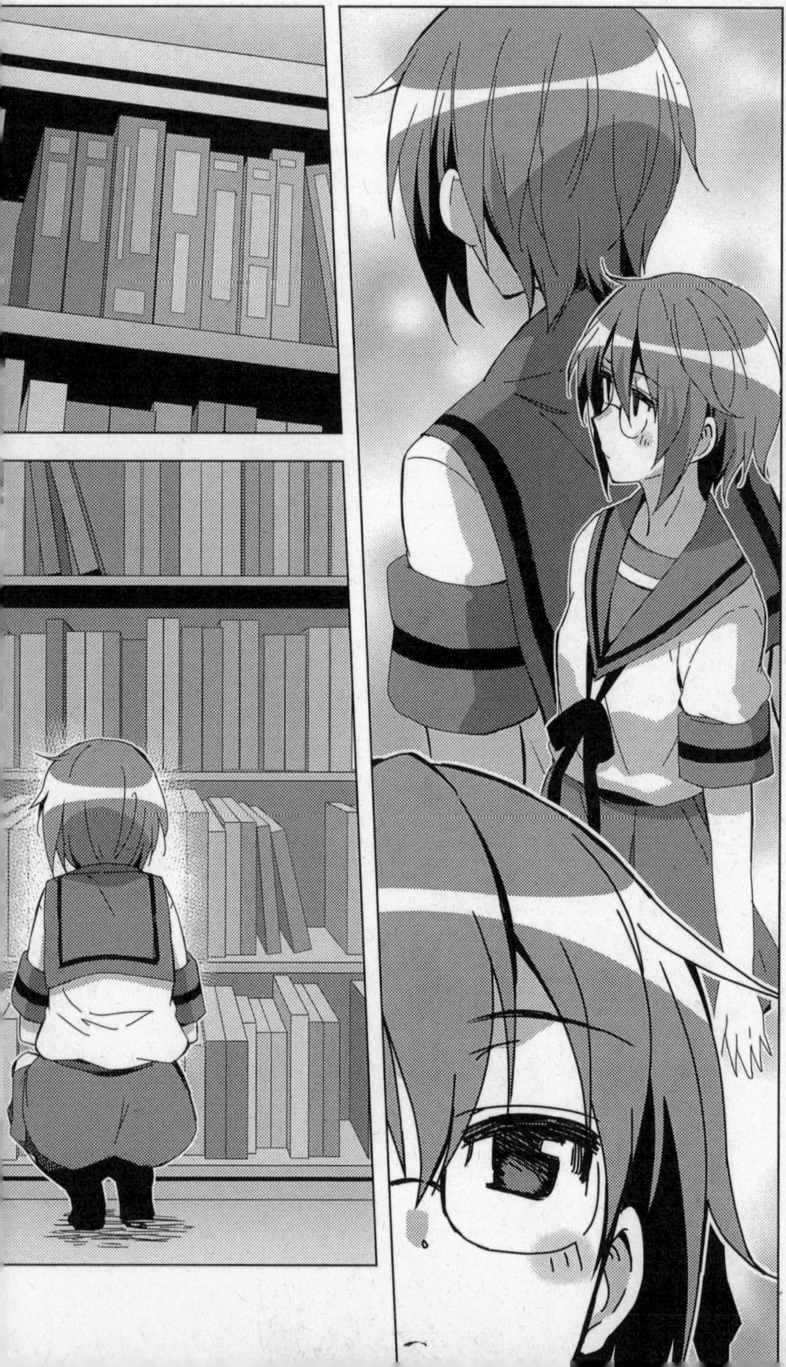

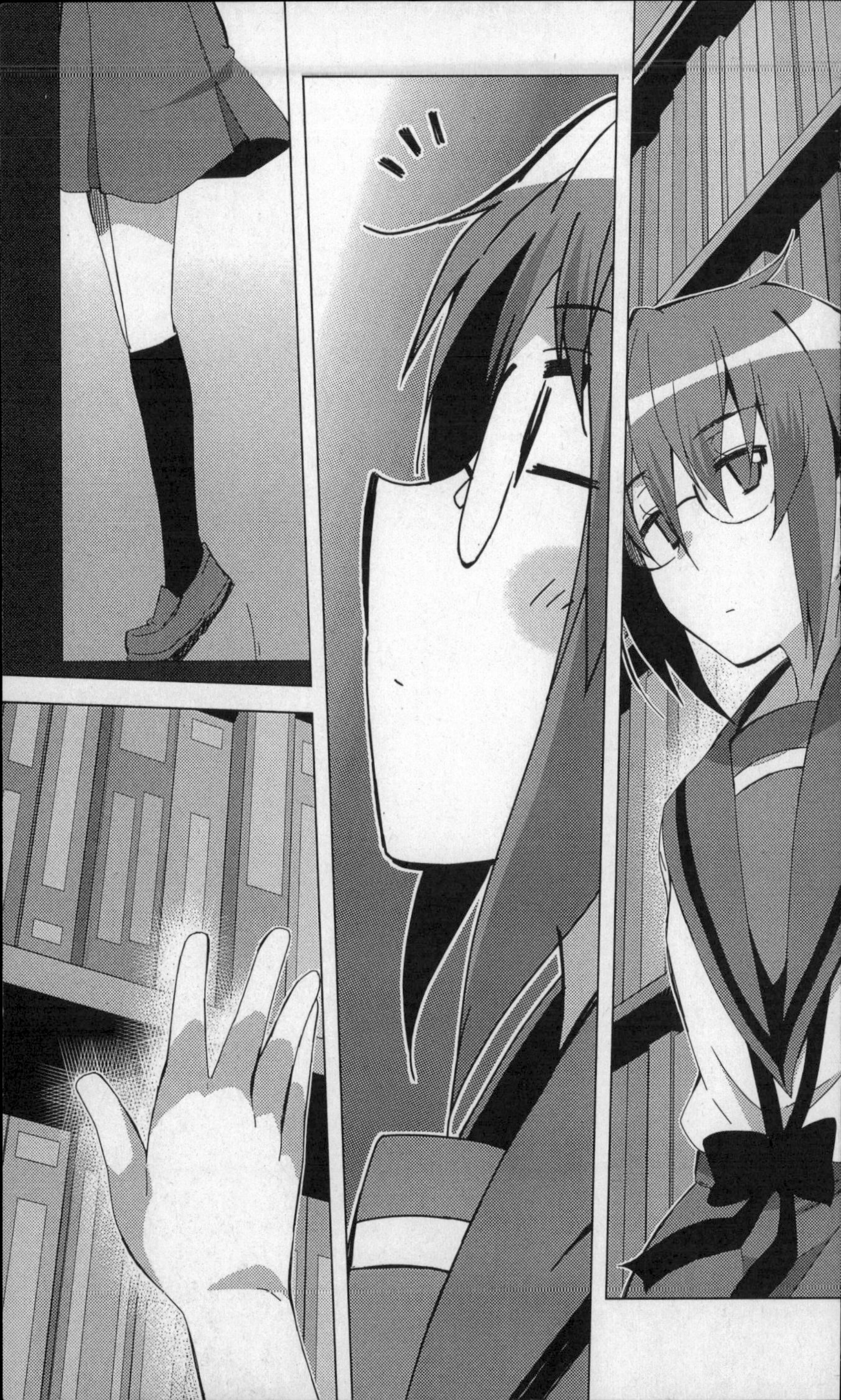

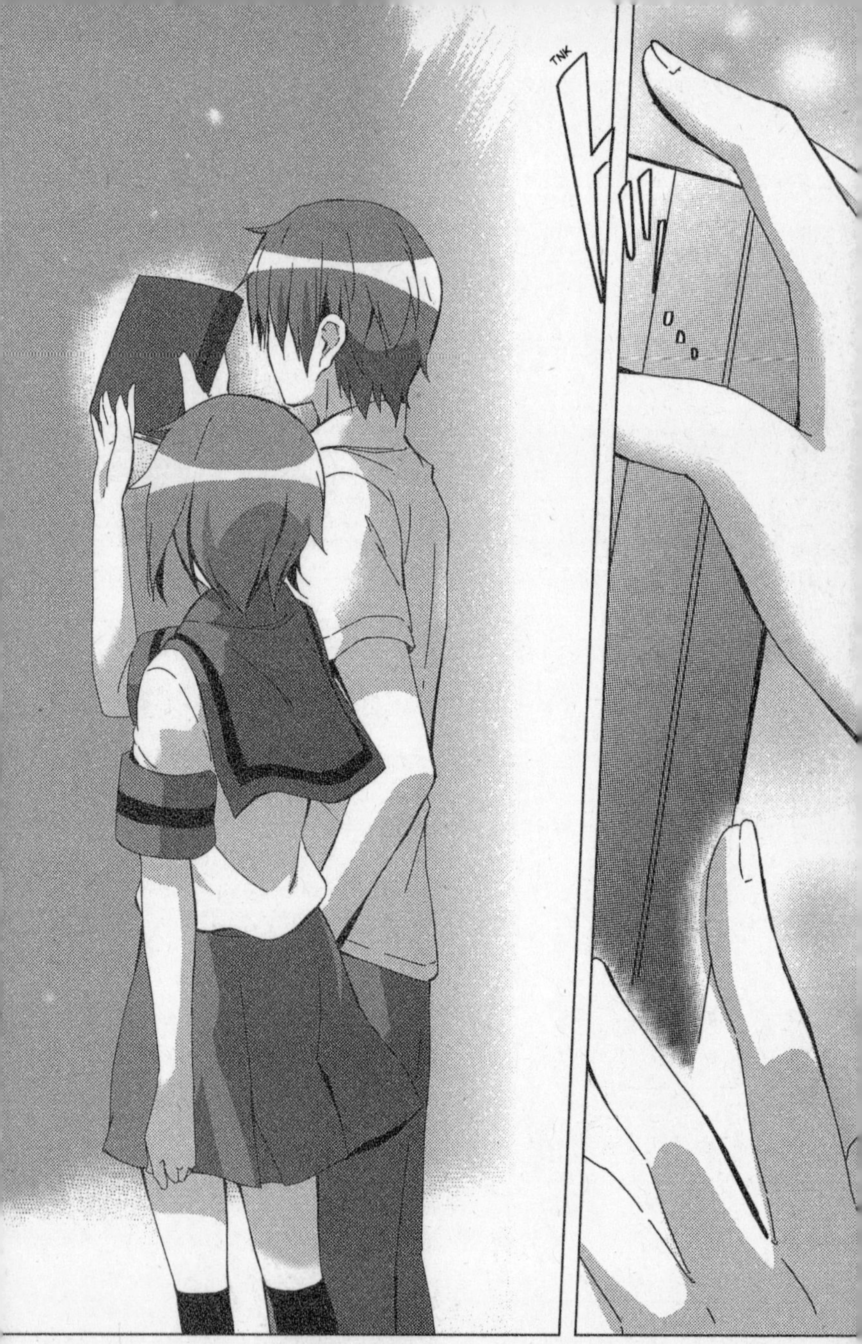
TNK

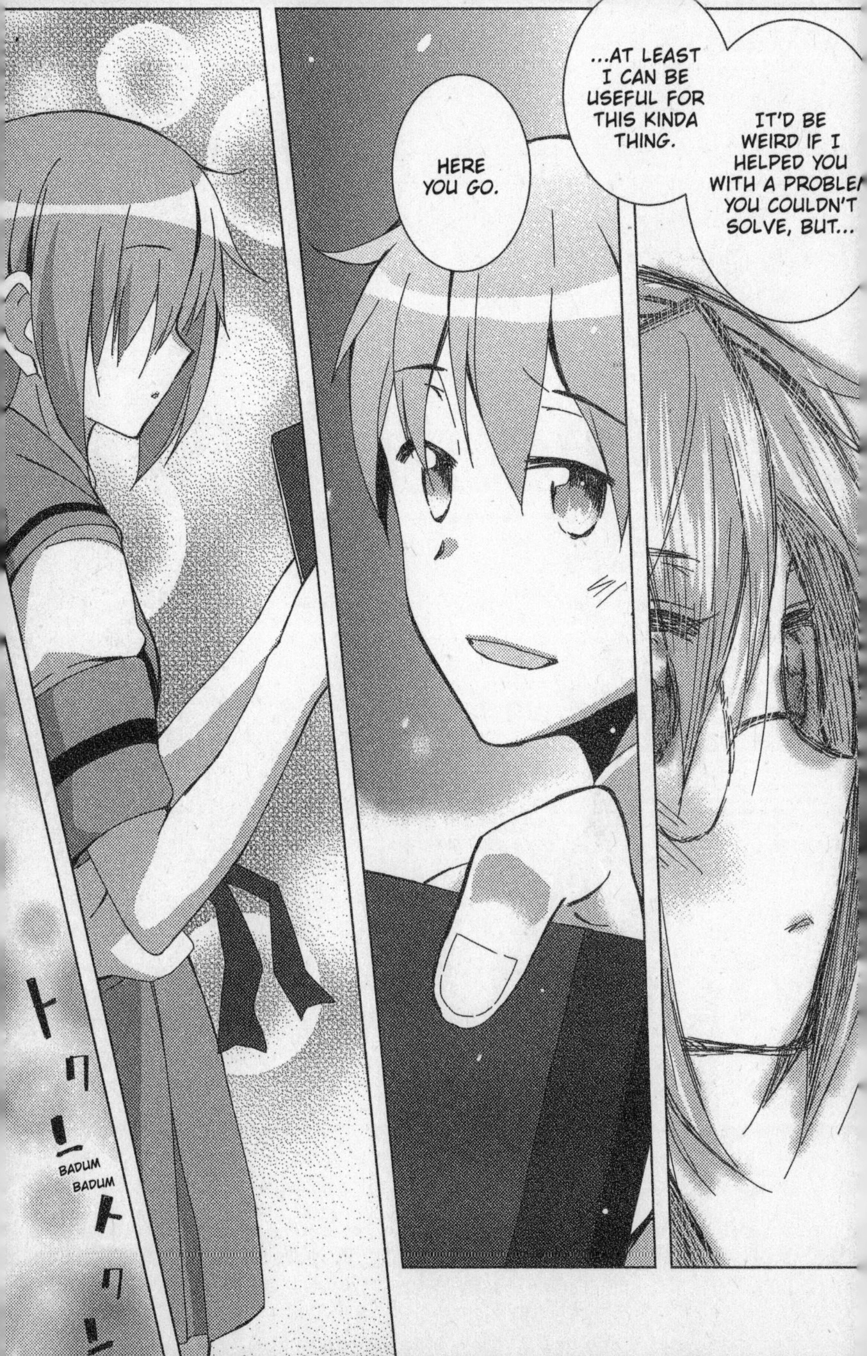
IT'D BE WEIRD IF I HELPED YOU WITH A PROBLEM YOU COULDN'T SOLVE, BUT...
...AT LEAST I CAN BE USEFUL FOR THIS KINDA THING.
HERE YOU GO.
トクン
BADUM BADUM
トクン

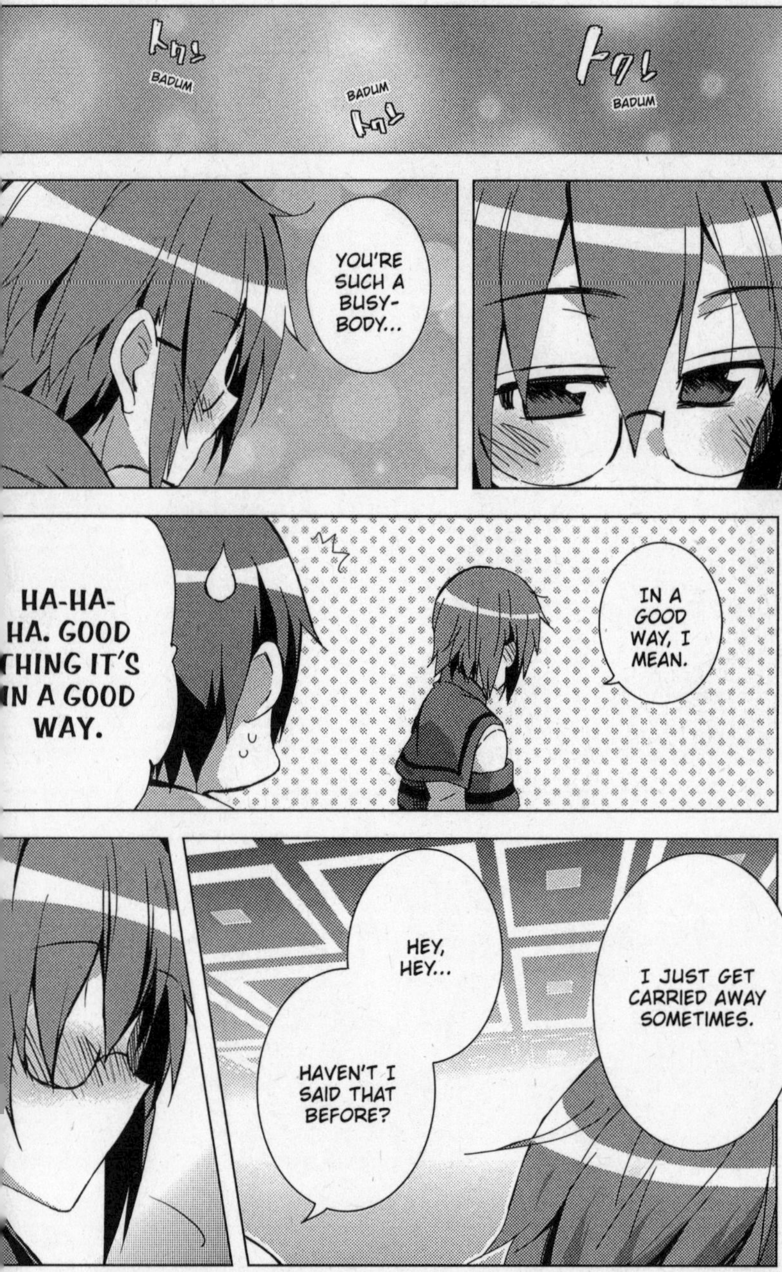
トクン
BADUM
BADUM
トクン
トクン
BADUM
YOU'RE SUCH A BUSY-BODY...
IN A GOOD WAY, I MEAN.
HA-HA-HA. GOOD THING IT'S IN A GOOD WAY.
I JUST GET CARRIED AWAY SOMETIMES.
HEY, HEY...
HAVEN'T I SAID THAT BEFORE?

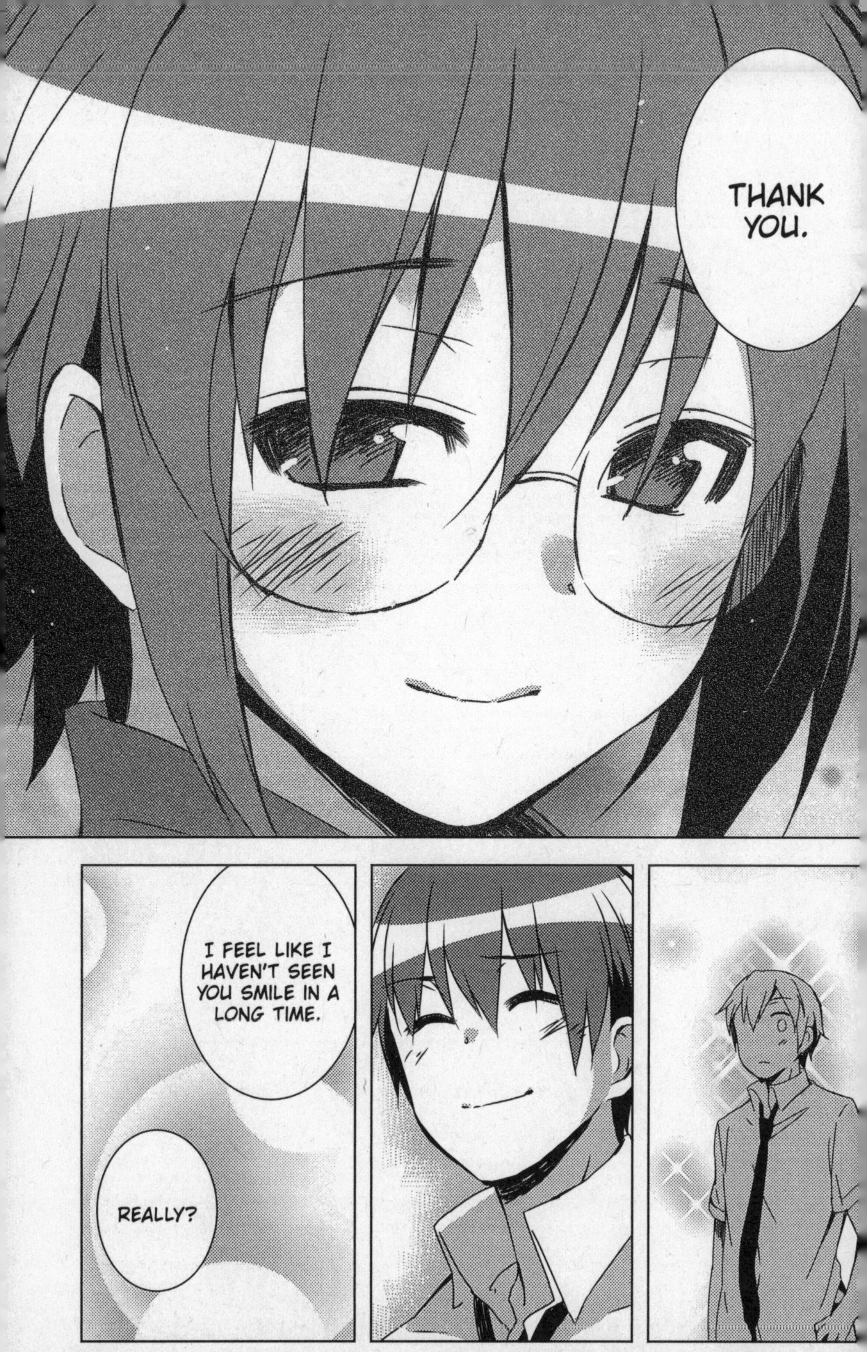
THANK YOU.
I FEEL LIKE I HAVEN'T SEEN YOU SMILE IN A LONG TIME.
REALLY?

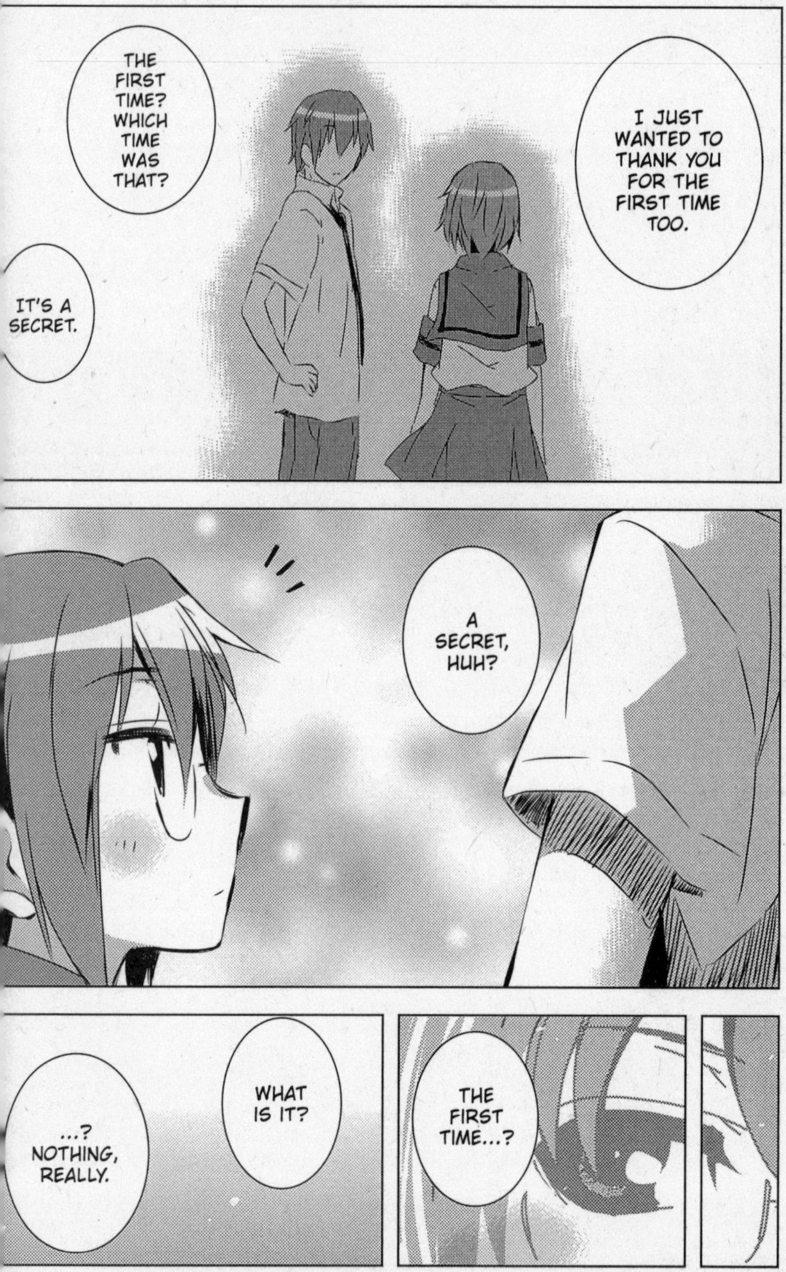
I JUST WANTED TO THANK YOU FOR THE FIRST TIME TOO.
THE FIRST TIME? WHICH TIME WAS THAT?
IT'S A SECRET.
A SECRET, HUH?
THE FIRST TIME...?
WHAT IS IT?
...? NOTHING, REALLY.

Epilogue 32>> End of Testing

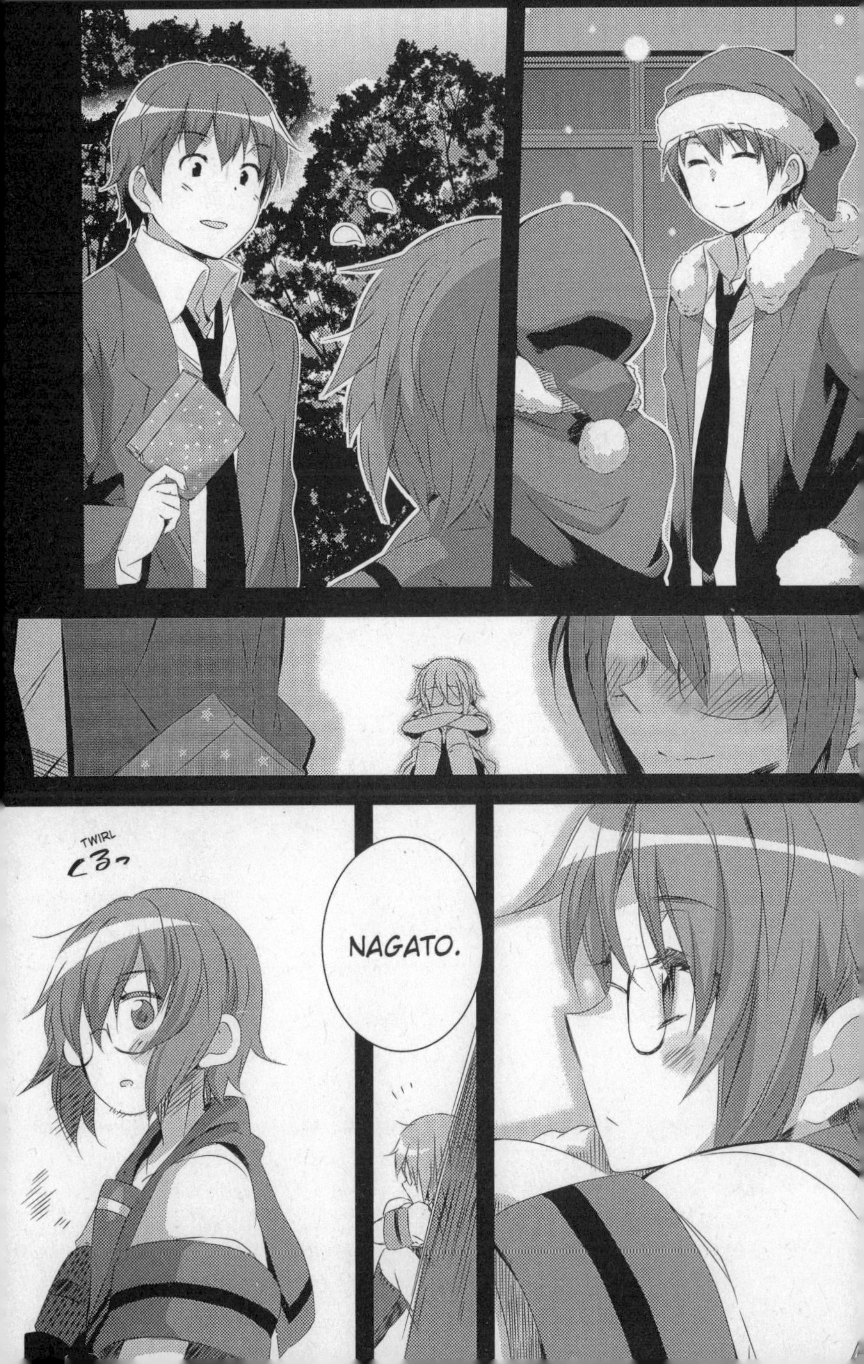
NAGATO.
TWIRL
くるっ

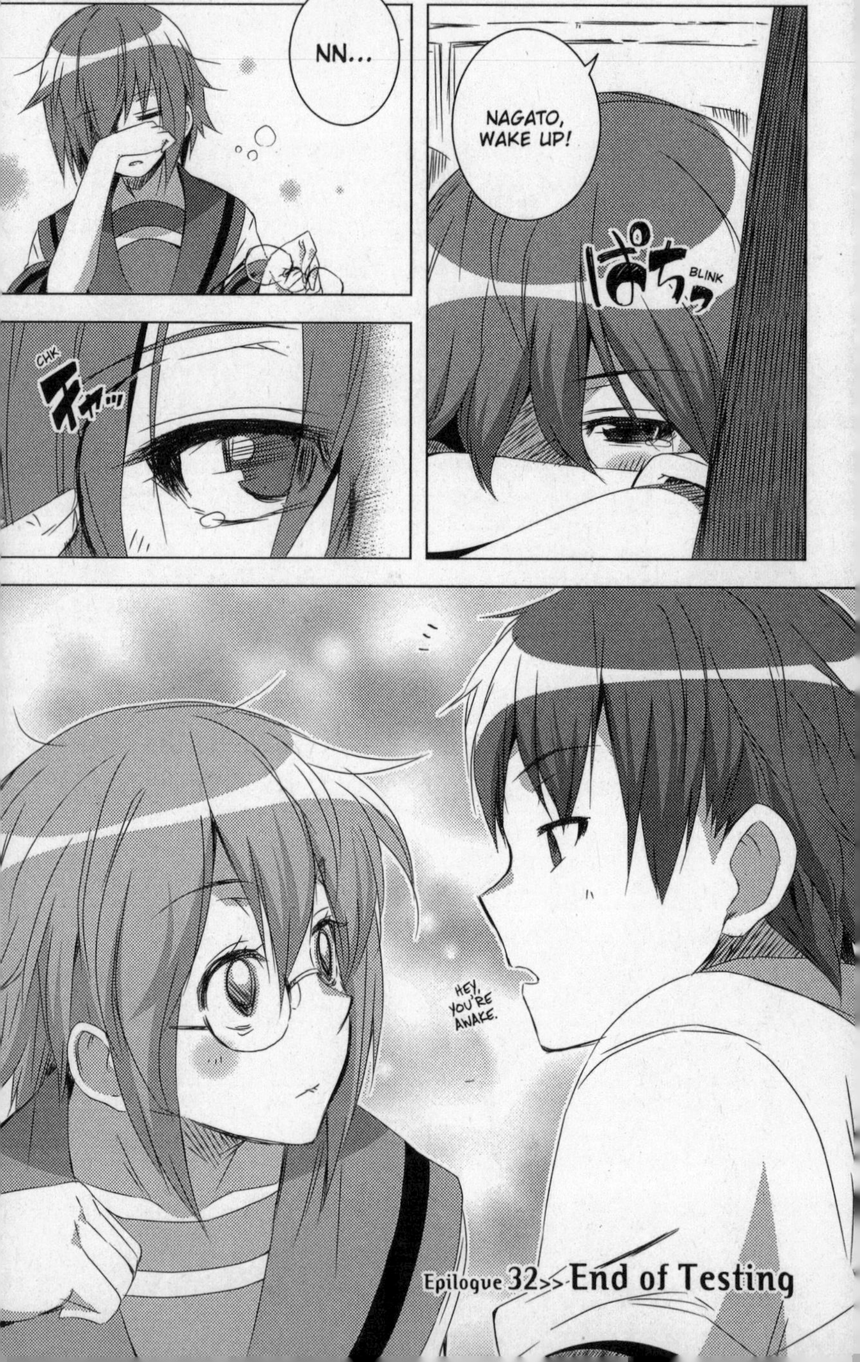
NAGATO, WAKE UP!
ぱちっ
BLINK
NN...
CHK
HEY, YOU'RE AWAKE.
Epilogue 32>> End of Testing

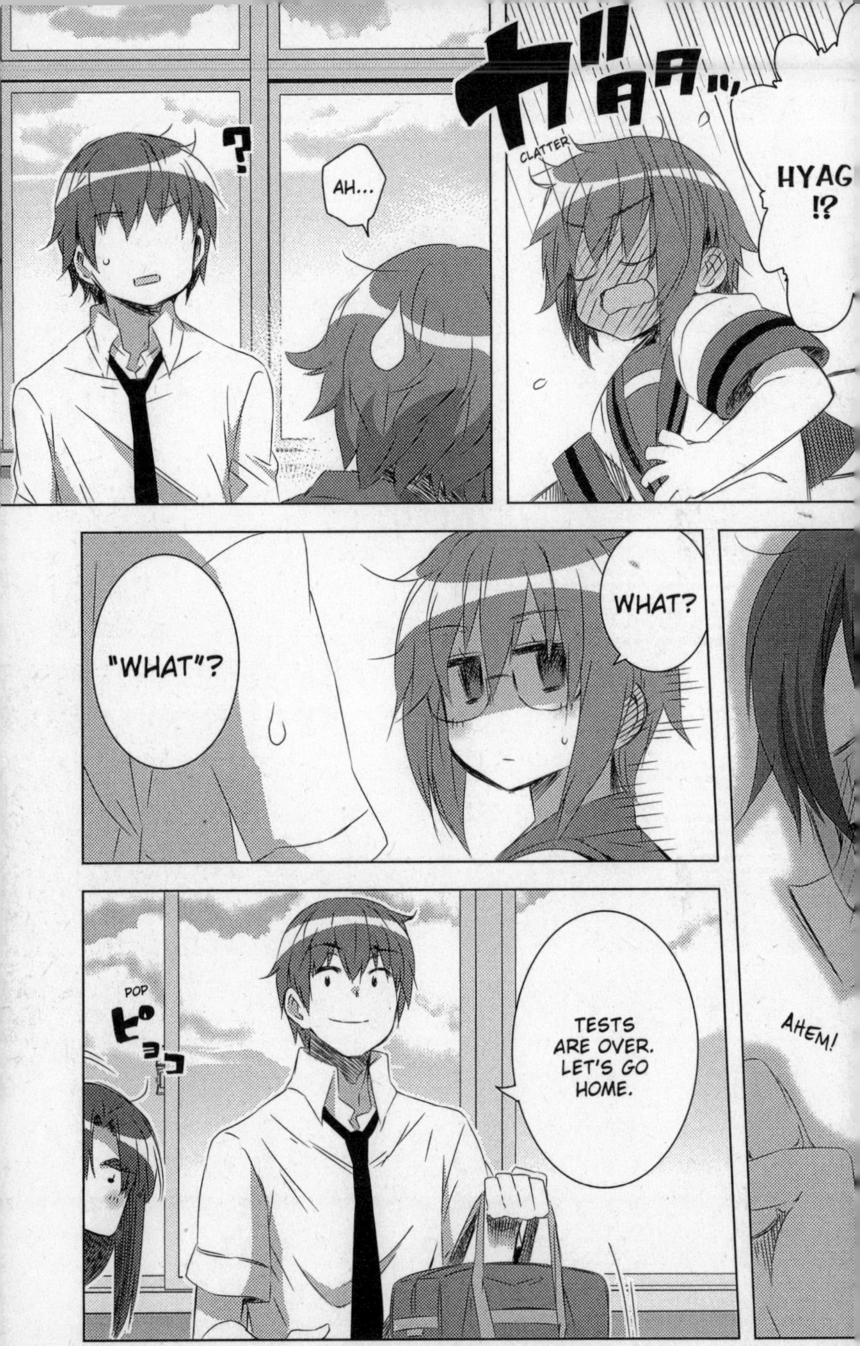

HYAG !?
CLATTER
AH...
?
AHEM!
WHAT?
"WHAT"?
TESTS ARE OVER. LET'S GO HOME.
POP
ピョコ

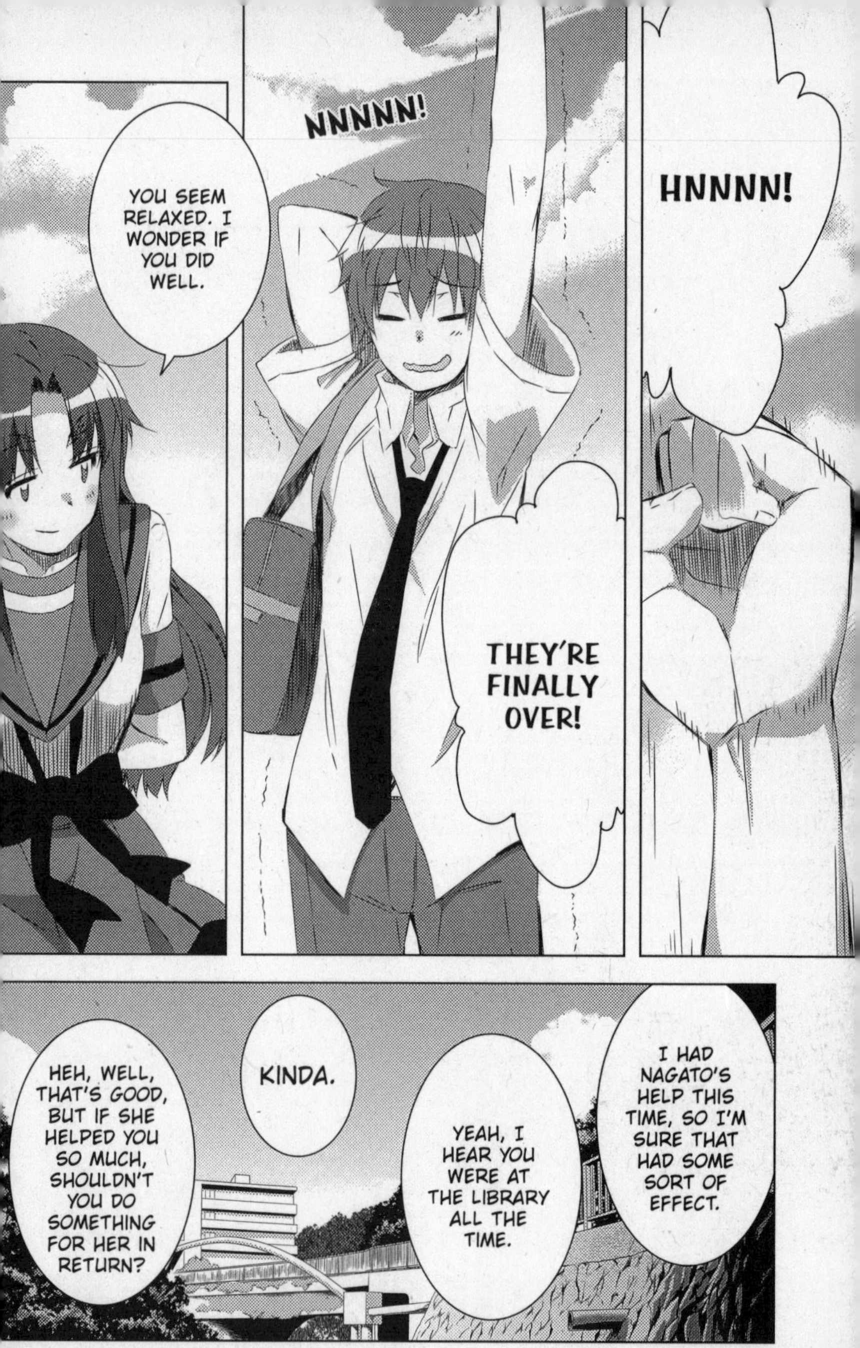
HNNNN!
NNNNN!
THEY'RE FINALLY OVER!
YOU SEEM RELAXED. I WONDER IF YOU DID WELL.
I HAD NAGATO'S HELP THIS TIME, SO I'M SURE THAT HAD SOME SORT OF EFFECT.
YEAH, I HEAR YOU WERE AT THE LIBRARY ALL THE TIME.
KINDA.
HEH, WELL, THAT'S GOOD, BUT IF SHE HELPED YOU SO MUCH, SHOULDN'T YOU DO SOMETHING FOR HER IN RETURN?

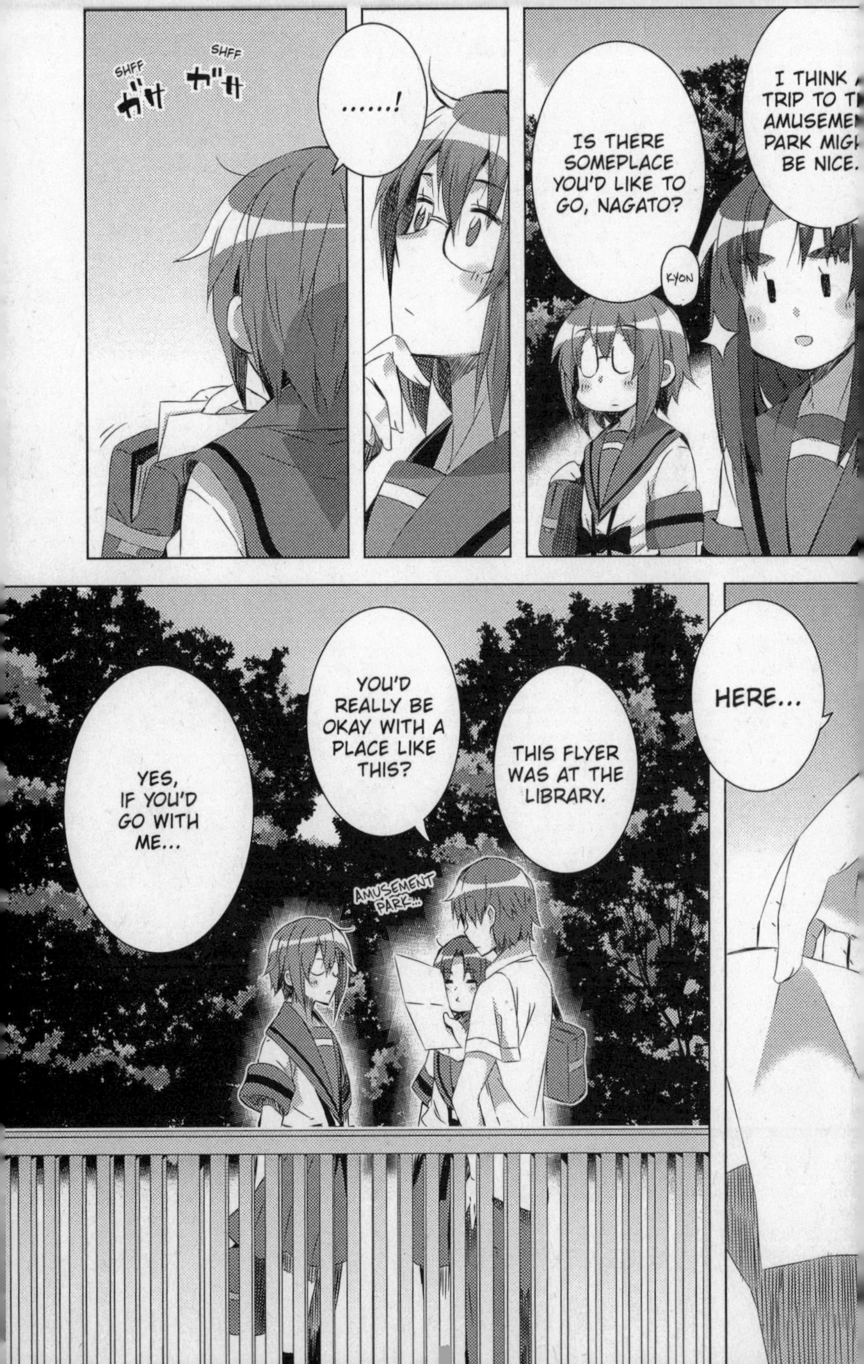
I THINK
TRIP TO T
AMUSEME
PARK MIGH
BE NICE.
IS THERE SOMEPLACE YOU'D LIKE TO GO, NAGATO?
KYON
......!
SHFF
ガサ
SHFF
ガサ
HERE...
THIS FLYER WAS AT THE LIBRARY.
YOU'D REALLY BE OKAY WITH A PLACE LIKE THIS?
YES, IF YOU'D GO WITH ME...
AMUSEMENT PARK...

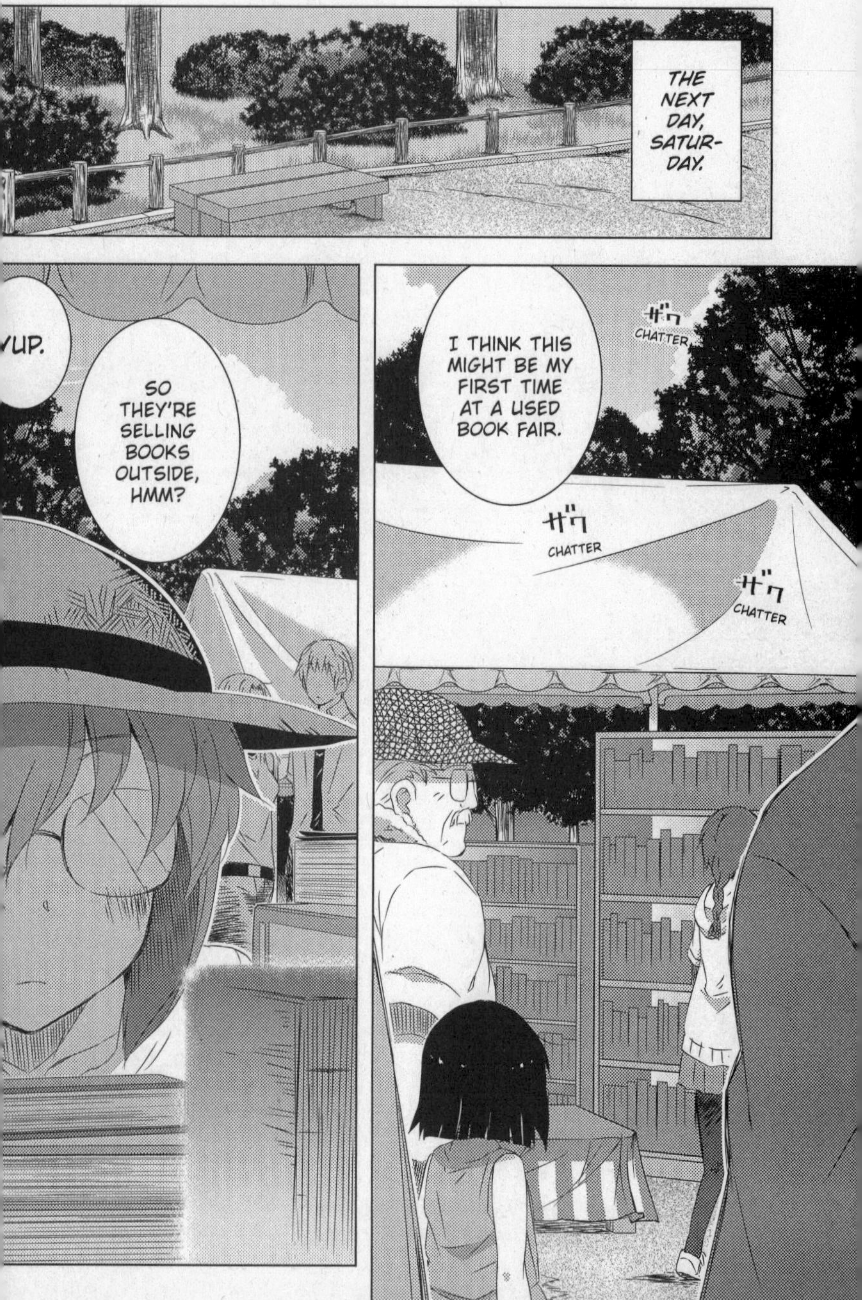
THE NEXT DAY, SATUR-DAY.
I THINK THIS MIGHT BE MY FIRST TIME AT A USED BOOK FAIR.
ザワ
CHATTER
ザワ
CHATTER
ザワ
CHATTER
YUP.
SO THEY'RE SELLING BOOKS OUTSIDE, HMM?

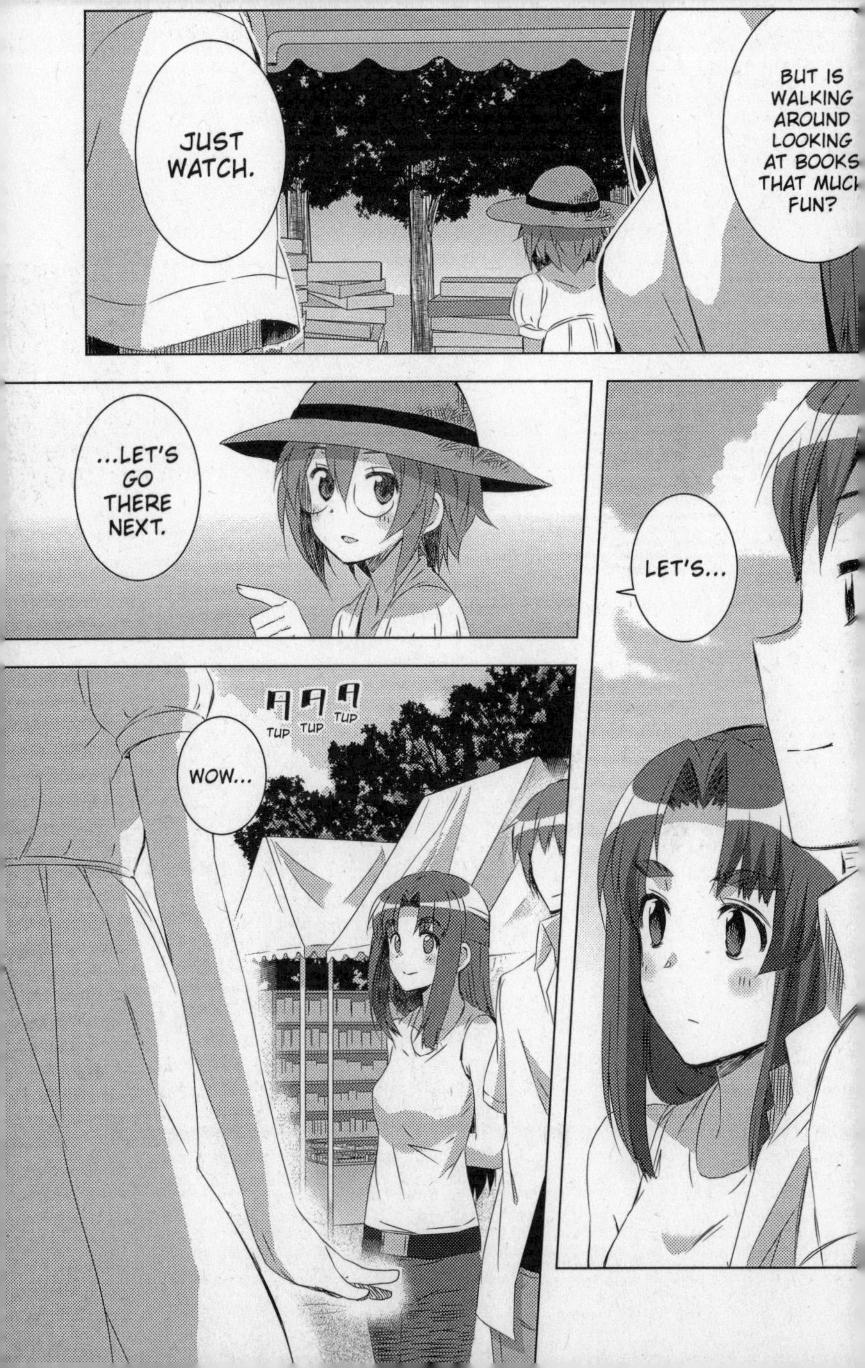
BUT IS WALKING AROUND LOOKING AT BOOKS THAT MUC FUN?
JUST WATCH.
LET'S...
...LET'S GO THERE NEXT.
TUP TUP TUP
WOW...

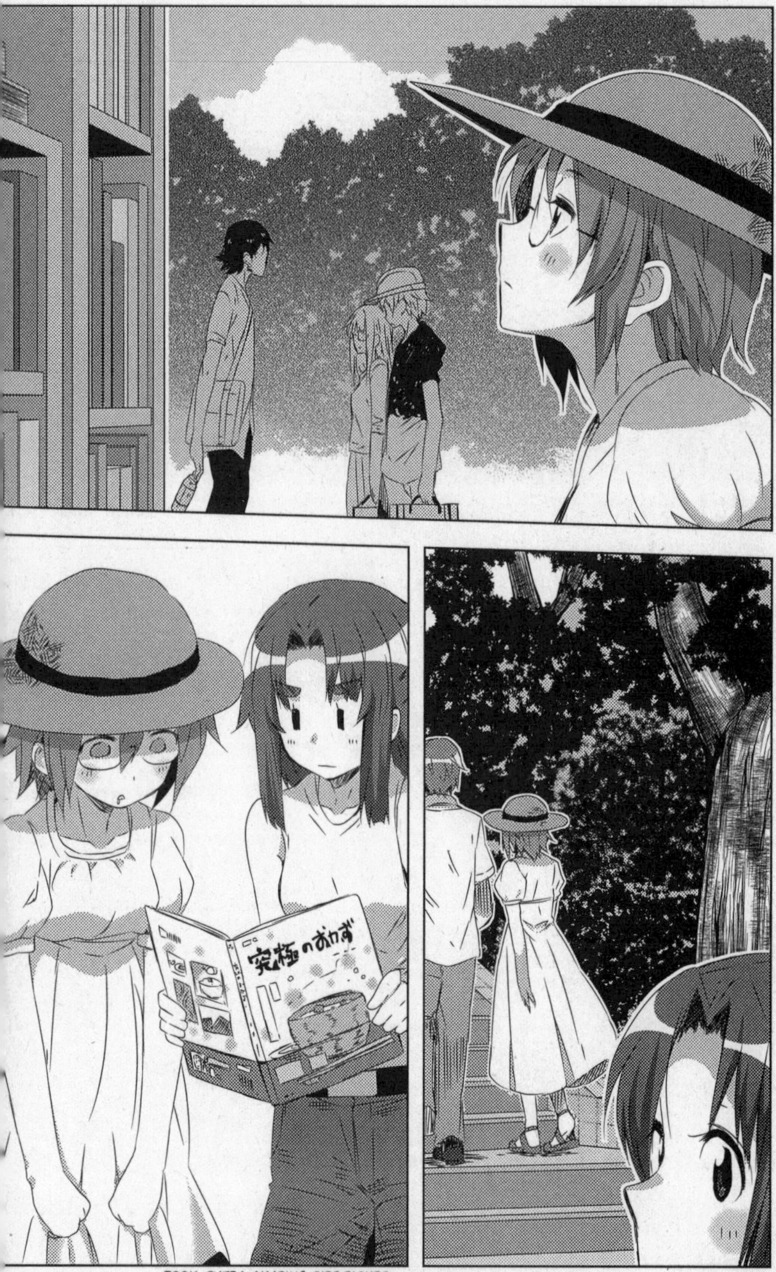
究極のおかず

BOOK: EXTRA-AMAZING SIDE DISHES

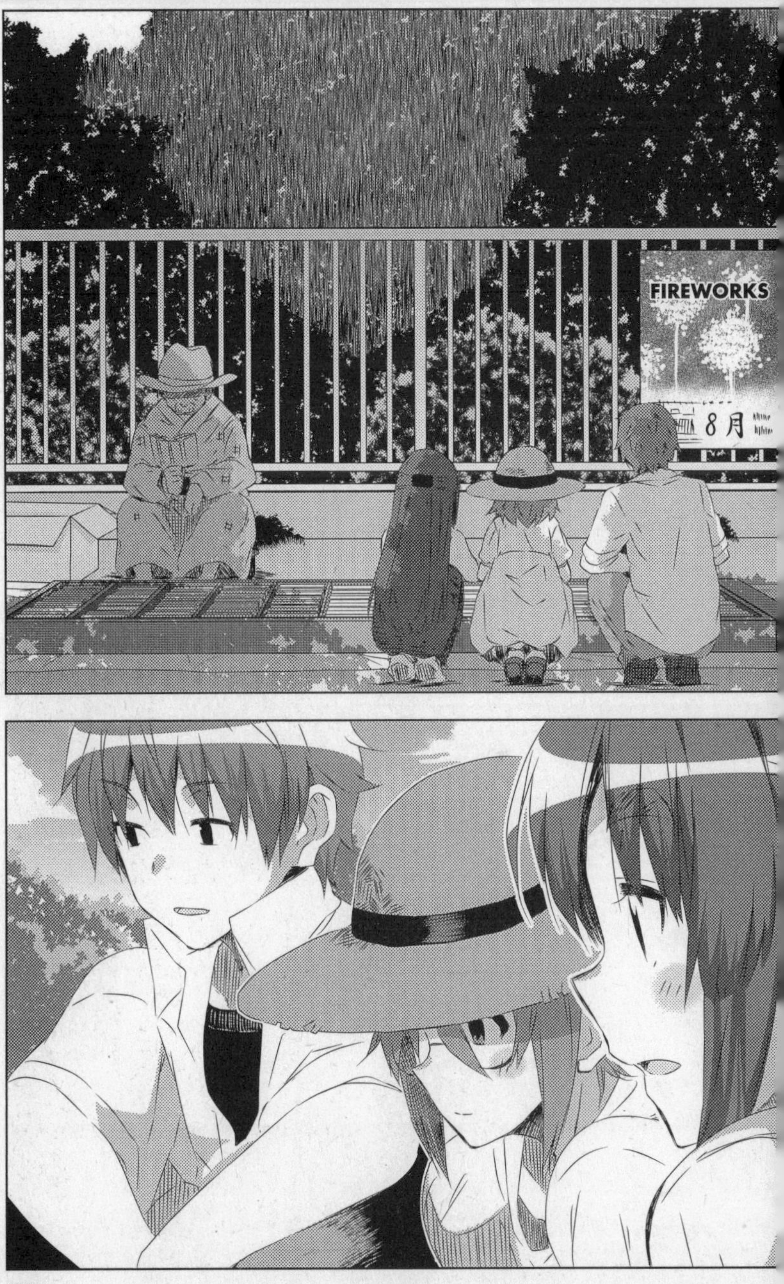
FIREWORKS
8月

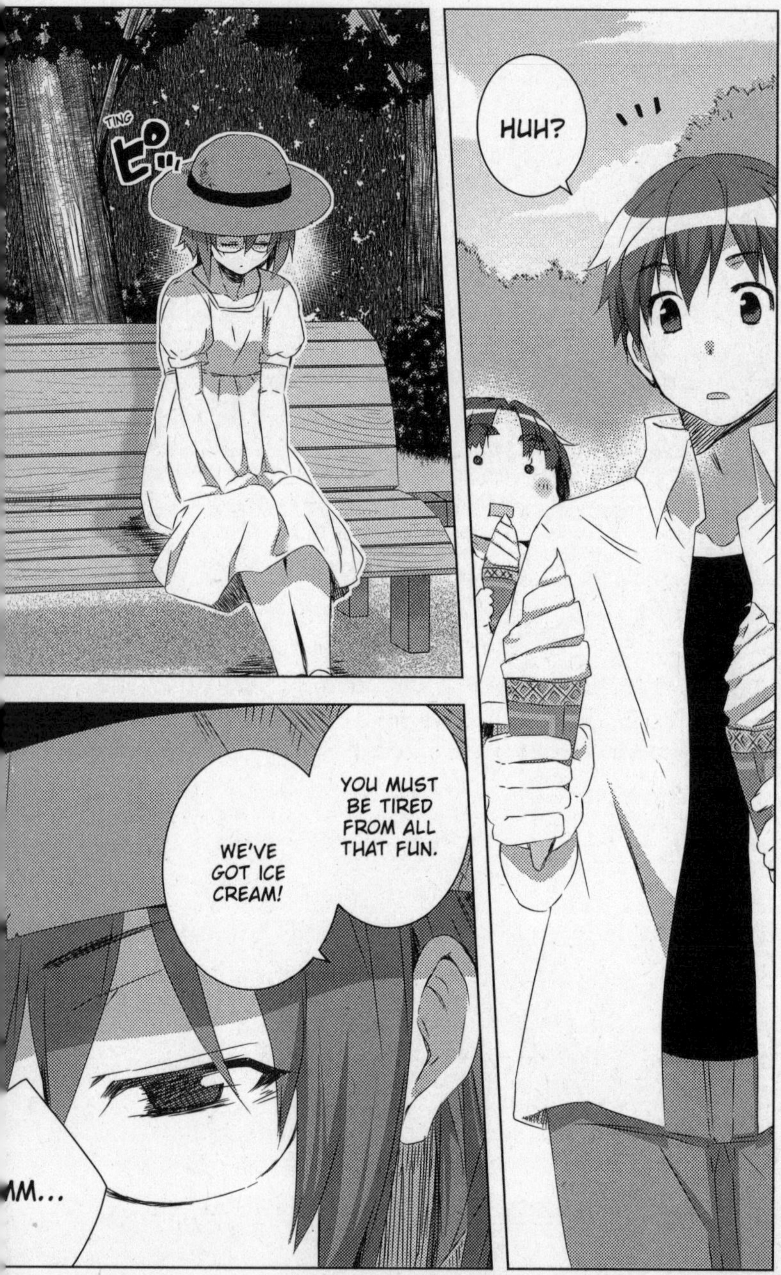
HUH?
TING
ピ
YOU MUST BE TIRED FROM ALL THAT FUN.
WE'VE GOT ICE CREAM!
MM...

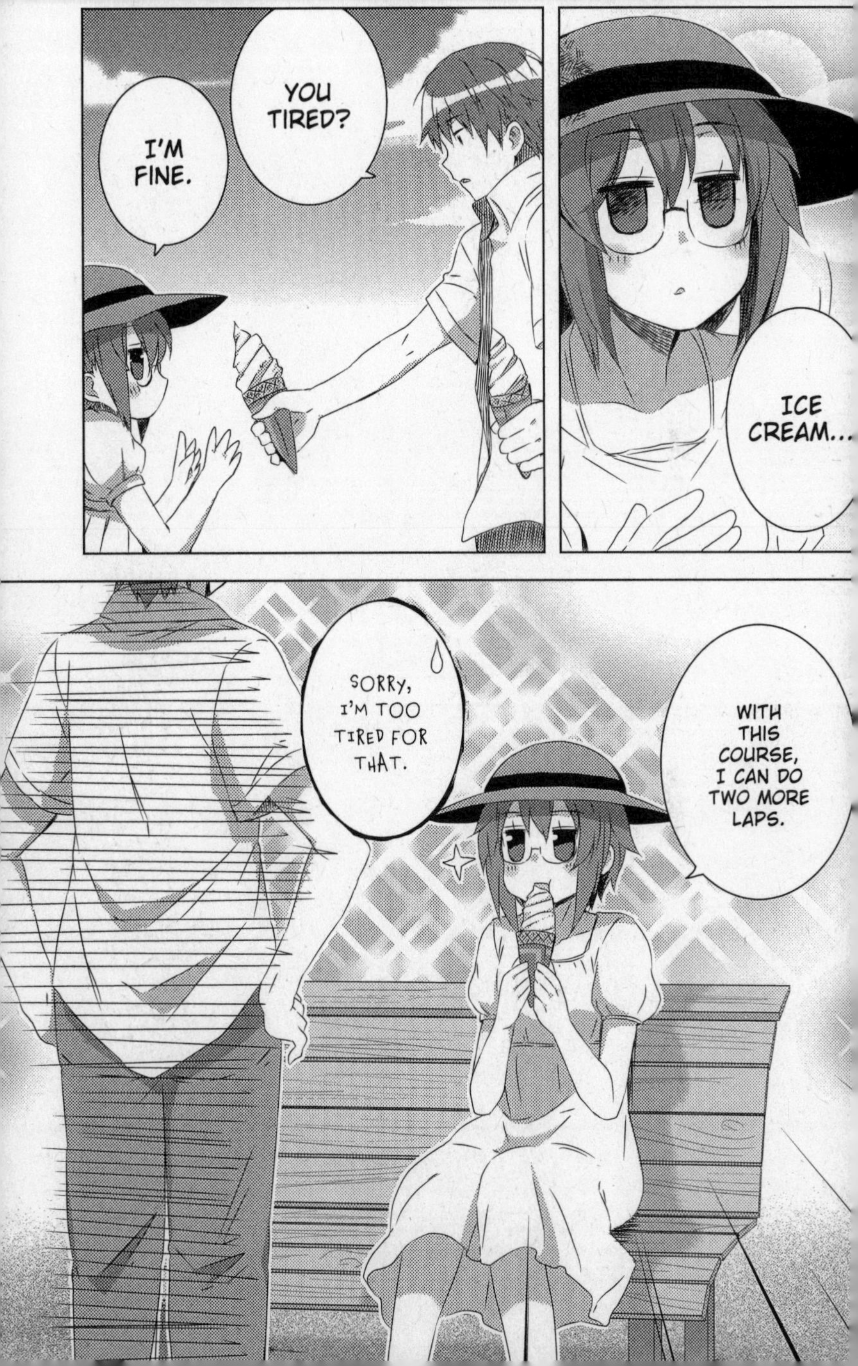
ICE CREAM...
YOU TIRED?
I'M FINE.
WITH THIS COURSE, I CAN DO TWO MORE LAPS.
SORRY, I'M TOO TIRED FOR THAT.

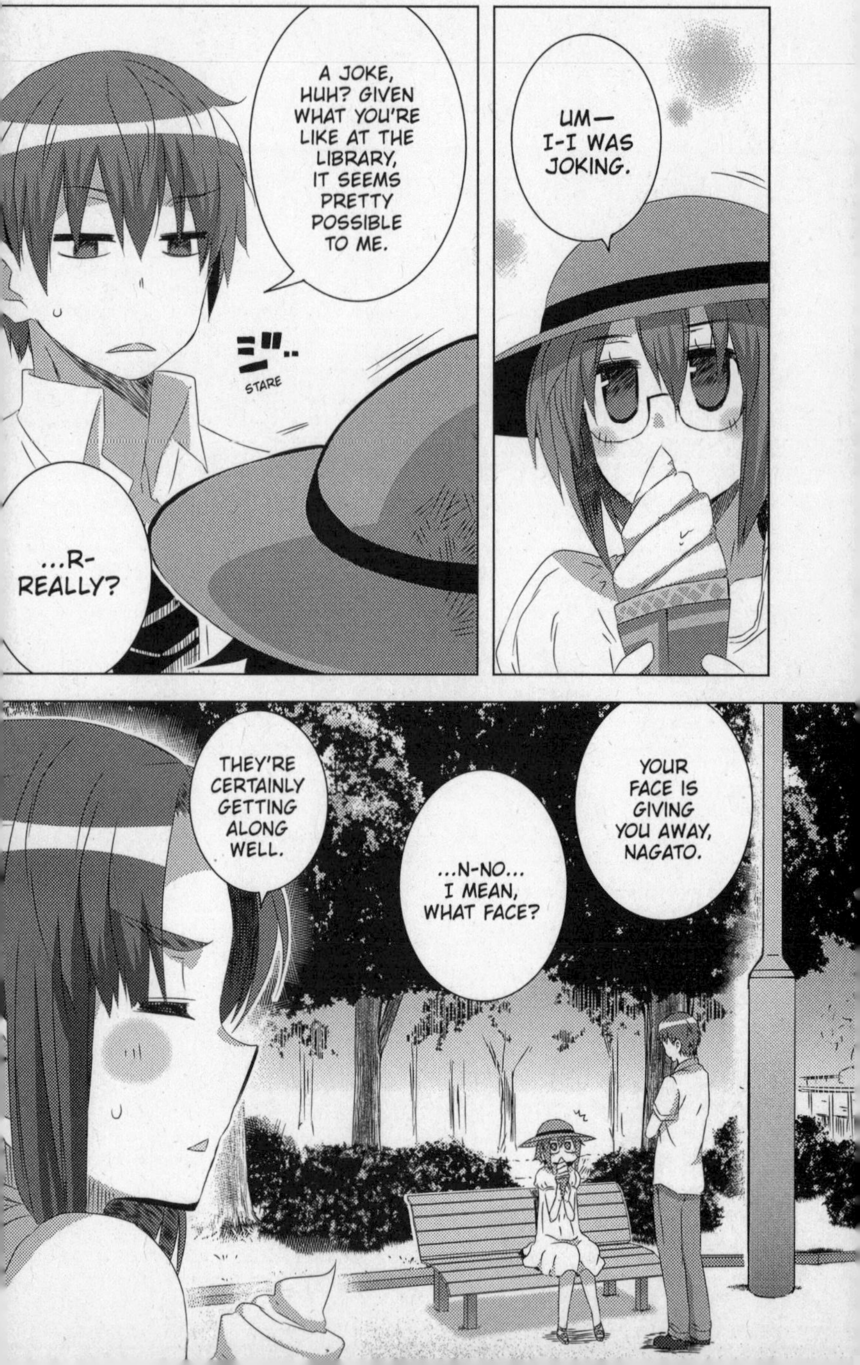
UM— I-I WAS JOKING.
A JOKE, HUH? GIVEN WHAT YOU'RE LIKE AT THE LIBRARY, IT SEEMS PRETTY POSSIBLE TO ME.
STARE
...R-REALLY?
YOUR FACE IS GIVING YOU AWAY, NAGATO.
...N-NO... I MEAN, WHAT FACE?
THEY'RE CERTAINLY GETTING ALONG WELL.

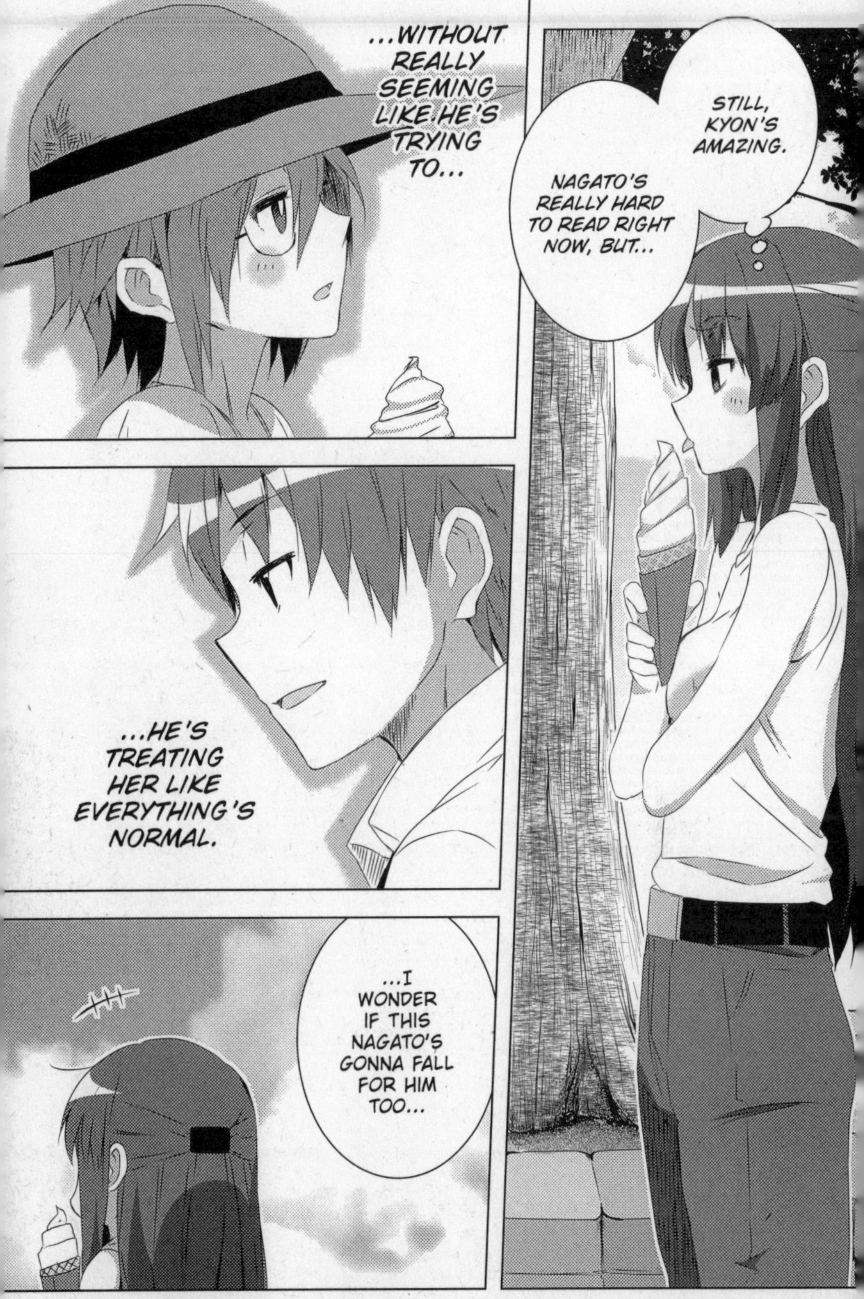
STILL, KYON'S AMAZING.
NAGATO'S REALLY HARD TO READ RIGHT NOW, BUT...
...WITHOUT REALLY SEEMING LIKE HE'S TRYING TO...
...HE'S TREATING HER LIKE EVERYTHING'S NORMAL.
...I WONDER IF THIS NAGATO'S GONNA FALL FOR HIM TOO...

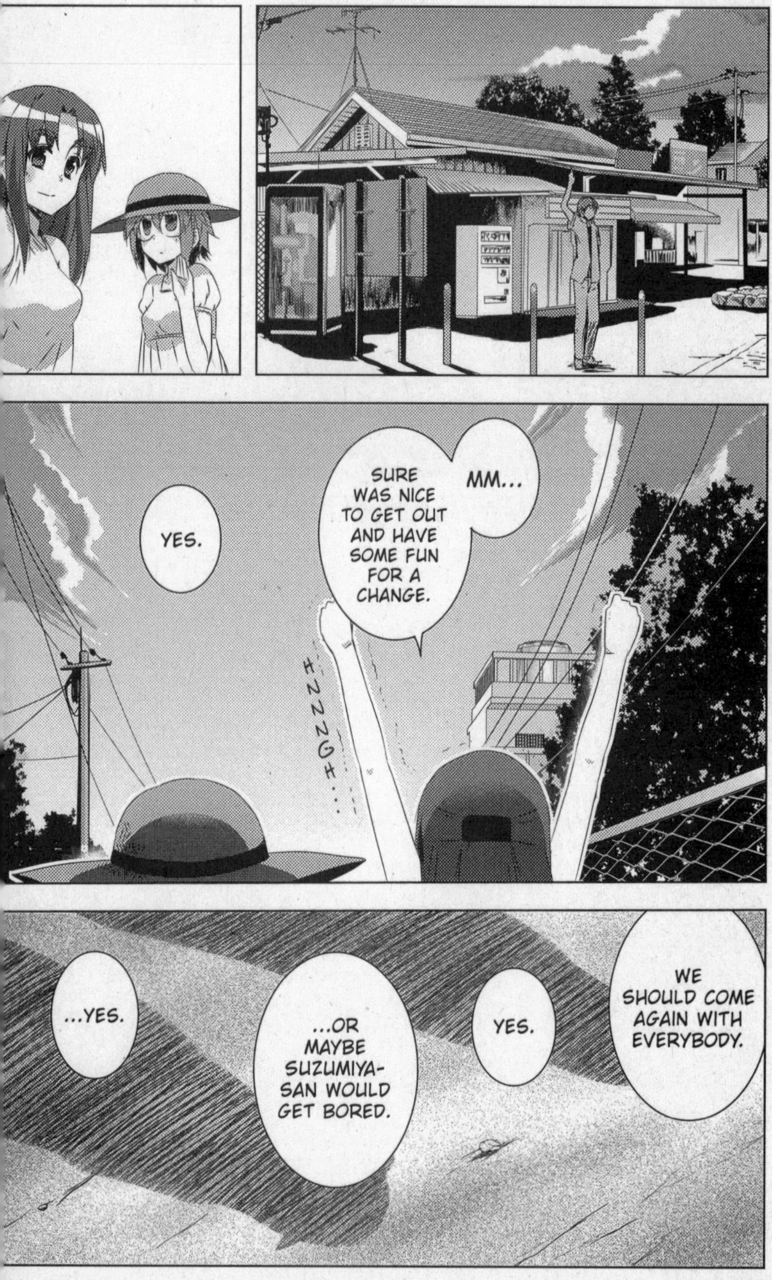
MM...
SURE WAS NICE TO GET OUT AND HAVE SOME FUN FOR A CHANGE.
HNNNGH...
YES.
WE SHOULD COME AGAIN WITH EVERYBODY.
YES.
...OR MAYBE SUZUMIYA-SAN WOULD GET BORED.
...YES.

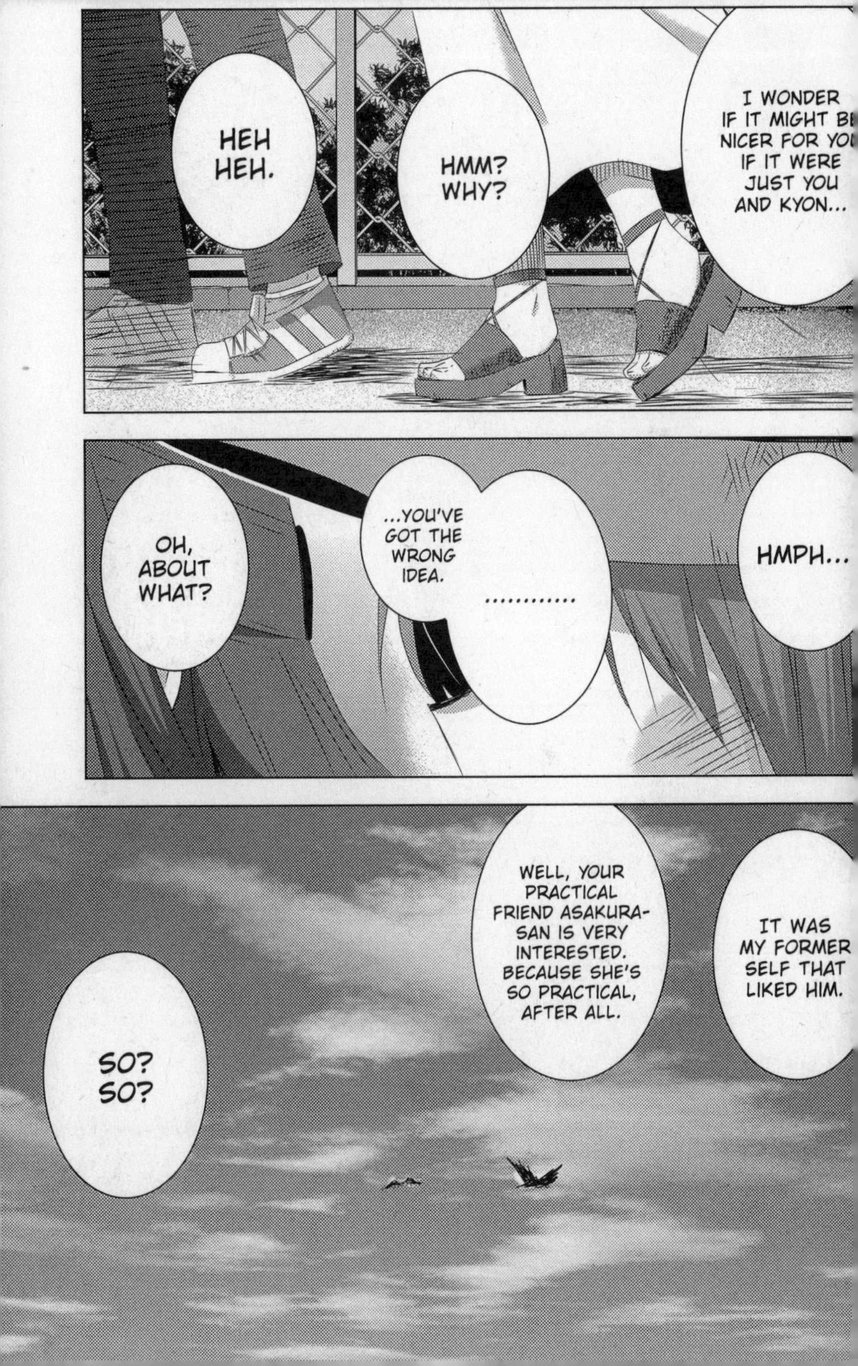
I WONDER IF IT MIGHT BE NICER FOR YOU IF IT WERE JUST YOU AND KYON...
HMM? WHY?
HEH HEH.
HMPH...
....
...YOU'VE GOT THE WRONG IDEA.
OH, ABOUT WHAT?
IT WAS MY FORMER SELF THAT LIKED HIM.
WELL, YOUR PRACTICAL FRIEND ASAKURA-SAN IS VERY INTERESTED. BECAUSE SHE'S SO PRACTICAL, AFTER ALL.
SO? SO?

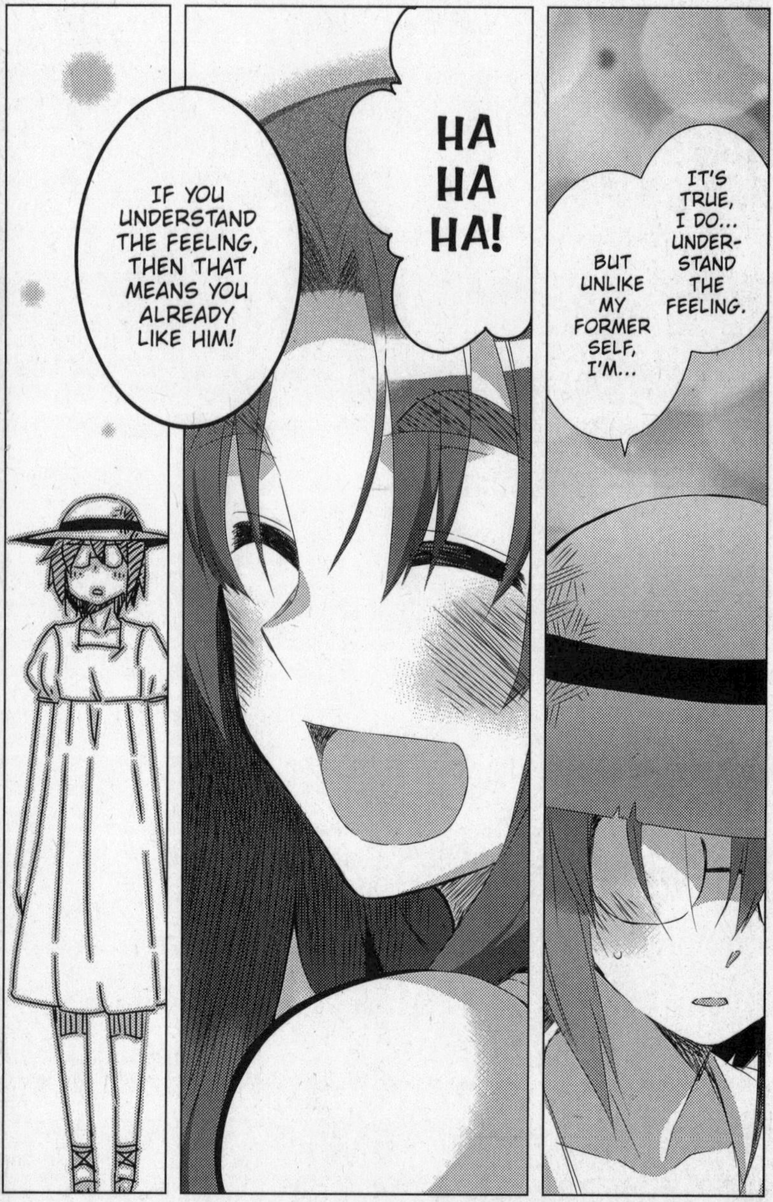
IT'S TRUE, I DO... UNDER-STAND THE FEELING.
BUT UNLIKE MY FORMER SELF, I'M...
HA HA HA!
IF YOU UNDERSTAND THE FEELING, THEN THAT MEANS YOU ALREADY LIKE HIM!

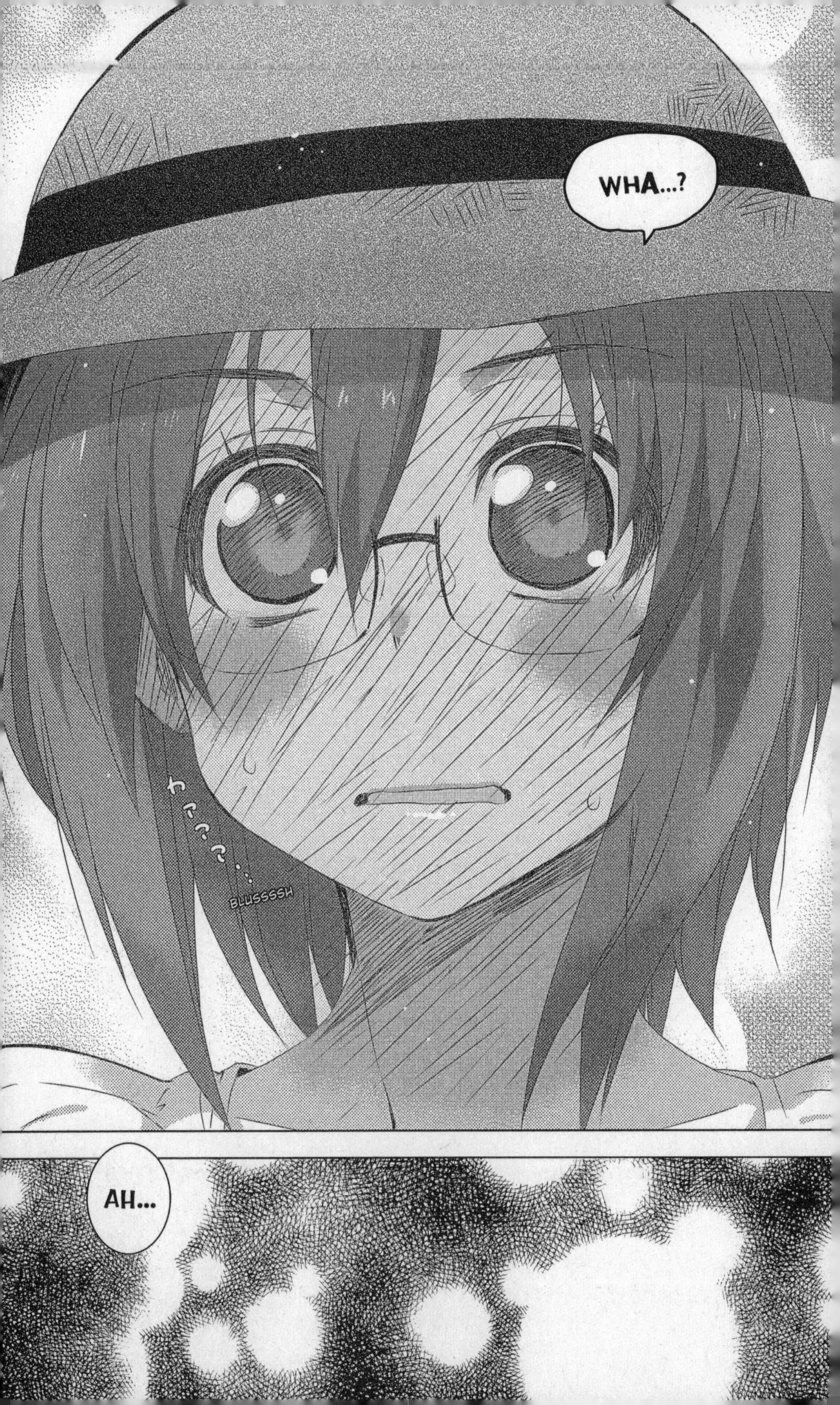
WHA...?
BLUSSSSH
AH...

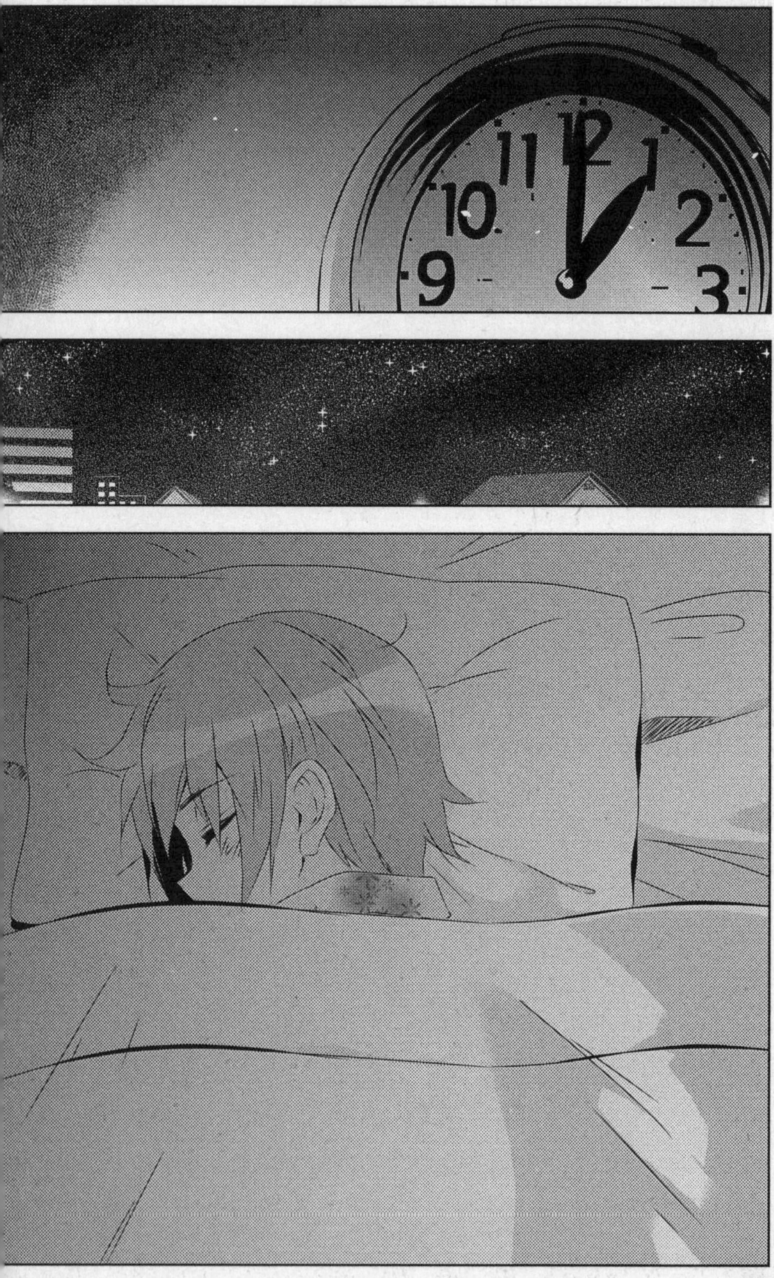

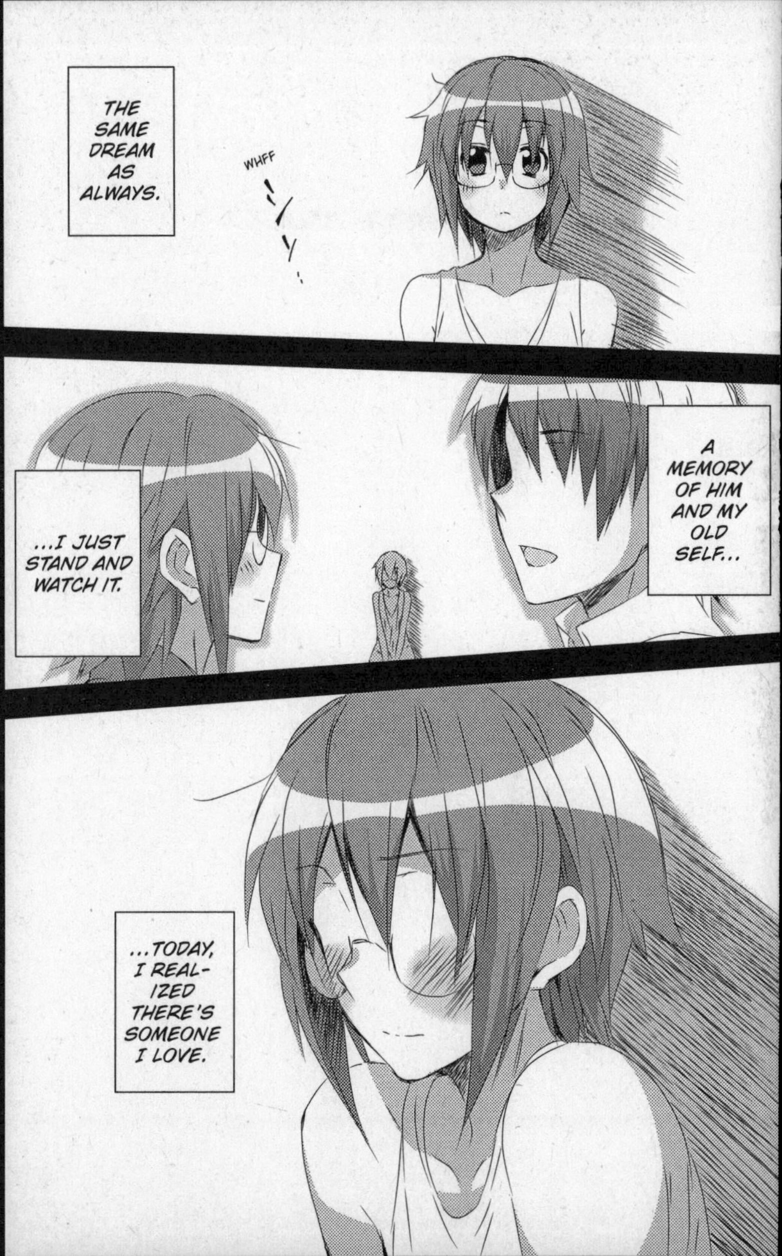
THE SAME DREAM AS ALWAYS.
WHFF
A MEMORY OF HIM AND MY OLD SELF...
...I JUST STAND AND WATCH IT.
...TODAY, I REAL-IZED THERE'S SOMEONE I LOVE.

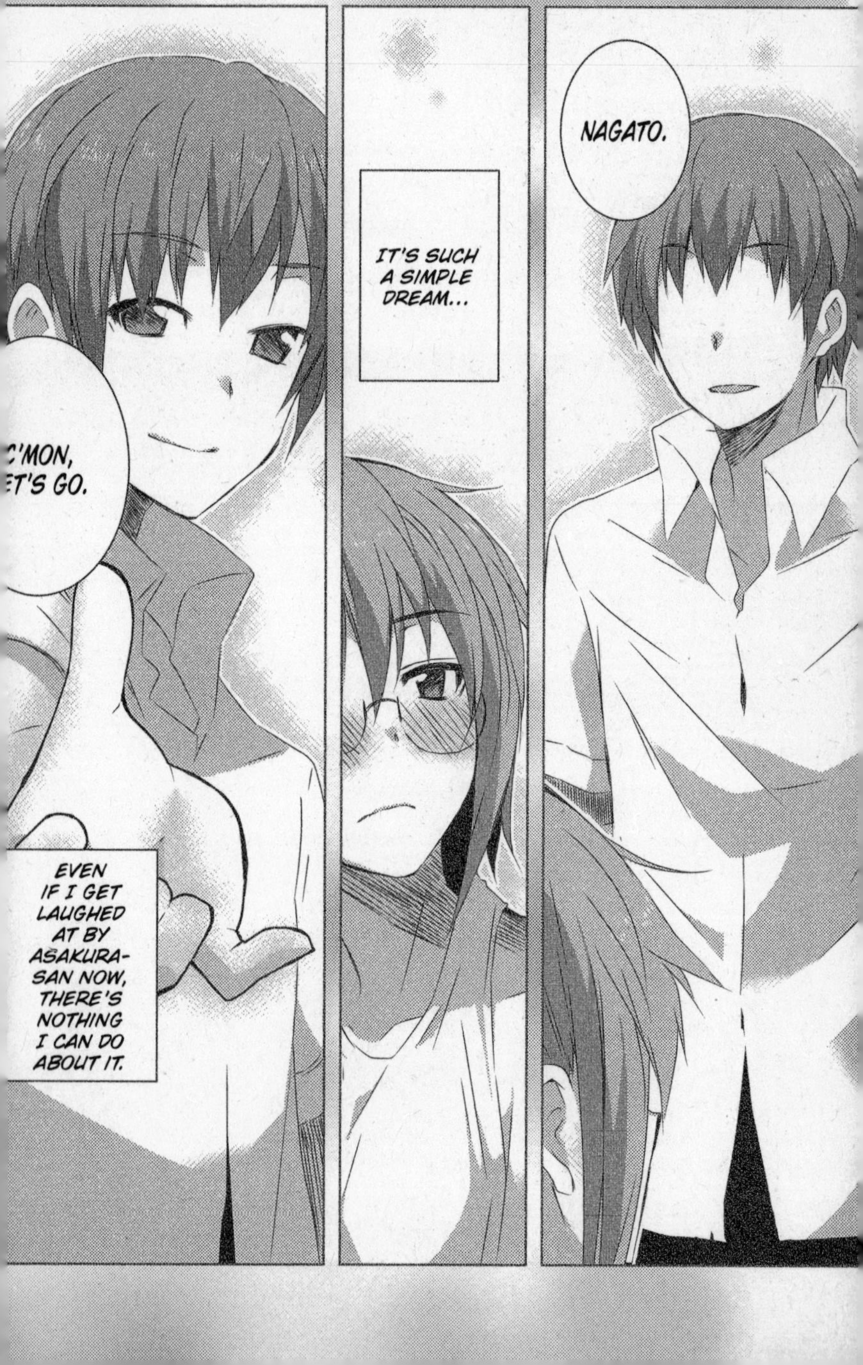
NAGATO.
IT'S SUCH A SIMPLE DREAM...
C'MON, ET'S GO.
EVEN IF I GET LAUGHED AT BY ASAKURA-SAN NOW, THERE'S NOTHING I CAN DO ABOUT IT.

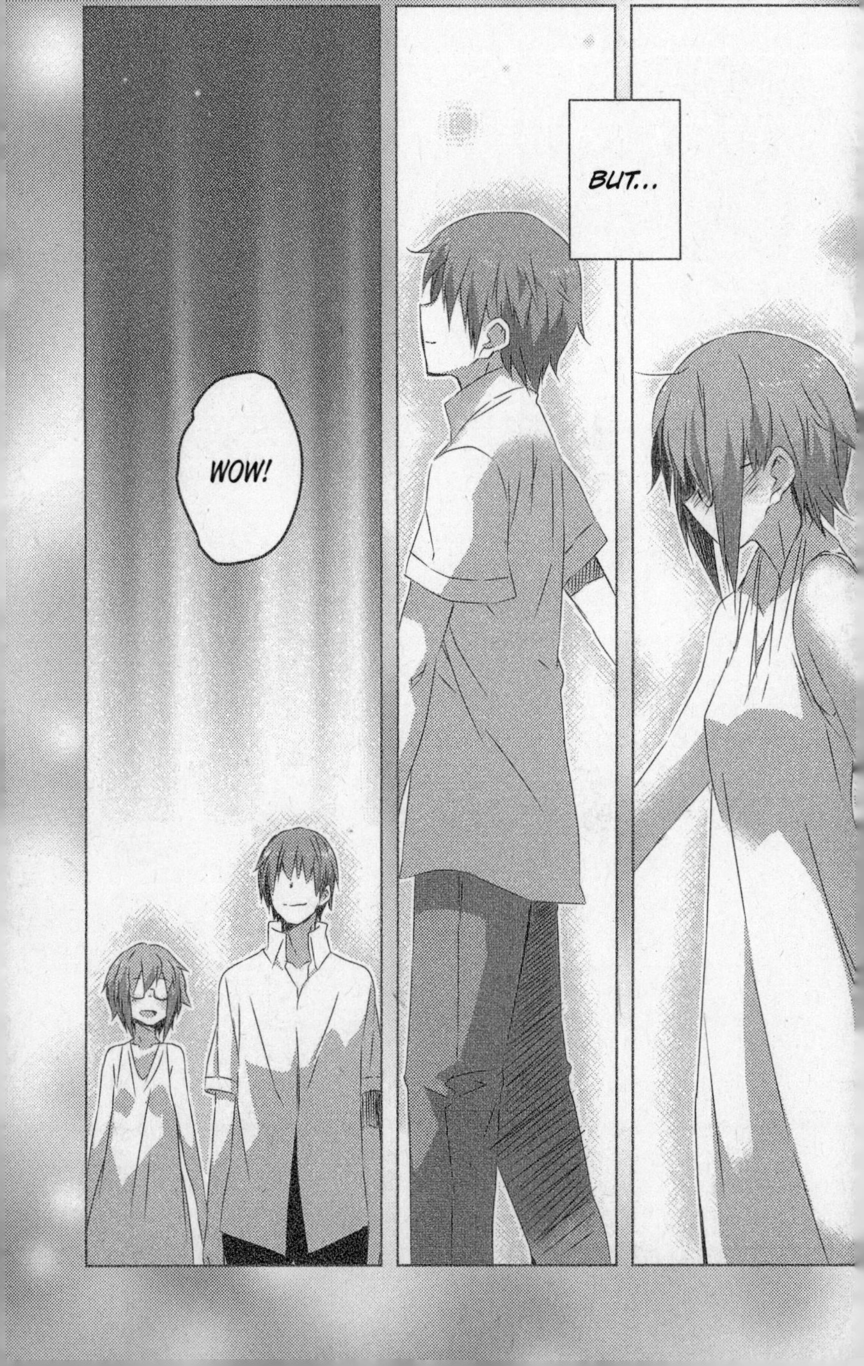
BUT...
WOW!

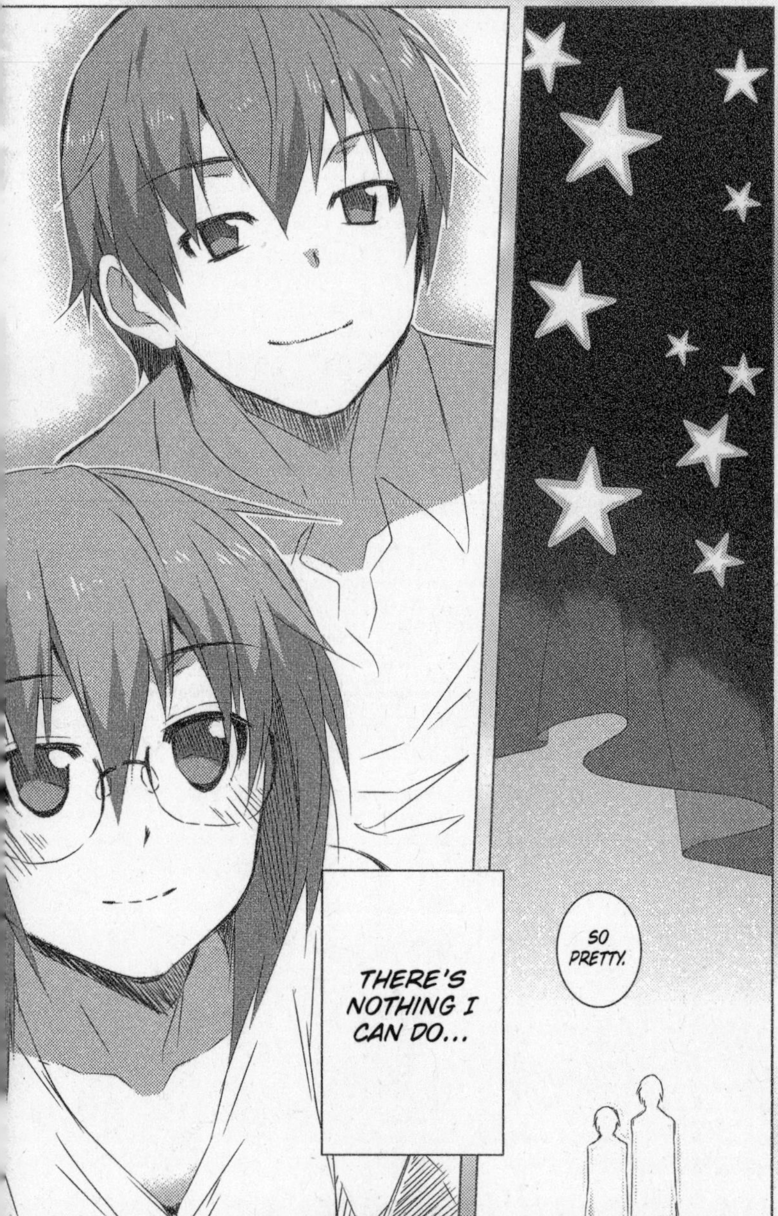
SO PRETTY.
THERE'S NOTHING I CAN DO...

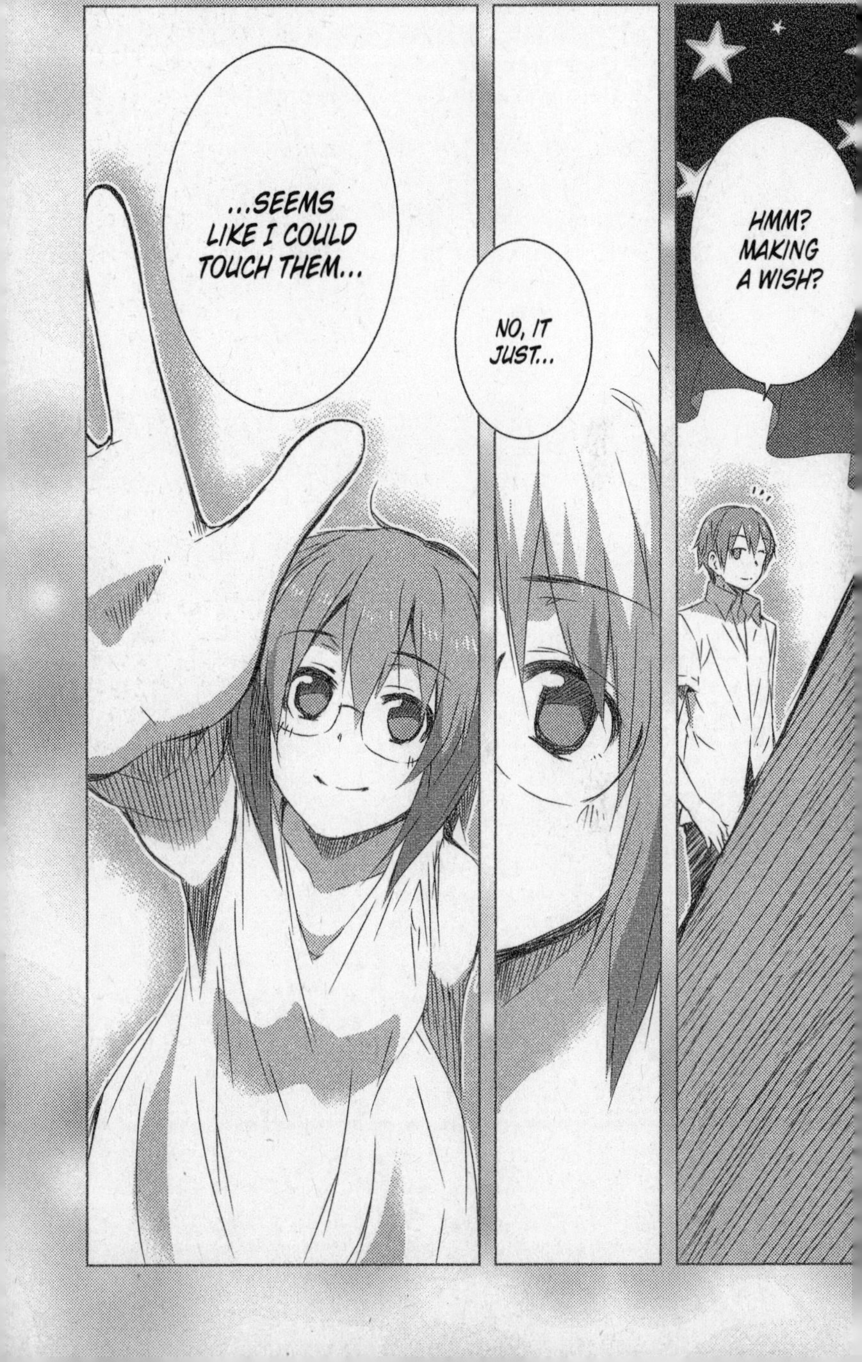
HMM? MAKING A WISH?
NO, IT JUST...
...SEEMS LIKE I COULD TOUCH THEM...

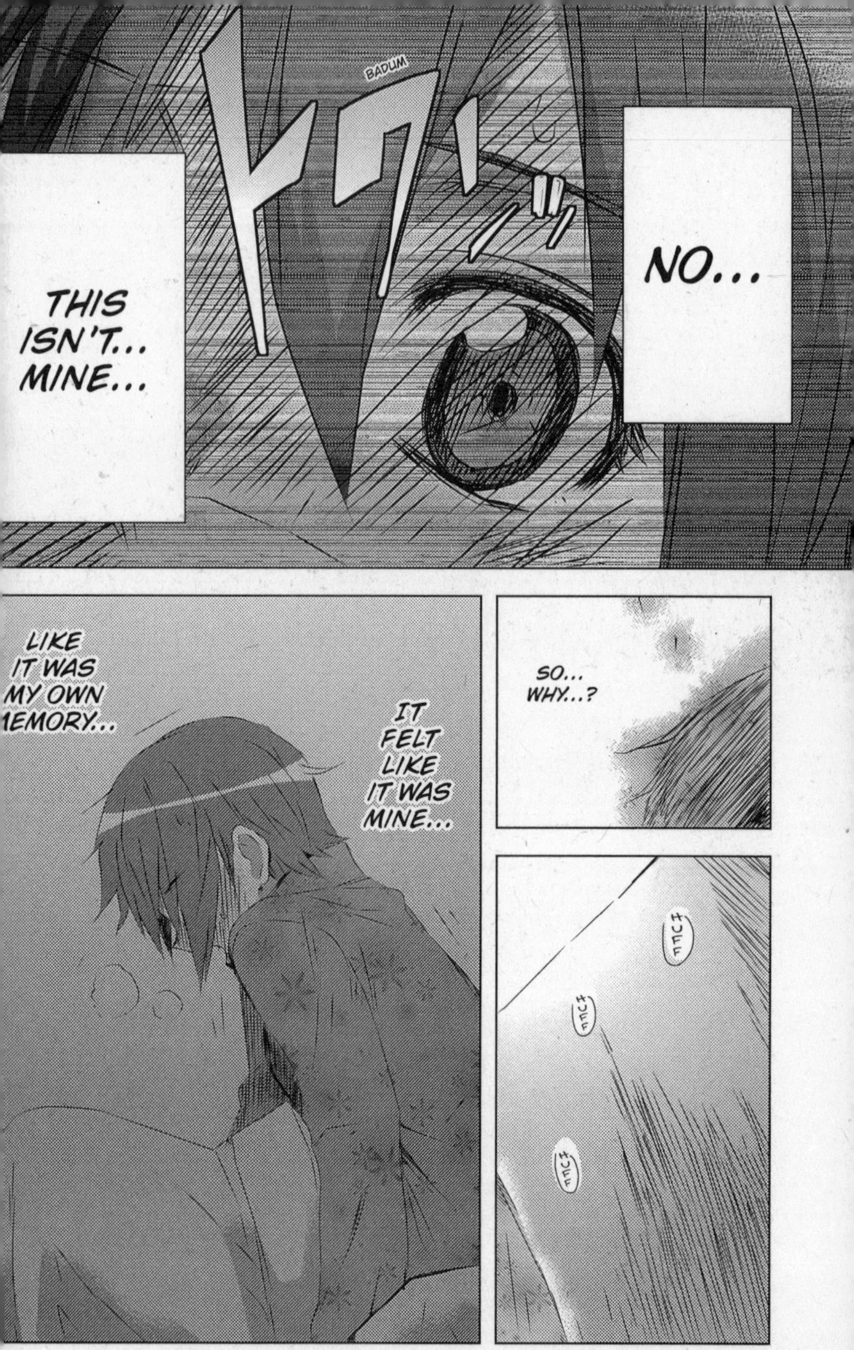
NO...
BADUM
THIS ISN'T... MINE...
SO... WHY...?
HUFF
HUFF
HUFF
IT FELT LIKE IT WAS MINE...
LIKE IT WAS MY OWN MEMORY...

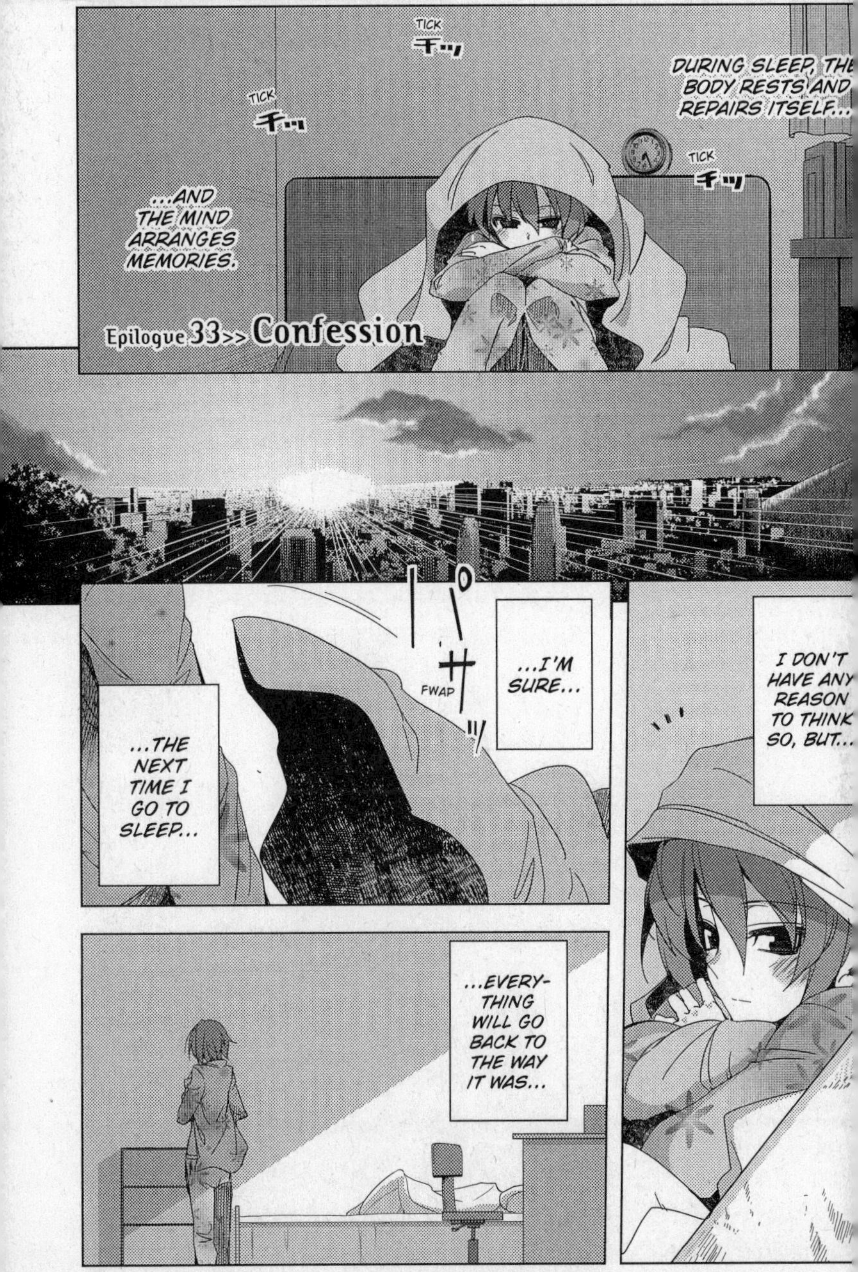
DURING SLEEP, THE BODY RESTS AND REPAIRS ITSELF...
TICK
チッ
TICK
チッ
TICK
チッ
...AND THE MIND ARRANGES MEMORIES.
Epilogue 33>> Confession
I DON'T HAVE ANY REASON TO THINK SO, BUT...
...
...I'M SURE...
パサッ
FWAP
...THE NEXT TIME I GO TO SLEEP...
...EVERY-THING WILL GO BACK TO THE WAY IT WAS...

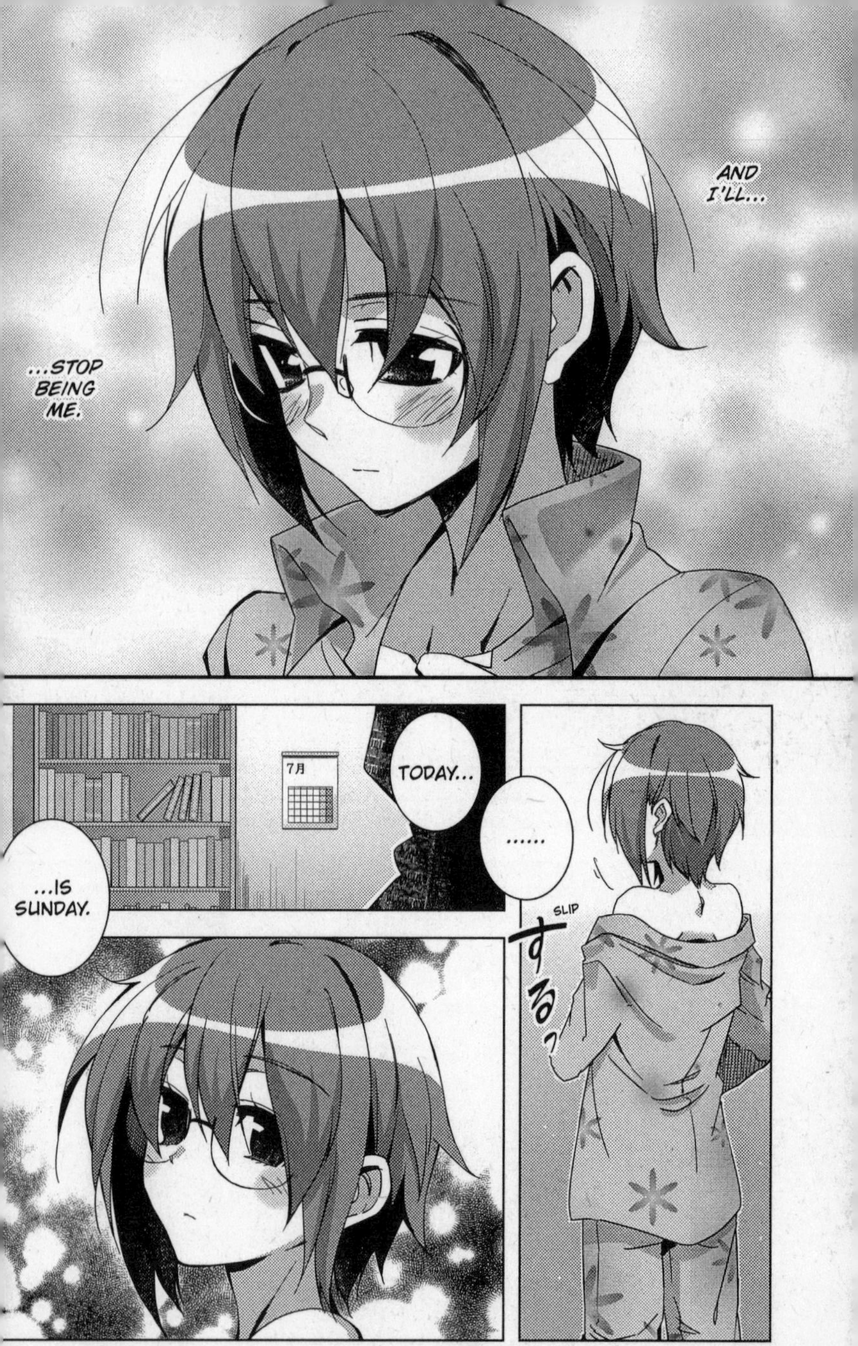
AND I'LL...
...STOP BEING ME.
......
SLIP
するっ
7月
TODAY...
...IS SUNDAY.

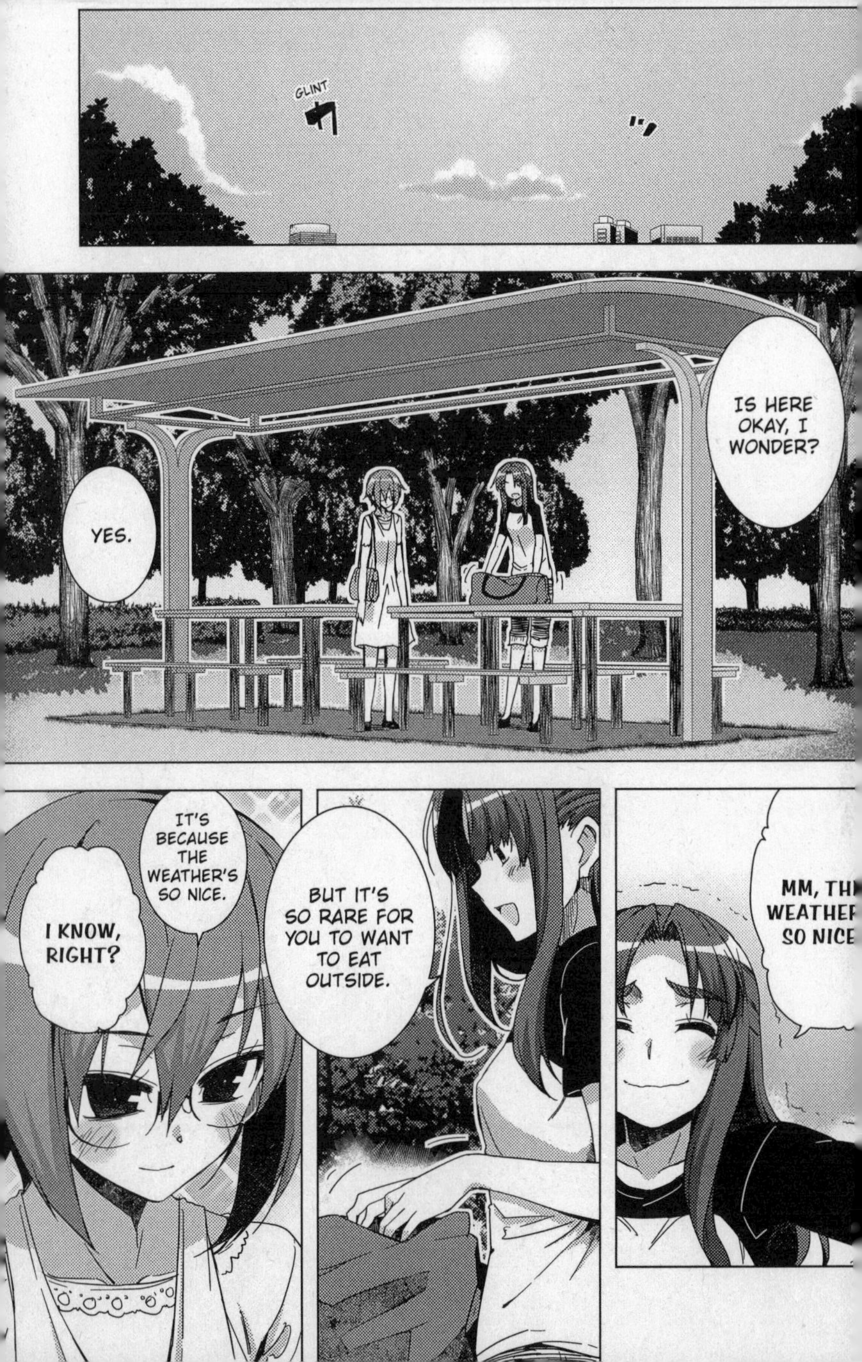
GLINT
IS HERE OKAY, I WONDER?
YES.
MM, TH WEATHER SO NICE
BUT IT'S SO RARE FOR YOU TO WANT TO EAT OUTSIDE.
IT'S BECAUSE THE WEATHER'S SO NICE.
I KNOW, RIGHT?

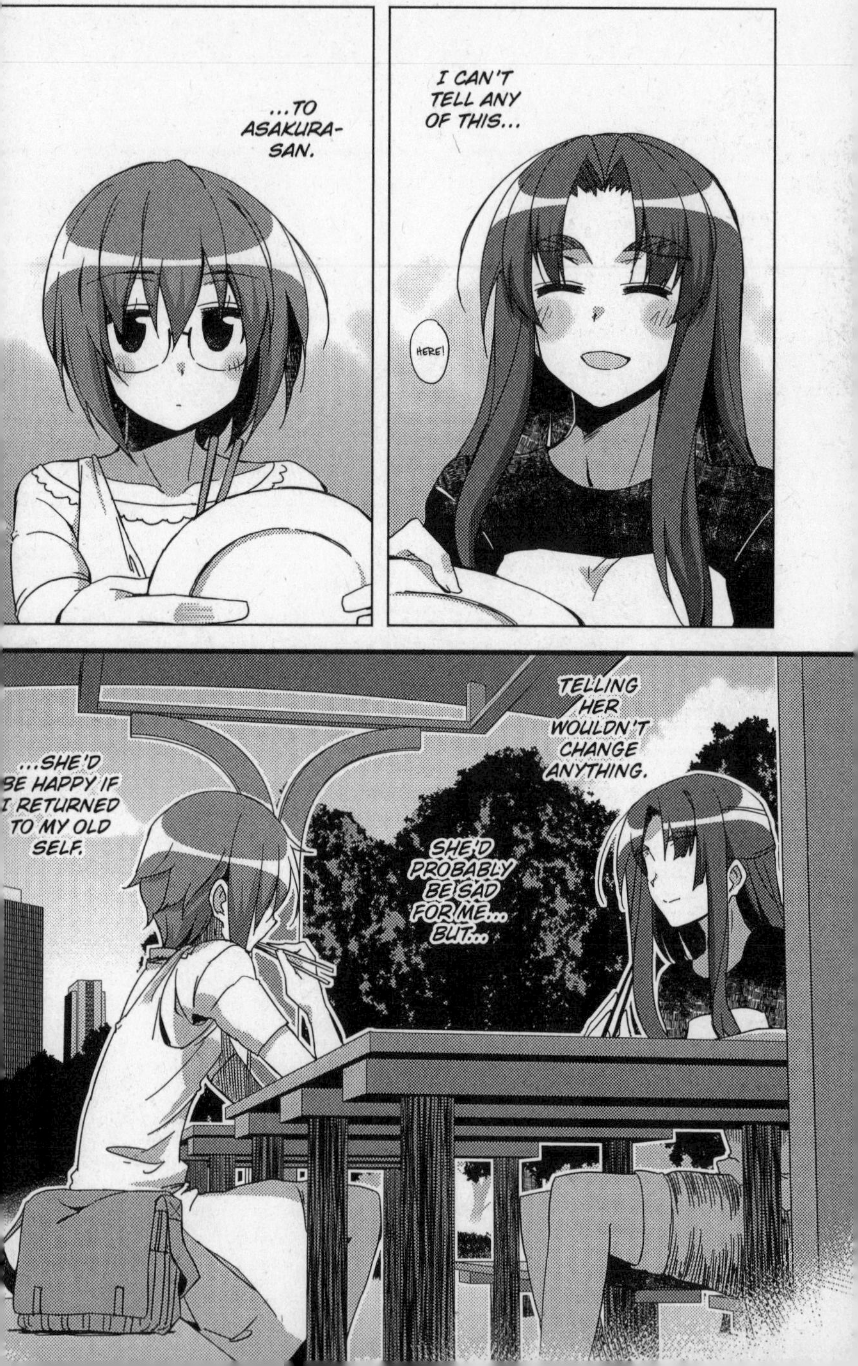
I CAN'T TELL ANY OF THIS...
HERE!
...TO ASAKURA-SAN.
TELLING HER WOULDN'T CHANGE ANYTHING.
SHE'D PROBABLY BE SAD FOR ME... BUT...
...SHE'D BE HAPPY IF I RETURNED TO MY OLD SELF.

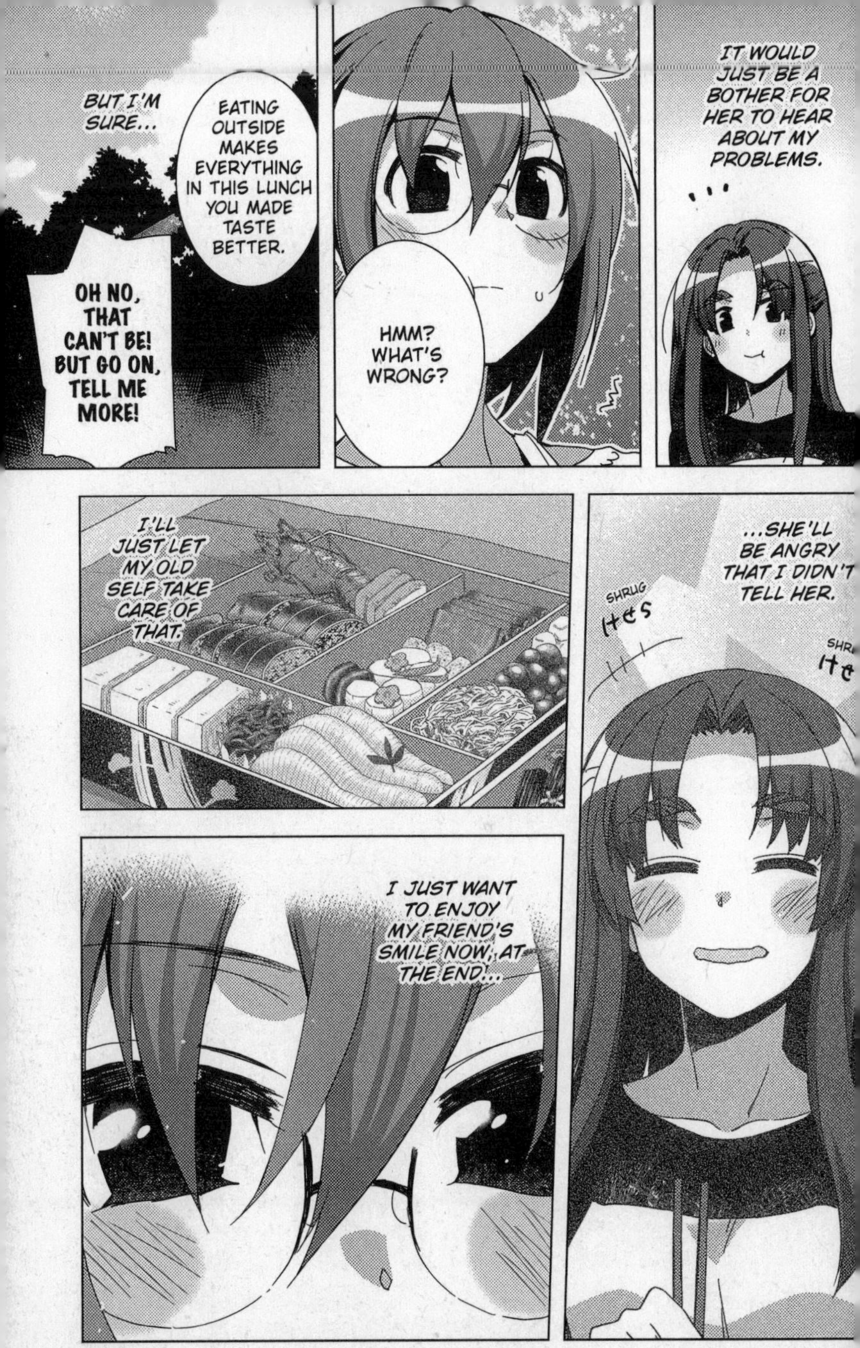

IT WOULD JUST BE A BOTHER FOR HER TO HEAR ABOUT MY PROBLEMS.
...
HMM? WHAT'S WRONG?
EATING OUTSIDE MAKES EVERYTHING IN THIS LUNCH YOU MADE TASTE BETTER.
BUT I'M SURE...
OH NO, THAT CAN'T BE! BUT GO ON, TELL ME MORE!
...SHE'LL BE ANGRY THAT I DIDN'T TELL HER.
SHRUG
けせら
I'LL JUST LET MY OLD SELF TAKE CARE OF THAT.
I JUST WANT TO ENJOY MY FRIEND'S SMILE NOW, AT THE END...

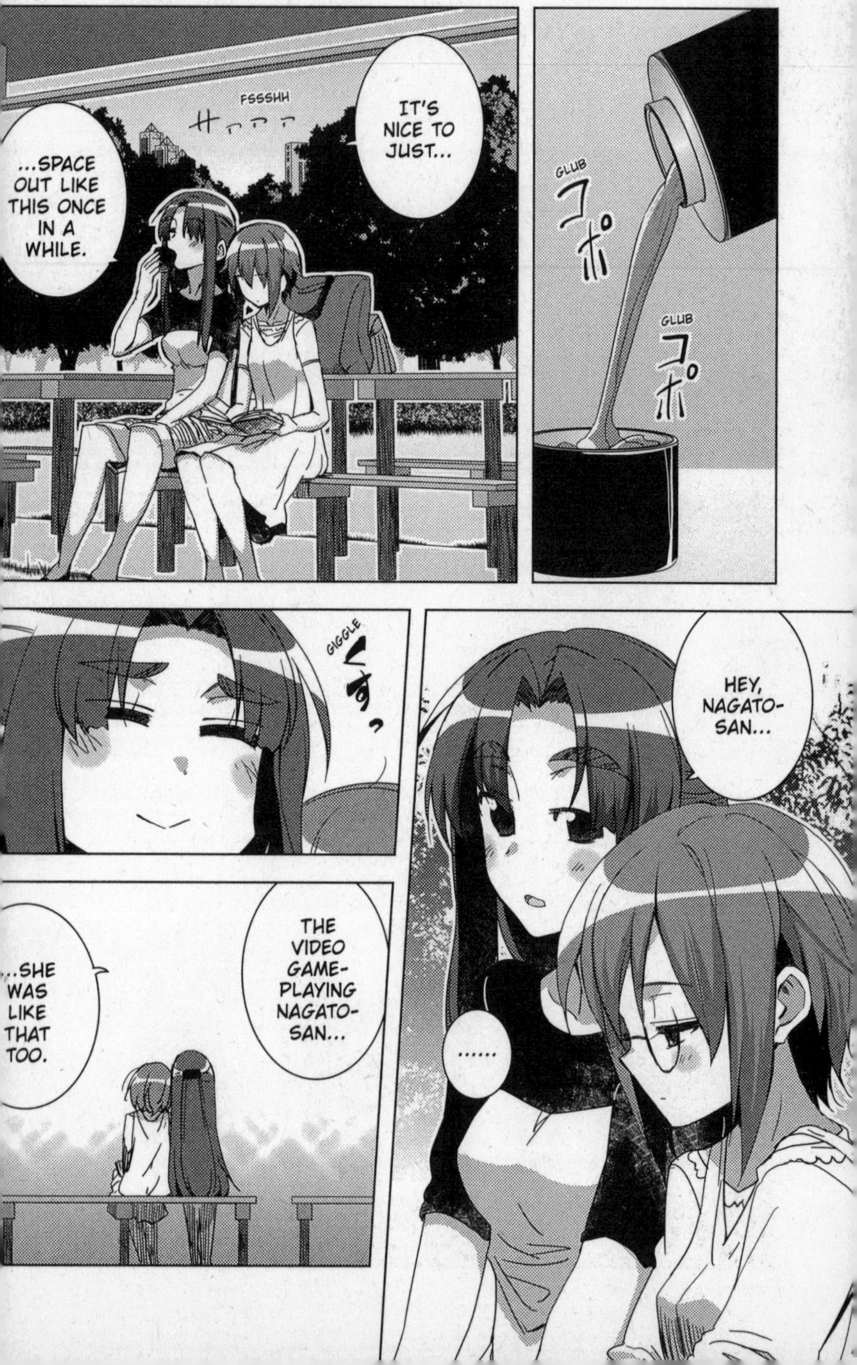
GLUB
コポ
GLUB
コポ
IT'S NICE TO JUST...
FSSSHH
サァァァ
...SPACE OUT LIKE THIS ONCE IN A WHILE.
HEY, NAGATO-SAN...
......
GIGGLE
くすっ
THE VIDEO GAME-PLAYING NAGATO-SAN...
...SHE WAS LIKE THAT TOO.

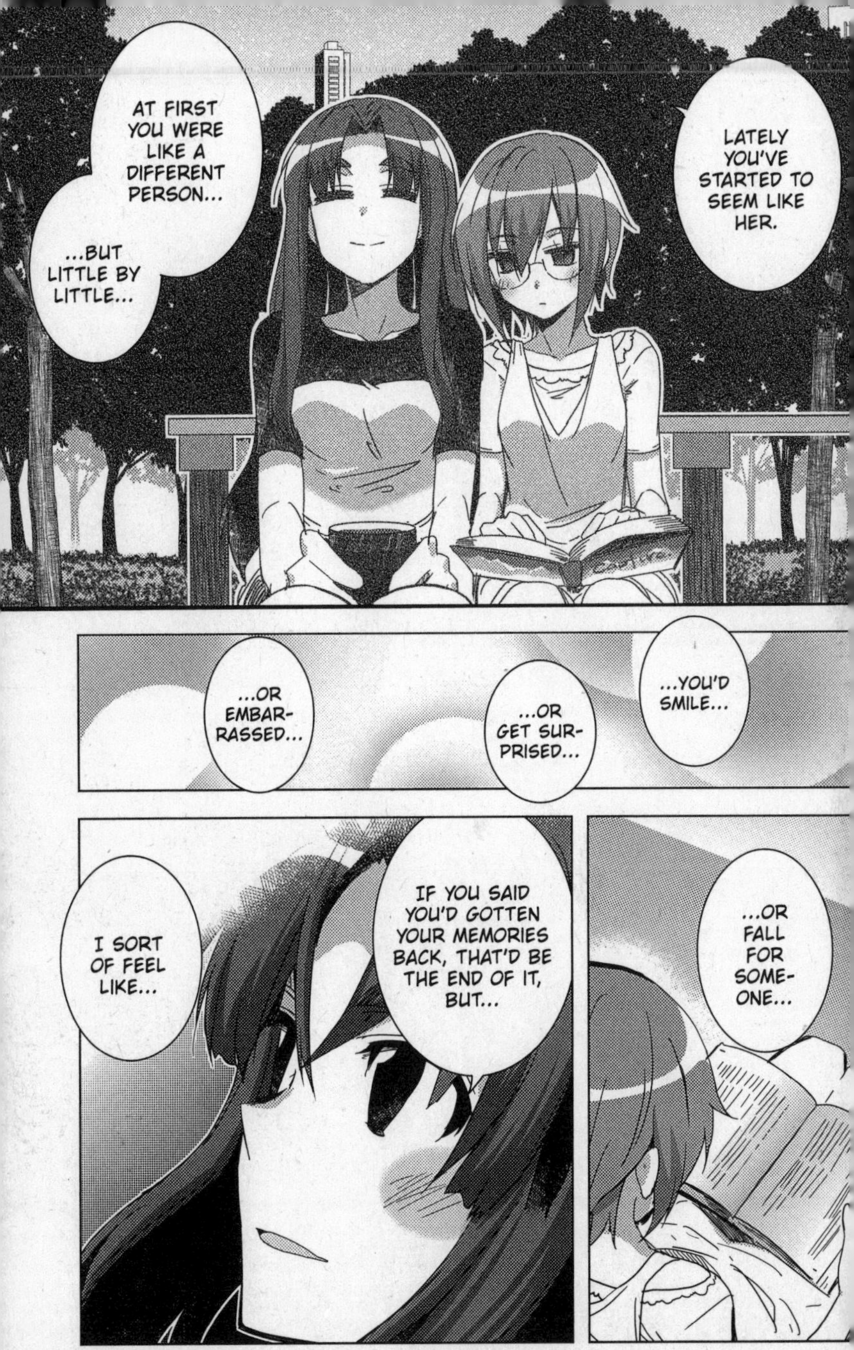
LATELY YOU'VE STARTED TO SEEM LIKE HER.
AT FIRST YOU WERE LIKE A DIFFERENT PERSON...
...BUT LITTLE BY LITTLE...
...YOU'D SMILE...
...OR GET SUR-PRISED...
...OR EMBAR-RASSED...
...OR FALL FOR SOME-ONE...
IF YOU SAID YOU'D GOTTEN YOUR MEMORIES BACK, THAT'D BE THE END OF IT, BUT...
I SORT OF FEEL LIKE...

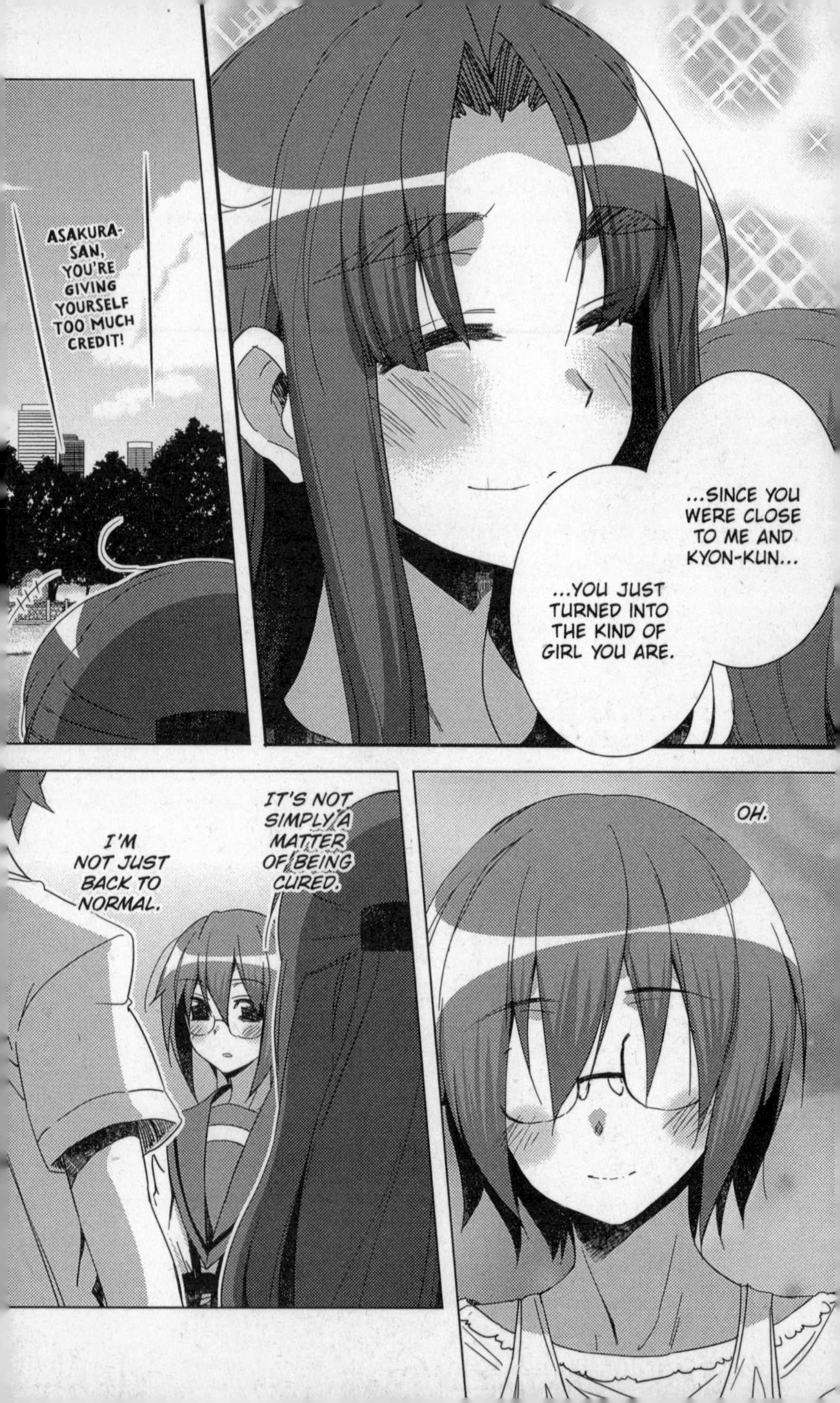
...SINCE YOU WERE CLOSE TO ME AND KYON-KUN...
...YOU JUST TURNED INTO THE KIND OF GIRL YOU ARE.
ASAKURA-SAN, YOU'RE GIVING YOURSELF TOO MUCH CREDIT!
OH.
IT'S NOT SIMPLY A MATTER OF BEING CURED.
I'M NOT JUST BACK TO NORMAL.

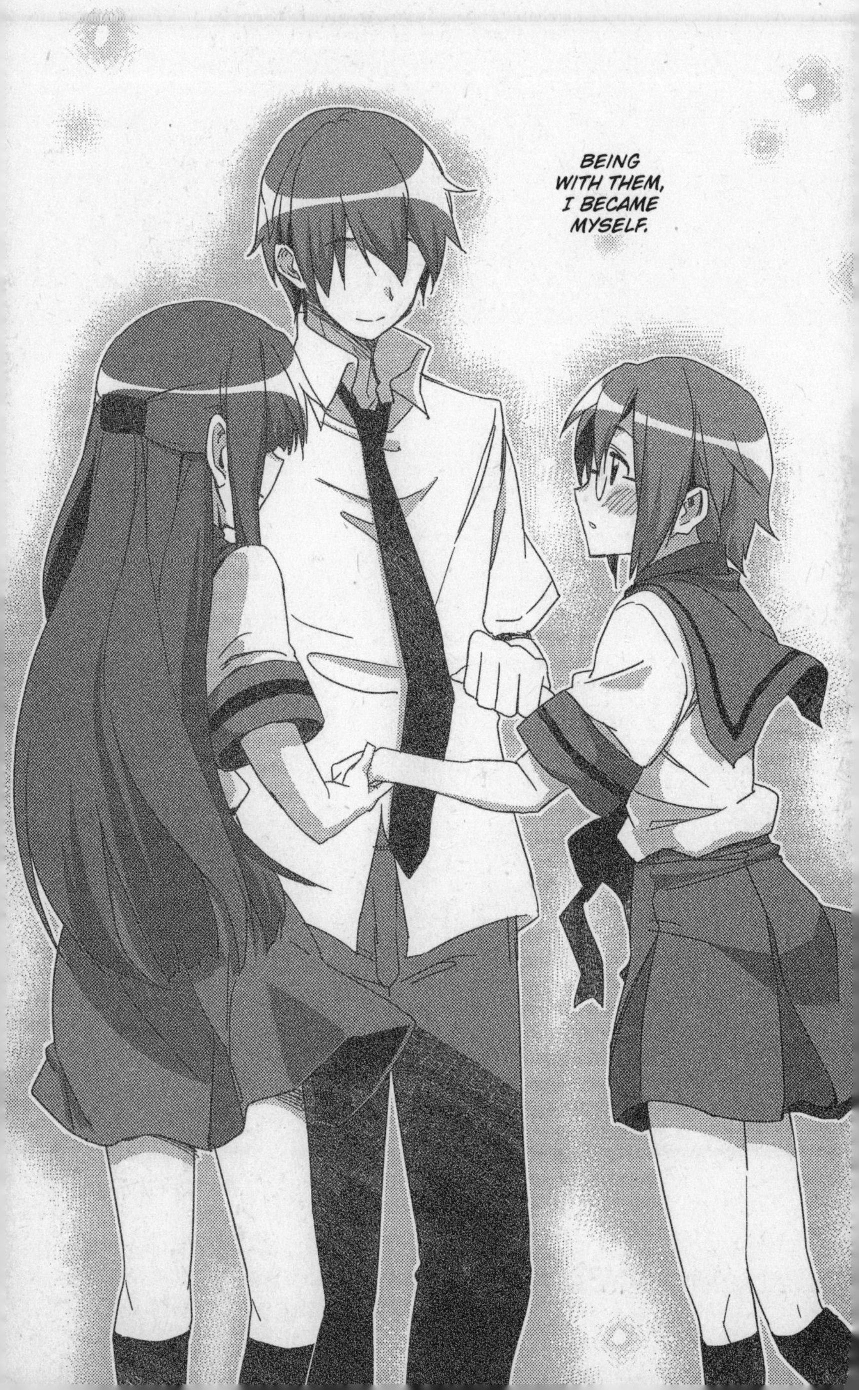
BEING WITH THEM, I BECAME MYSELF.

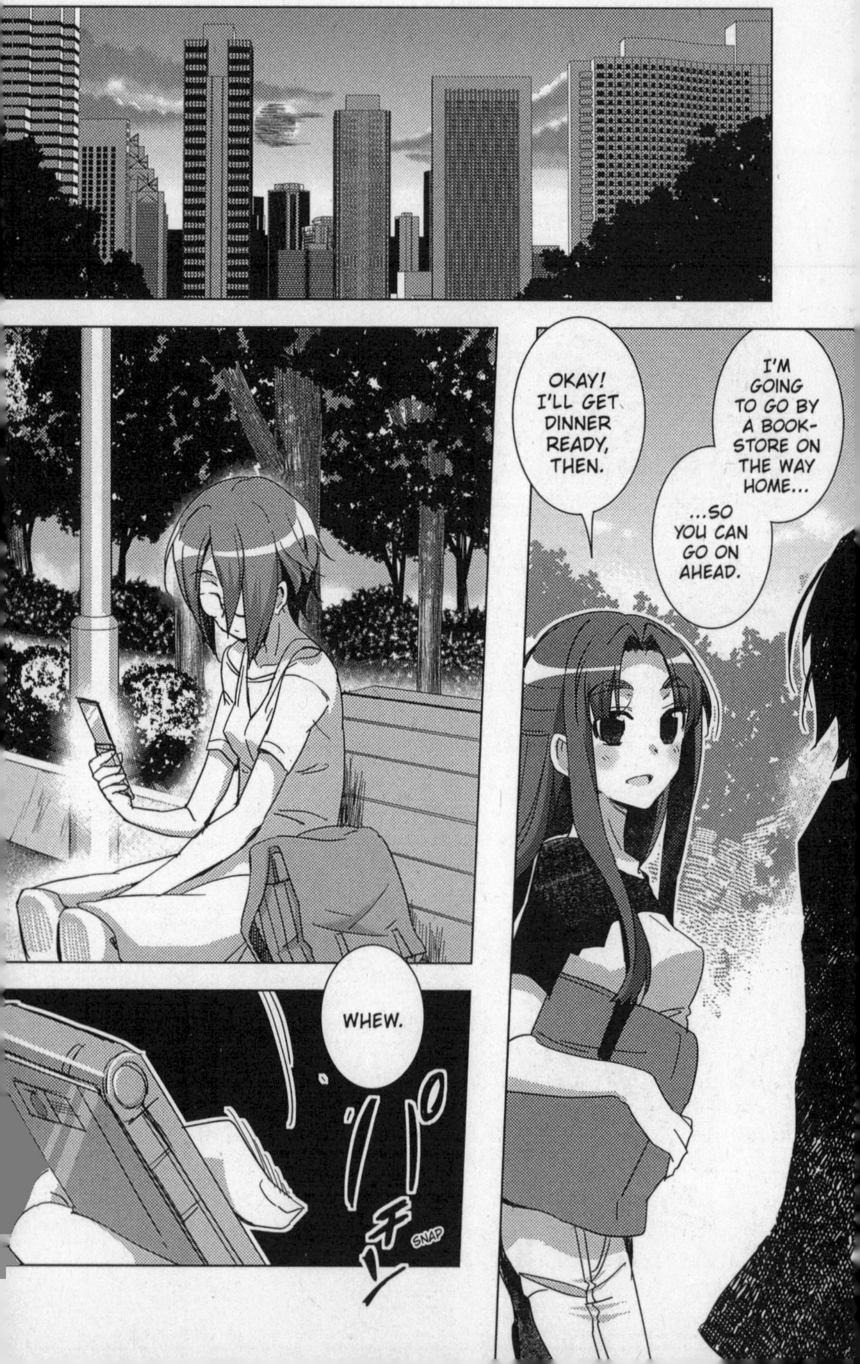
I'M GOING TO GO BY A BOOK-STORE ON THE WAY HOME...
...SO YOU CAN GO ON AHEAD.
OKAY! I'LL GET DINNER READY, THEN.
WHEW.
SNAP

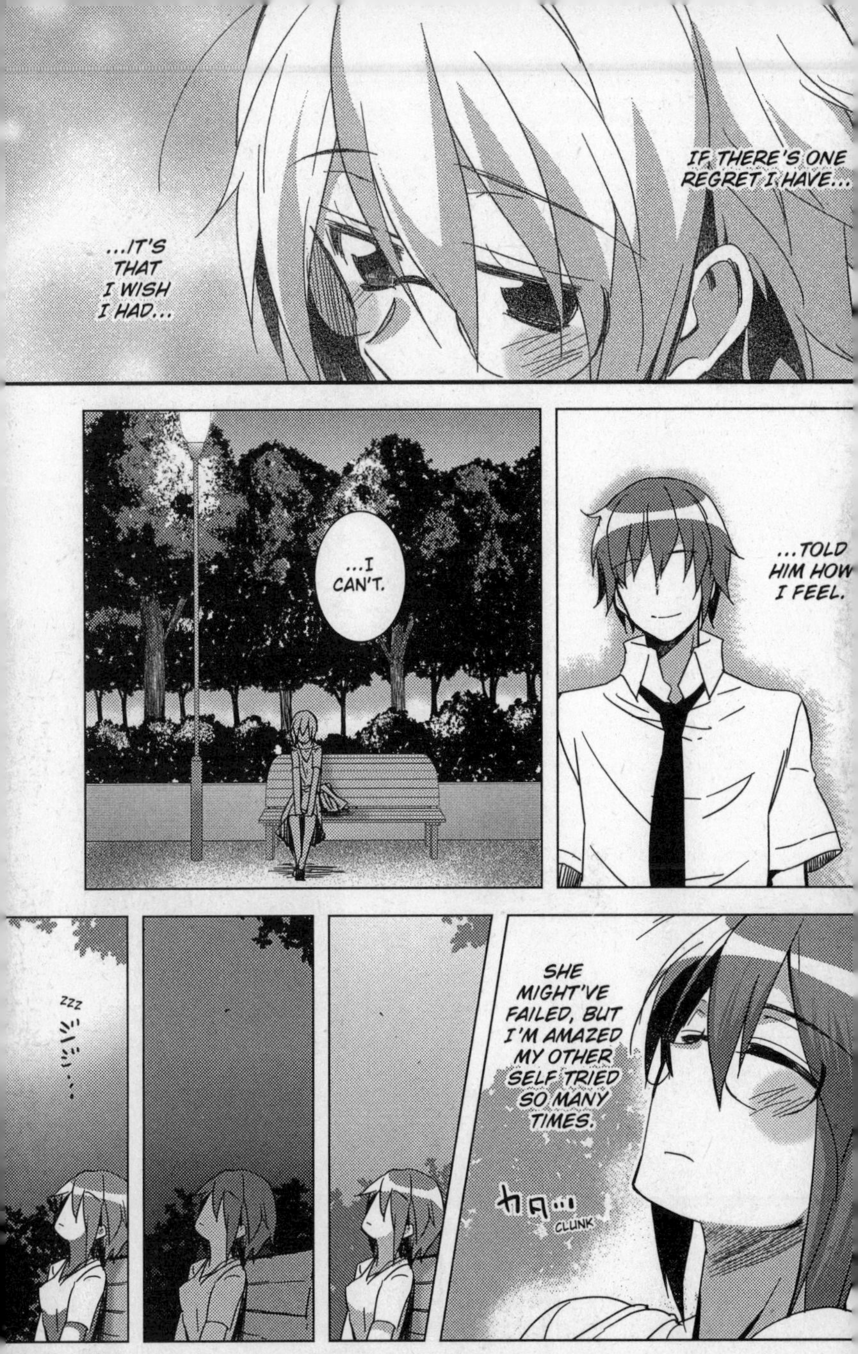
IF THERE'S ONE REGRET I HAVE...
...IT'S THAT I WISH I HAD...
...TOLD HIM HOW I FEEL.
...I CAN'T.
SHE MIGHT'VE FAILED, BUT I'M AMAZED MY OTHER SELF TRIED SO MANY TIMES.
CLUNK
ZZZ

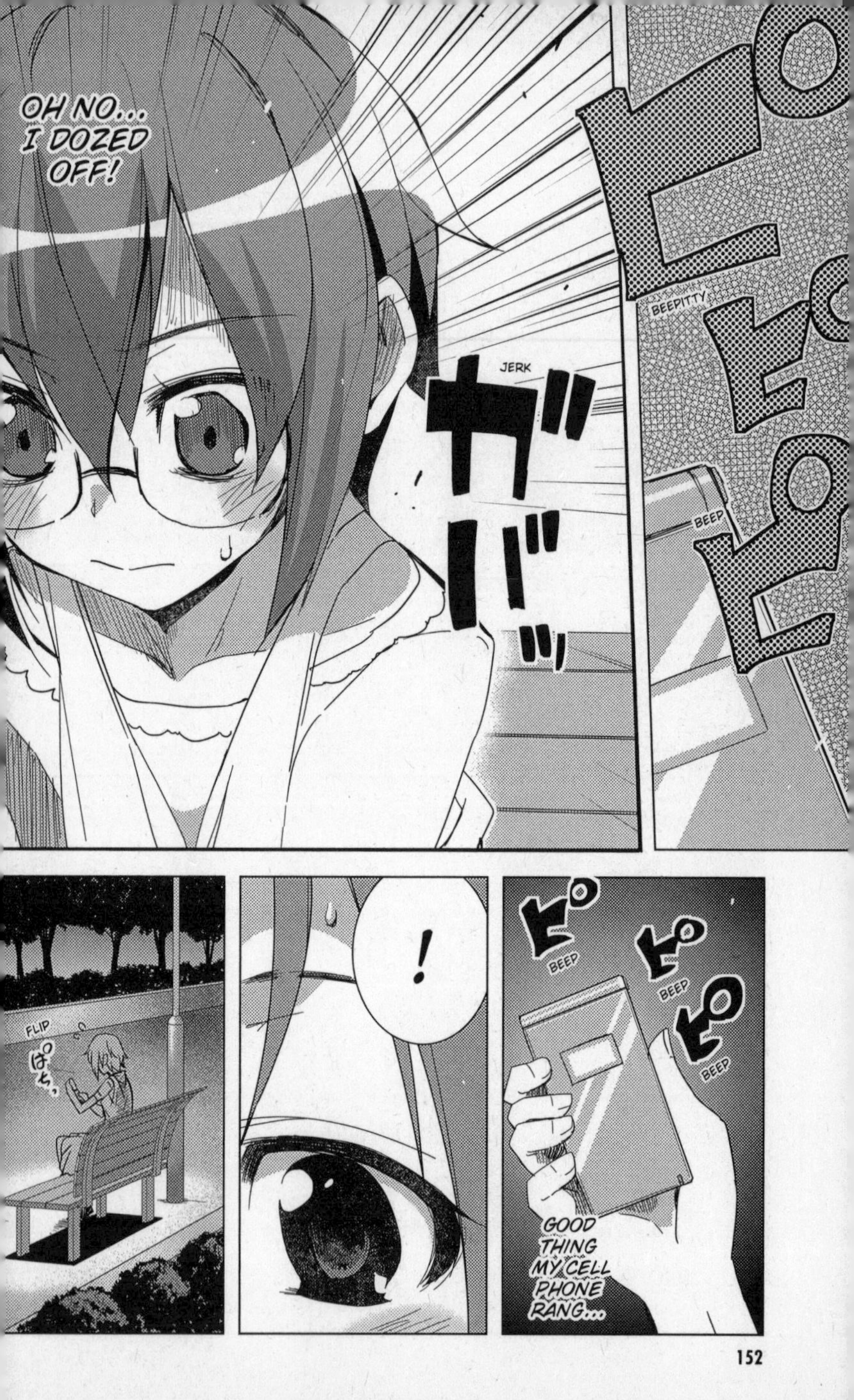
BEEPITTY
BEEP
OH NO... I DOZED OFF!
JERK
ピ
BEEP
ピ
BEEP
ピ
BEEP
GOOD THING MY CELL PHONE RANG...
!
FLIP
ぱち。

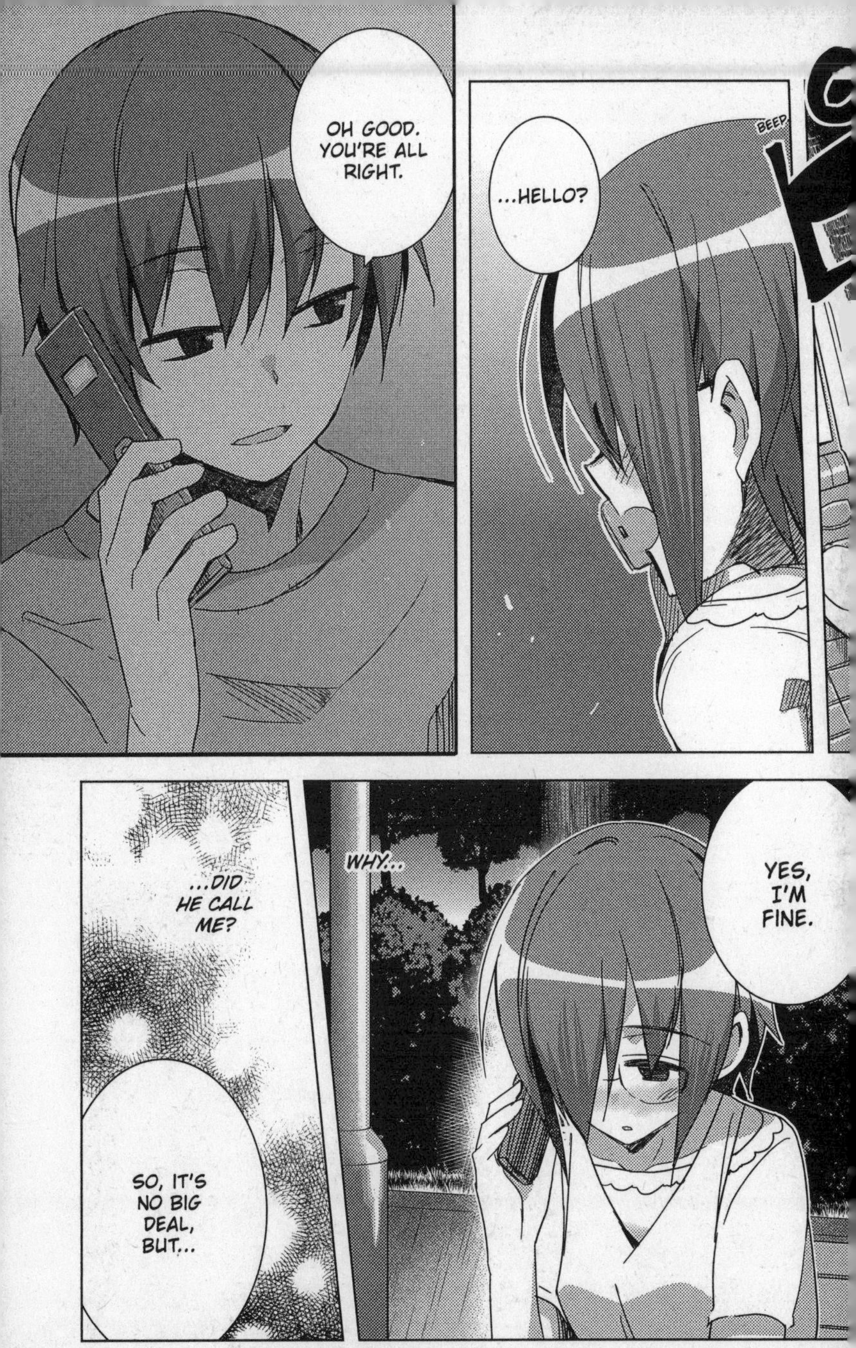
BEEP
...HELLO?
OH GOOD. YOU'RE ALL RIGHT.
YES, I'M FINE.
WHY...
...DID HE CALL ME?
SO, IT'S NO BIG DEAL, BUT...

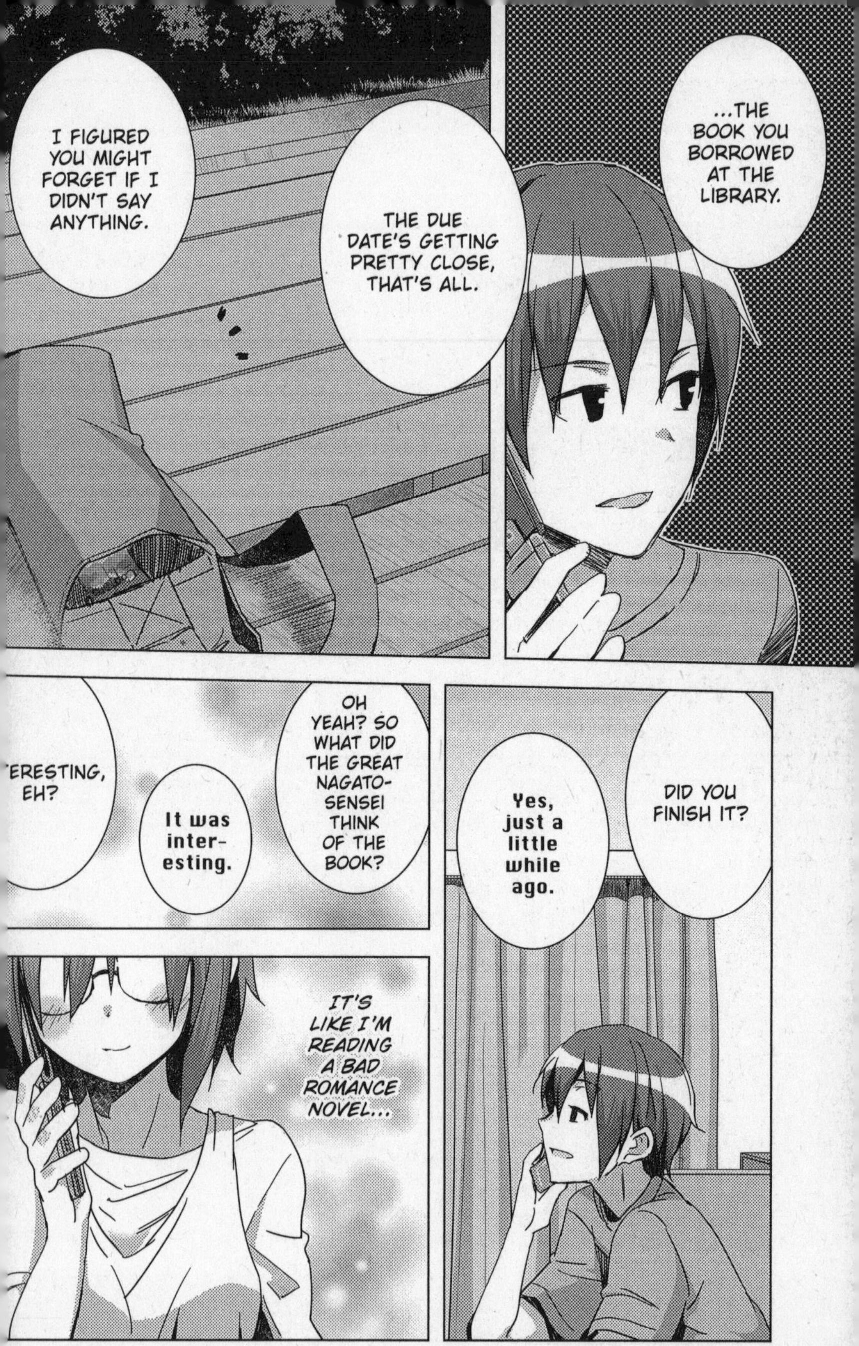

...THE BOOK YOU BORROWED AT THE LIBRARY.
THE DUE DATE'S GETTING PRETTY CLOSE, THAT'S ALL.
I FIGURED YOU MIGHT FORGET IF I DIDN'T SAY ANYTHING.
DID YOU FINISH IT?
Yes, just a little while ago.
OH YEAH? SO WHAT DID THE GREAT NAGATO-SENSEI THINK OF THE BOOK?
It was inter-esting.
ERESTING, EH?
IT'S LIKE I'M READING A BAD ROMANCE NOVEL...

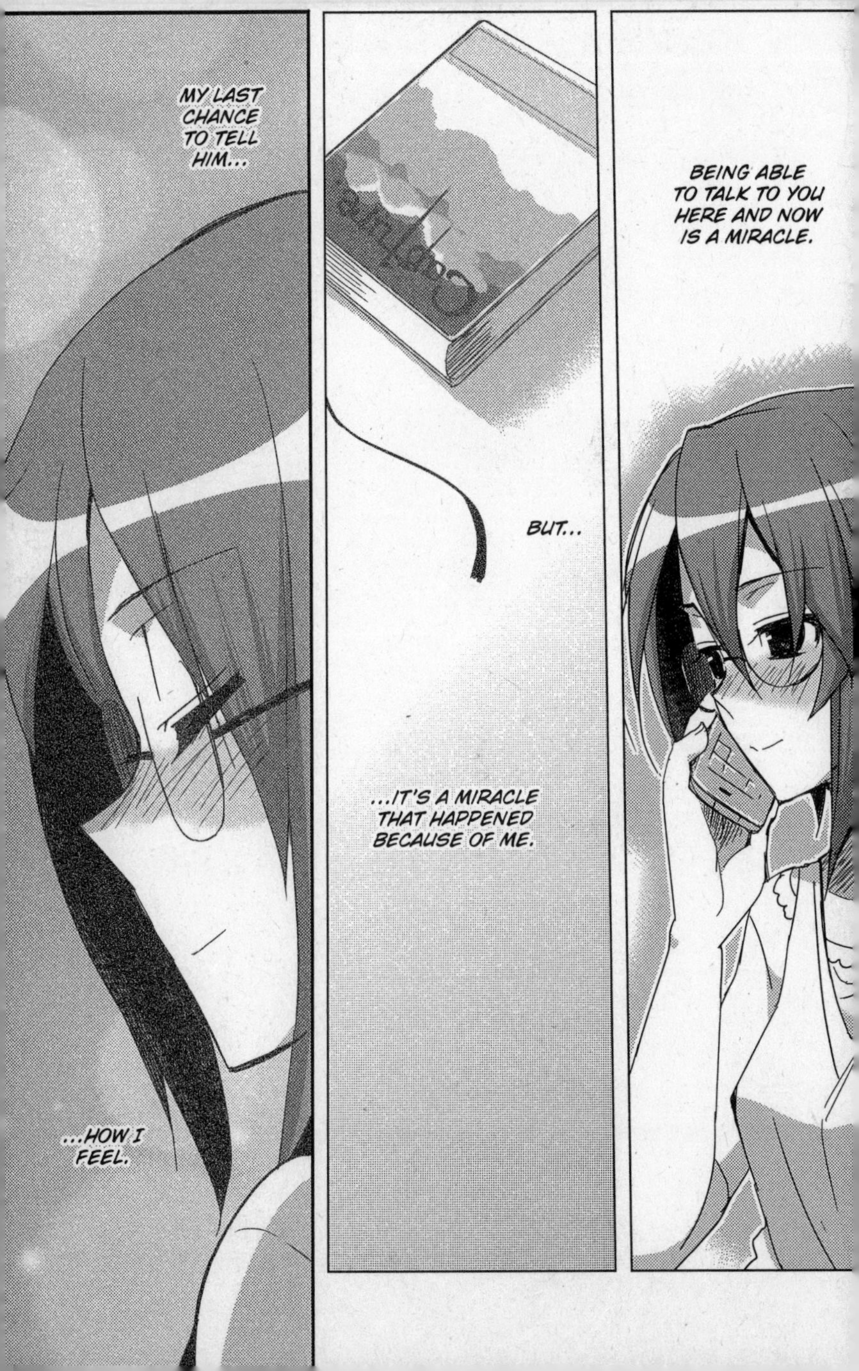
BEING ABLE TO TALK TO YOU HERE AND NOW IS A MIRACLE.
BUT...
...IT'S A MIRACLE THAT HAPPENED BECAUSE OF ME.
MY LAST CHANCE TO TELL HIM...
...HOW I FEEL.

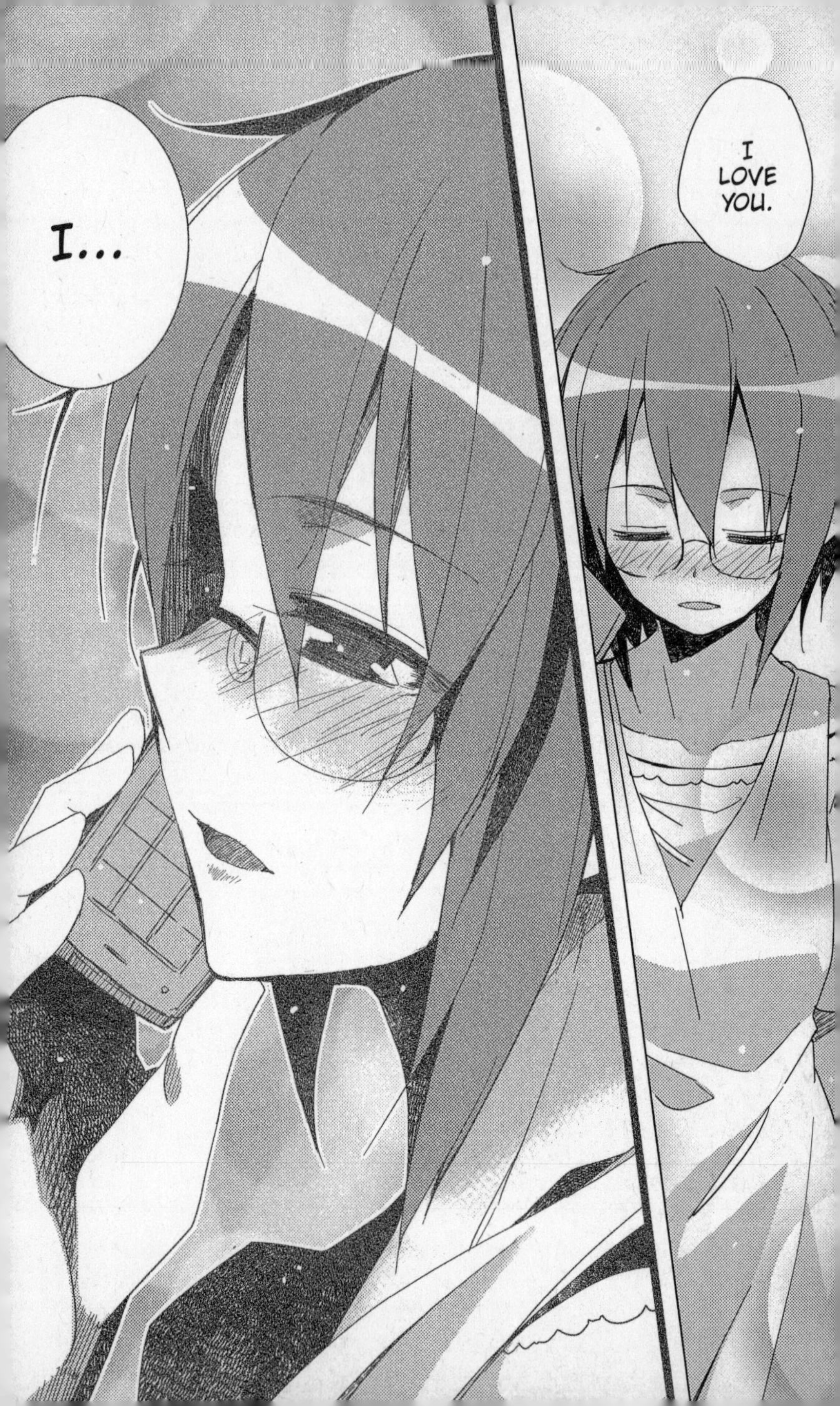
I LOVE YOU.
I...

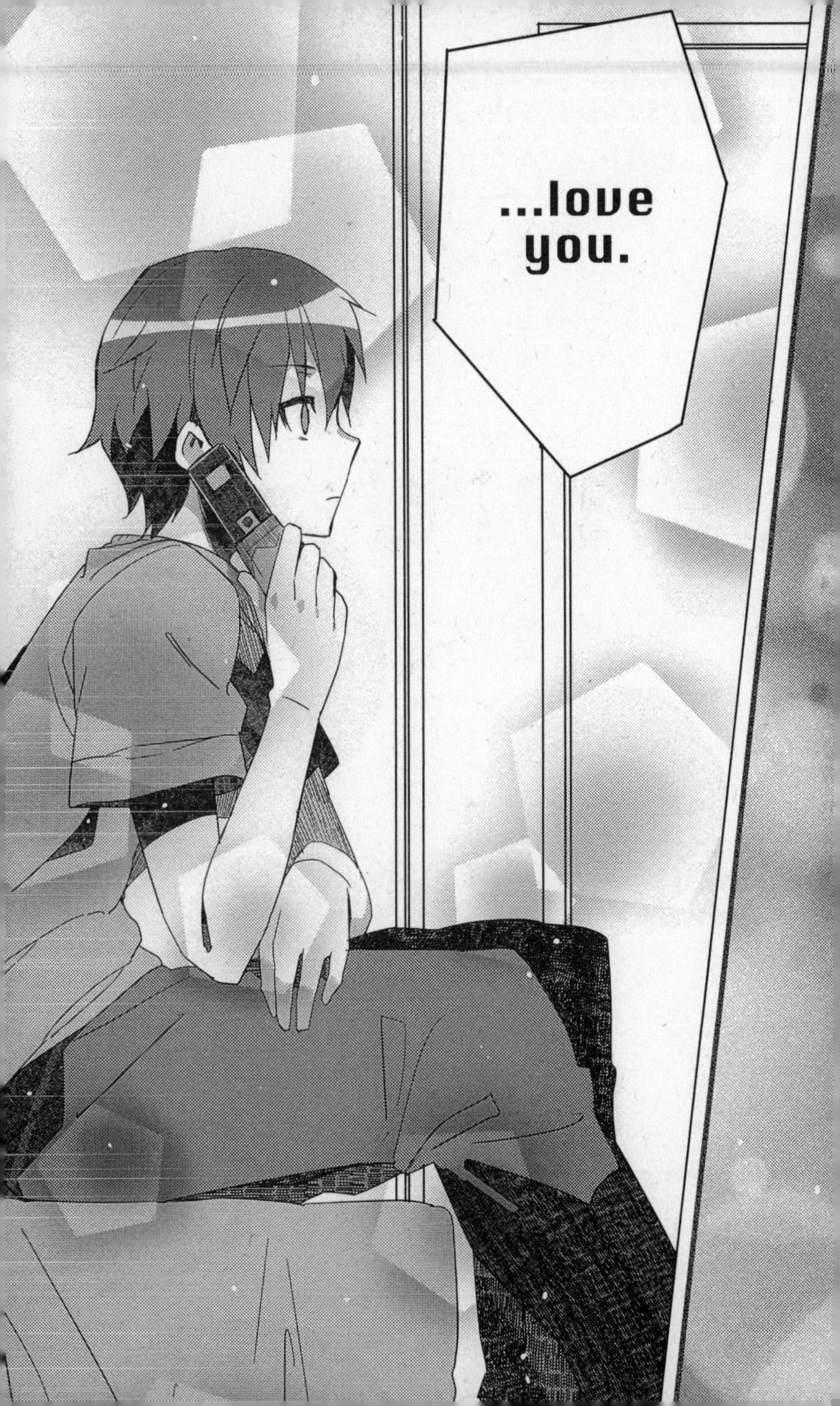
...love you.

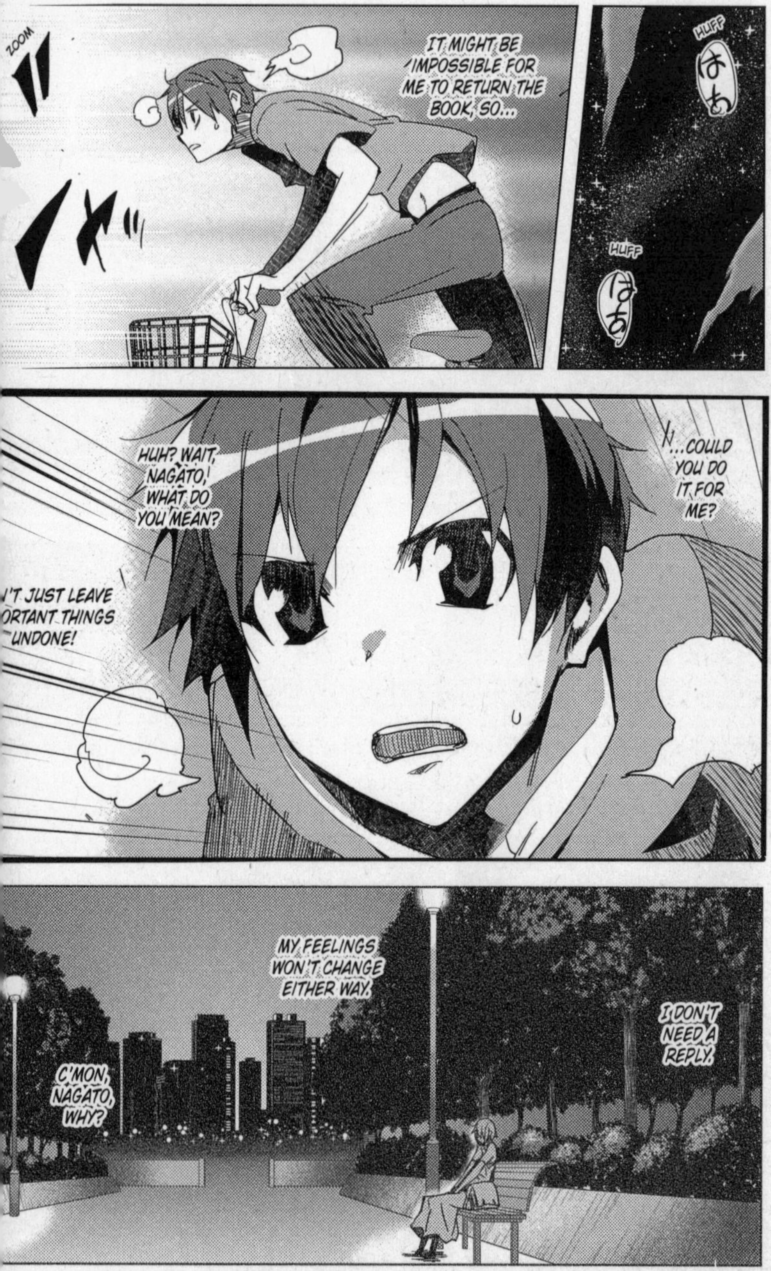
HUFF
はあ
HUFF
はあ
ZOOM
IT MIGHT BE IMPOSSIBLE FOR ME TO RETURN THE BOOK, SO...
...COULD YOU DO IT FOR ME?
HUH? WAIT, NAGATO, WHAT DO YOU MEAN?
'T JUST LEAVE ORTANT THINGS UNDONE!
MY FEELINGS WON'T CHANGE EITHER WAY.
I DON'T NEED A REPLY.
C'MON, NAGATO, WHY?

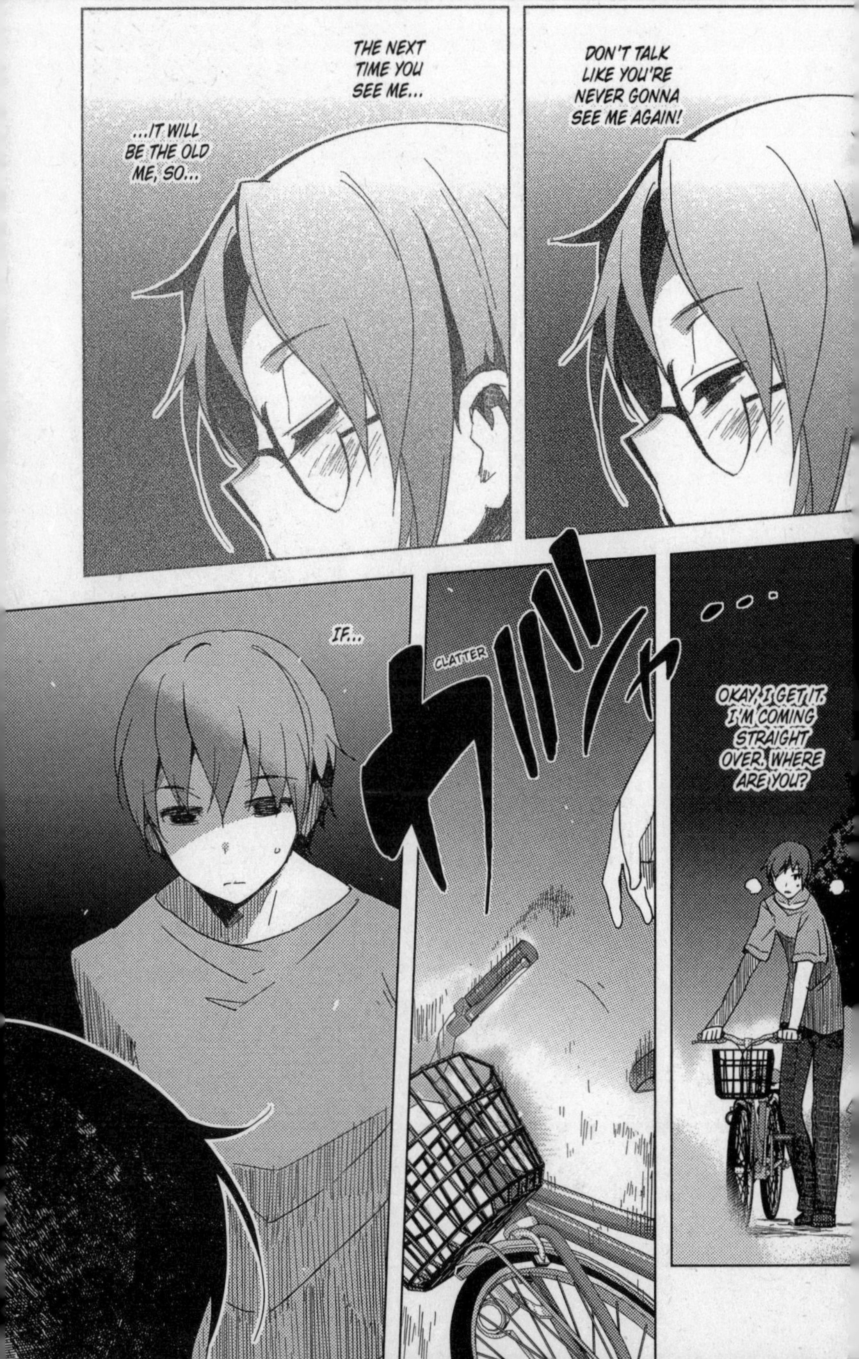
DON'T TALK LIKE YOU'RE NEVER GONNA SEE ME AGAIN!
THE NEXT TIME YOU SEE ME...
...IT WILL BE THE OLD ME, SO...
OKAY, I GET IT. I'M COMING STRAIGHT OVER. WHERE ARE YOU?
CLATTER
IF...

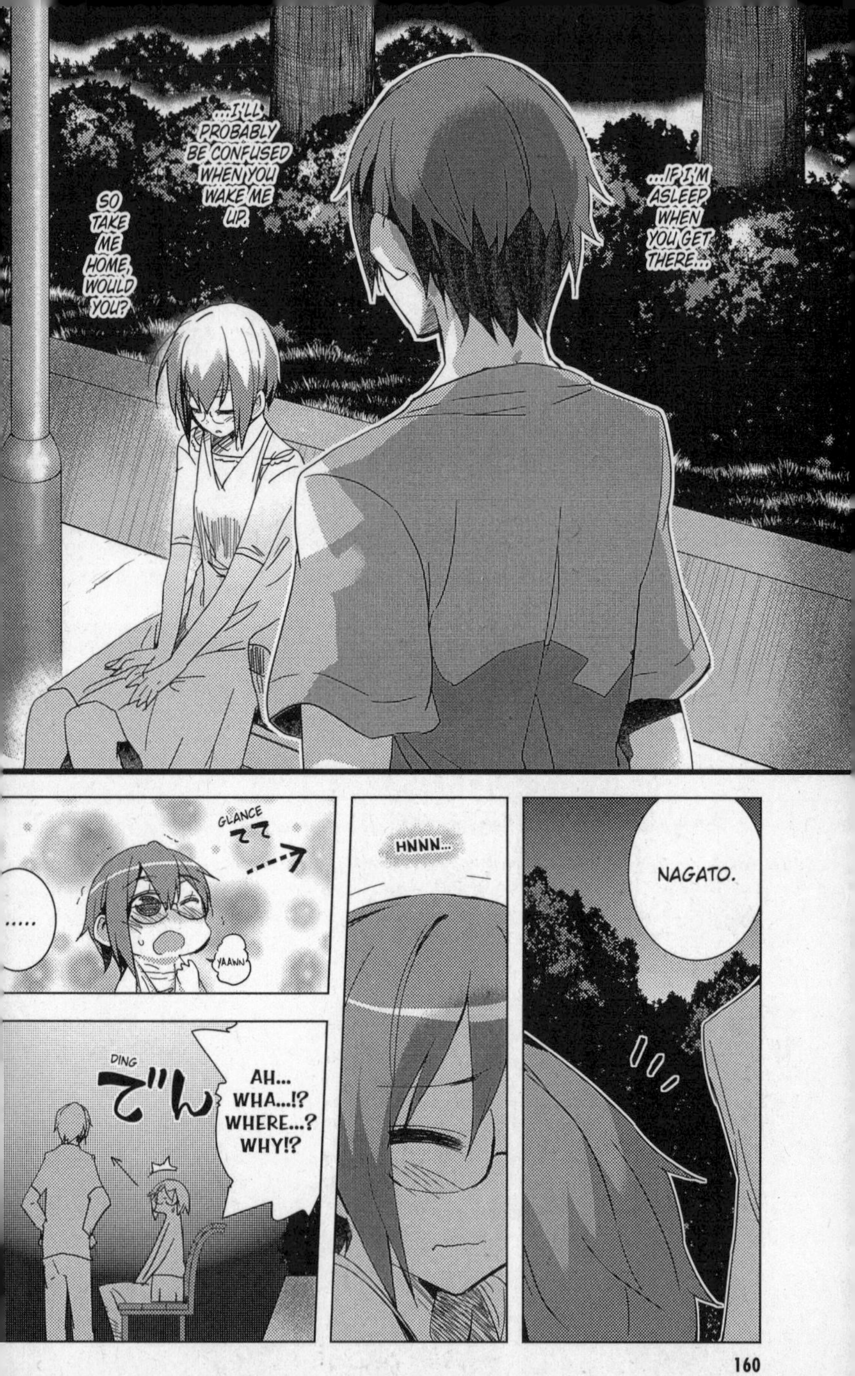
...IF I'M ASLEEP WHEN YOU GET THERE...
...I'LL PROBABLY BE CONFUSED WHEN YOU WAKE ME UP.
SO TAKE ME HOME, WOULD YOU?
NAGATO.
HNNN...
GLANCE
......
YAAWN
DING
でん
AH... WHA...!? WHERE...? WHY!?

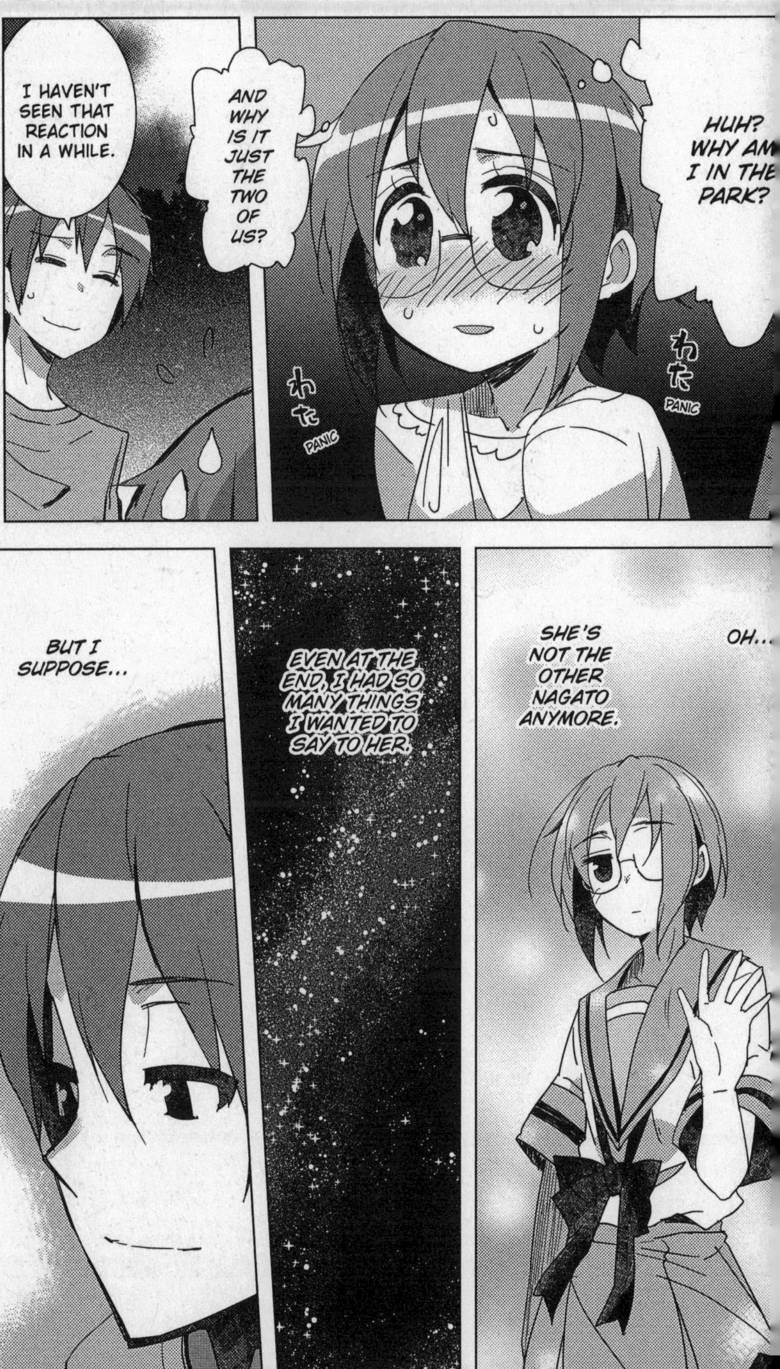
HUH? WHY AM I IN THE PARK?
わた
PANIC
AND WHY IS IT JUST THE TWO OF US?
わた
PANIC
I HAVEN'T SEEN THAT REACTION IN A WHILE.
OH...
SHE'S NOT THE OTHER NAGATO ANYMORE.
EVEN AT THE END, I HAD SO MANY THINGS I WANTED TO SAY TO HER.
BUT I SUPPOSE...

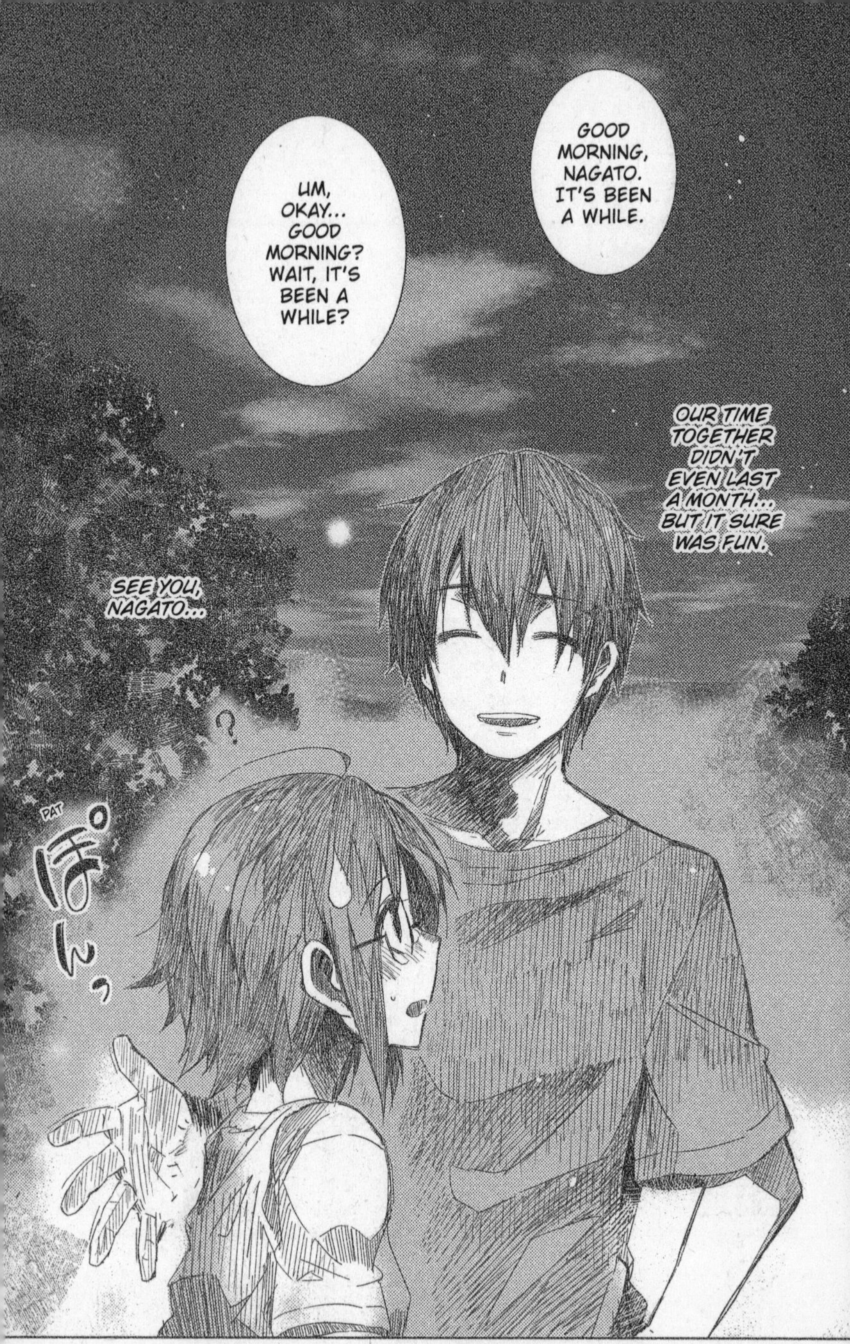
GOOD MORNING, NAGATO. IT'S BEEN A WHILE.
UM, OKAY... GOOD MORNING? WAIT, IT'S BEEN A WHILE?
OUR TIME TOGETHER DIDN'T EVEN LAST A MONTH... BUT IT SURE WAS FUN.
SEE YOU, NAGATO...
?
PAT
ぽん

AFTERWORD FANTASY EPISODE

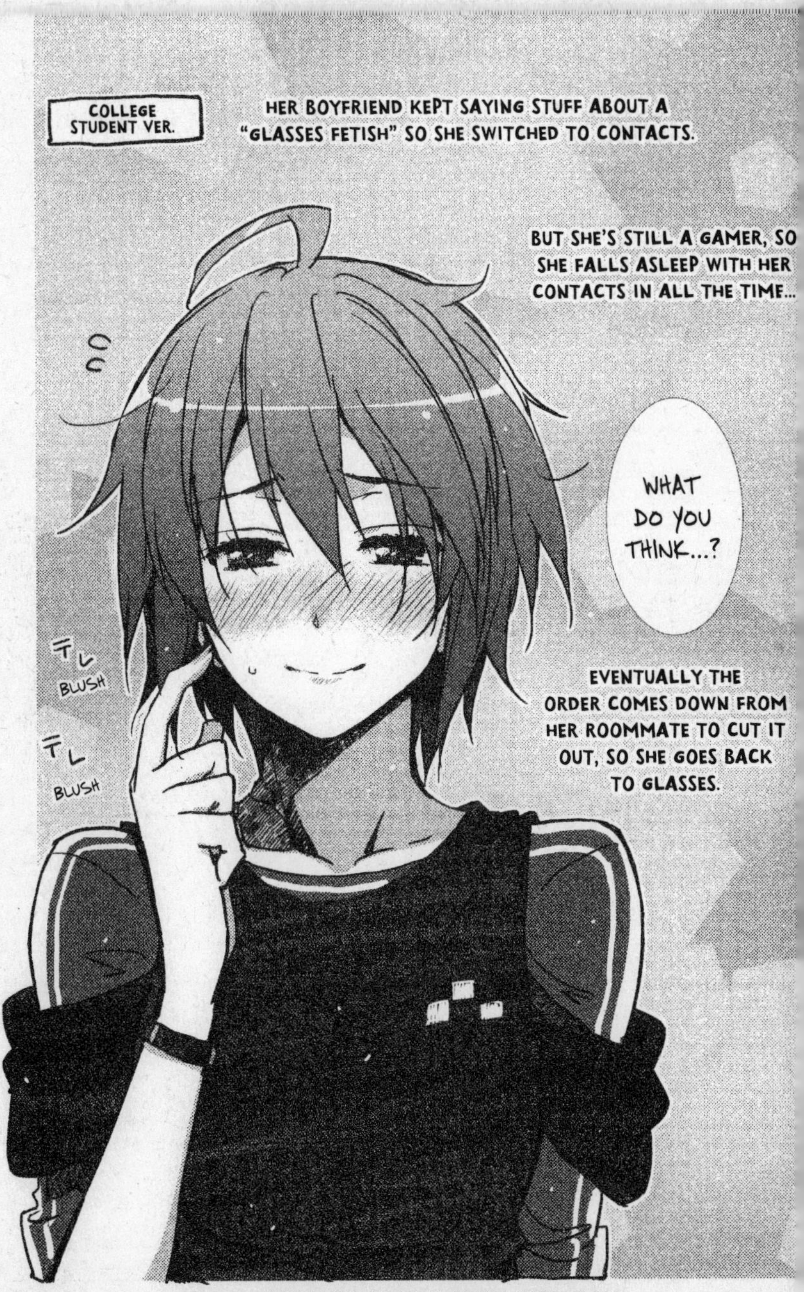
HER BOYFRIEND KEPT SAYING STUFF ABOUT A "GLASSES FETISH" SO SHE SWITCHED TO CONTACTS.
COLLEGE STUDENT VER.
BUT SHE'S STILL A GAMER, SO SHE FALLS ASLEEP WITH HER CONTACTS IN ALL THE TIME...
WHAT DO YOU THINK...?
EVENTUALLY THE ORDER COMES DOWN FROM HER ROOMMATE TO CUT IT OUT, SO SHE GOES BACK TO GLASSES.
BLUSH
BLUSH

SEE YOU IN THE NEXT VOLUME!

THE DISAPPEARANCE OF NAGATO
YUKI-CHAN
❹

Original Story: Nagaru Tanigawa
Manga: PUYO
Character Design: Noizi Ito

Translation: Paul Starr
Lettering: Jennifer Skarupa

NAGATO YUKI CHAN NO SHOSHITSU Volume 4 © Nagaru TANIGAWA • Noizi ITO 2012 © PUYO 2012. First published in Japan in 2012 by KADOKAWA SHOTEN Co., Ltd., Tokyo. English translation rights arranged with KADOKAWA SHOTEN Co., Ltd., Tokyo through TUTTLE-MORI AGENCY, INC., Tokyo.

English translation © 2013 by Hachette Book Group, Inc.

Yen Press
Hachette Book Group
237 Park Avenue, New York, NY 10017

www.HachetteBookGroup.com
www.YenPress.com

Yen Press is an imprint of Hachette Book Group, Inc.
The Yen Press name and logo are trademarks of Hachette Book Group, Inc.

First Yen Press Edition: May 2013

ISBN: 978-0-316-25088-7

10 9 8 7 6 5 4 3 2 1

BVG

Printed in the United States of America